Praise for John Grisham and Jim McCloskey's

FRAMED

"Grisham does a service by elevating Jim McCloskey, who can inspire all of us to use our privilege in the service of those ensnared in the moral scandal we call a criminal justice system."

—*The New York Times*

"The flaws and lethal errors that condemn innocent people in the American legal system have caused too many for too long to needlessly suffer. Jim McCloskey and John Grisham are towering figures in law and literature shining an urgent, compelling, and critically important light on the heartbreaking wrongful convictions that compromise our legal system and remain a national tragedy."   —Bryan Stevenson, author of *Just Mercy*

"*Framed* should come with a warning label: Be prepared never to look at the justice system the same way again. How grateful we all should be to John Grisham and Jim McCloskey—for raising the alarm and crusading for true justice."

—Robert Kolker, author of *Hidden Valley Road*

"In this essential collaboration, John Grisham and Jim McCloskey vividly demonstrate the need to run just as fast, if not faster, to exonerate the innocent as to punish the guilty. In ten shocking true stories, they not only convey the devastating impact of wrongful convictions on each affected person but also sound the alarm for all of us—there but for the grace of God go I. These are remarkable stories of injustice that need to be told. And retold."

—Preet Bharara, former U.S. Attorney
and author of *Doing Justice*

"These ten stories—bitter, gritty, and heartbreaking—will astound you, will inspire you, will bring your blood up to a roiling boil. Grisham and McCloskey, writing in crisp, propulsive prose, remind us how much hard and thoughtful work we still have to do to make America's legal system equitable, transparent, and fair."   —Hampton Sides, author of *The Wide Wide Sea*

JOHN GRISHAM and JIM McCLOSKEY

FRAMED

John Grisham is the author of numerous #1 bestsellers, which have been translated into nearly fifty languages. His recent books include *The Exchange* and *The Boys from Biloxi*. Grisham serves on the board of directors of the Innocence Project and Centurion Ministries, two national organizations dedicated to exonerating those who have been wrongfully convicted. Much of his fiction explores deep-seated problems in our criminal justice system. He lives on a farm in central Virginia.

jgrisham.com

Jim McCloskey founded Centurion Ministries, the first organization in the world devoted to freeing the wrongly convicted. Since he began this work forty-five years ago, Centurion has freed seventy-one individuals, all of whom spent decades in prison serving life or death sentences for the crimes of others. McCloskey has a Master of Divinity from Princeton Theological Seminary and an Honorary Doctorate of Humane Letters from John Jay College of Criminal Justice. His memoir, *When Truth Is All You Have*, was published by Doubleday in 2020.

centurion.org

FRAMED

JOHN GRISHAM

FRAMED

ASTONISHING TRUE STORIES OF WRONGFUL CONVICTIONS

JIM McCLOSKEY

VINTAGE BOOKS

A DIVISION OF PENGUIN RANDOM HOUSE LLC

NEW YORK

Published by Vintage Books, a division of Penguin Random House LLC, 1745 Broadway, New York, NY 10019. Originally published in hardcover in the United States by Doubleday, a division of Penguin Random House LLC, New York, in 2024.

Vintage and colophon are registered trademarks of Penguin Random House LLC.

The Library of Congress has cataloged the Doubleday edition as follows:
Names: Grisham, John, author. | McCloskey, Jim (Minister), author.
Title: Framed : astonishing true stories of wrongful convictions /
John Grisham and Jim McCloskey.
Description: First edition. | New York : Doubleday, 2024.
Identifiers: LCCN 2024012479 (print) | LCCN 2024012480 (ebook)
Subjects: LCSH: Judicial error—United States. | Criminal justice, Administration—
United States. | Racism in criminal justice administration—United States. |
Discrimination in criminal justice administration—United States.
Classification: LCC HV7419.3 .G75 2024 (print) | LCC HV7419.3 (ebook) |
DDC 345/.0122—dc23/eng/20240419
LC record available at https://lccn.loc.gov/2024012479
LC ebook record available at https://lccn.loc.gov/2024012480

Vintage Books Trade Paperback ISBN: 978-0-593-68723-9
eBook ISBN: 978-0-385-55045-1

Grisham author photograph © Michael Lionstar
McCloskey author photograph © Andrew Wilkinson
Book design by Casey Hampton

penguinrandomhouse.com | vintagebooks.com

Printed in the United States of America
10 9 8 7 6 5 4 3 2 1

The authorized representative in the EU for product safety and compliance is
Penguin Random House Ireland, Morrison Chambers, 32 Nassau Street,
Dublin D02 YH68, Ireland, https://eu-contact.penguin.ie.

TO KATE GERMOND AND PAUL CASTELEIRO:
For the last forty-plus years and counting, your steadfast devotion to Centurion and those we work to free is unequaled in persistence and achievement. Centurion owes its life to your unparalleled service to the wrongly convicted.

—JIM McCLOSKEY

TO PETER NEUFELD AND BARRY SCHECK,
cofounders of the Innocence Project;
and to the warriors who labor there

—JOHN GRISHAM

CONTENTS

PREFACE

JOHN GRISHAM

In 2006, I published *The Innocent Man,* a true story about the wrongful conviction and near execution of Ron Williamson. Before then, I had never considered nonfiction—I was having too much fun with the novels—but Ron's story captivated me. From a pure storytelling point of view, it was irresistible. Filled with tragedy, suffering, corruption, loss, near death, a measure of redemption, and an ending that could not be considered happy but could have been much worse, the story was just waiting for an author. I soon learned that every wrongful conviction deserves its own book.

Since then I've met many exonerees, along with their families, lawyers, advocates, and old cellmates. As a group, they are amazing because they somehow survived nightmares that the rest of us cannot begin to comprehend. Most enjoy telling their stories. All are determined to change a broken judicial system and prevent more wrongful convictions. Dozens have written about their ordeals. More than a few have asked me to do the writing.

For a long time I've thought about a collection of some of the best stories, but the research got in the way. It is daunting. Thousands of pages of trial transcripts, police reports, witness statements that always seem to vary from one stage to the next, prison records, forensic tests, and petitions, motions, pleadings, and orders written by lawyers and judges and filed, seemingly, by the pound. Novelists can be lazy because we simply make up stuff. Nonfiction is brutal because the research has to be meticulous. You can't afford to make mistakes.

I met Jim McCloskey about fifteen years ago when he asked me to speak at a Centurion Ministries annual gala at Princeton. Within ten minutes of first shaking hands we were telling war stories of the wrongfully convicted. Jim's stories are always better, because he lived them. He is part of them. He made the exonerations happen by pounding the streets from coast to coast in search of the truth. Centurion has been involved in about seventy exonerations, and Jim was usually there, outside the prisons, when his innocent clients walked out and into the arms of their loved ones. He was there when they tasted freedom, and he was the reason for it.

At some point a few years back, we began talking about this collection. The idea was simple. I would select five of my favorite stories, and so would Jim. The first challenge was to pick only ten, because there are so many. The second challenge was to limit each story to about 10,000 words. Since each story could fill a library, we knew the task would be formidable. We agreed that each would do his own writing with limited input from the other.

And so we wrote.

Our goal with this book is to raise awareness of wrongful convictions and in some small way help to prevent more of them. It is an effort to shine light on some of the terrible and abusive tactics used by the authorities to convict innocent people.

If we as a society had the political gumption to change unfair laws, practices, and procedures, we could avoid virtually all wrongful convictions.

JIM McCLOSKEY

As John points out, our association and friendship go back fifteen years. We were drawn together by our mutual concern and compassion for those men and women across America who fell victim to a deeply flawed criminal justice system and were falsely convicted and sentenced to a life sentence or to death. John generously volunteered to write the foreword to my memoir, *When Truth Is All You Have,* published by Doubleday in 2020. That book recounts the forty-year history of Centurion Ministries' encounters with our nation's judicial system on behalf of the convicted innocent as well as the personal journey that led me into this work.

Naturally, I was honored when John invited me to cowrite *Framed* with him. We quickly agreed that each of us would write five stories of real-life cases in which innocent defendants, much to their shock and disbelief, were found guilty of crimes they had absolutely nothing to do with. The five written by me are cases I personally worked on as case manager and lead investigator. Selecting these five from among the seventy or so individuals Centurion successfully freed was a challenge worthy of Solomon. I was fortunate in writing to be able to draw upon Centurion's voluminous in-house archival records collected during the many years of work on each case. These source materials include, but are not limited to, trial transcripts, police reports, legal briefs, judicial opinions, court records, and Centurion investigative reports.

The subtitle of *Framed* is *Astonishing True Stories of Wrongful Convictions.* I can assure readers, no matter what their background, that their response after reading each of these stories will be, "Did this really happen?" To which we the authors answer, "Yes, it did, and it happens far more often than you can imagine." It is our intention and hope that these stories are not only a compelling read but at the same time serve as a microcosm of what is occurring throughout our nation's halls of justice. It is our attempt to bring to light systemic flaws in the justice system's infrastructure that cause untold tens of thousands of innocent souls to interminably languish in prison.

The twenty-three defendants caught in the web of these ten wrongful convictions needlessly spent decades in prison until the truth of their innocence finally emerged and set them free. Four landed on death row, two of whom came within days of execution, while one was tragically executed. Perhaps it will surprise readers that the racial makeup of the twenty-three is almost evenly split, ten white and thirteen black, demonstrating that this kind of injustice easily occurs across racial lines.

Often the real killers were under the nose of the police from the outset of the crime, and in two cases they were the star witnesses for the prosecution. DNA played an important role in several cases but not in most. Perjury by police and civilian witnesses was pervasive in these stories. These convictions were not caused by unintentional mistakes by local law enforcement or misidentification by well-meaning eyewitnesses or honest but erroneous forensic analysis.

No, they were rooted in law enforcement misconduct and chicanery, men and women hell-bent on clearing cases or gaining a conviction through a wide variety of illicit means—subornation of perjury, secret deals with criminals in exchange for their fabricated testimony, coercing witnesses into false testimony or suspects to falsely confess, use of discredited or inept forensic analysts, suppression of exculpatory evidence from the defense, or other acts that obstructed justice and resulted in the ruination of innocent lives to the relief of the actual perpetrators.

Each of the stories takes the reader on a roller-coaster ride, most of which end with truth and justice ultimately prevailing, although at great and unimaginable personal cost to the exonerees and their loved ones. Once freed, the released face the formidable challenge of starting life all over again. It is a testament to the human spirit that so many of them have the will and capability to do so, unburdened with the anger and hate of years past, now filled with a forgiving heart, an enhanced appreciation for the everyday things of life that most of us take for granted, and a desire for a peaceful and quiet existence.

Our hope is that you find this book to be both interesting and informative, and that it provides you with a new perspective on the fallibility of our criminal justice system—a perspective that perhaps you didn't have prior to reading *Framed*.

FRAMED

THE NORFOLK FOUR

JOHN GRISHAM

O mar Ballard's mother was a black prostitute and drug addict who worked the mean streets of Newark, New Jersey. He never knew his father, who was white. His mother showed little interest in things maternal and almost no interest in the kid. He went from one foster home to another and naturally gravitated to the streets from whence he came. He was an angry kid who blamed his mother for his problems. His temper was explosive and often aimed at women. He found the life of a street thug appealing and quickly became part of the crime and violence of his neighborhood. He loved it all: the drugs and drug dealing, drinking, guns, sex, robberies, shootings, beatings, murders, gang fights, the thrill of running from the police. He got busted a few times for drugs and drunkenness, but nothing serious.

Ballard dropped out of school, and at the age of nineteen left New Jersey. He was broke, unemployed, and, as always, looking for trouble. He eventually took up with an old friend from home,

Tamika Taylor, an eighteen-year-old unwed mother of two who lived in a low-rent section of Norfolk, Virginia. The neighborhood was favored by thousands of young sailors stationed at the nearby naval base and was not considered unreasonably dangerous. That changed dramatically with the arrival of Omar Ballard.

His first known victim in Norfolk was a young white woman named Melissa Morse. He assaulted her, beat her with a baseball bat, and when her screams got the attention of others, a mob formed and gave chase. Ballard fled and sought refuge in the nearby apartment of Billy and Michelle Bosko, a young navy couple from Pittsburgh. The Boskos had been married for six weeks and just recently had met Omar through friends. They welcomed Omar, offered him a drink, and were having a pleasant visit when the mob appeared outside their apartment. The Boskos could not believe that their new friend Omar would assault anyone, and Billy bravely refused to hand over his guest. The mob dispersed, and Billy later told the police that Omar was not guilty.

Two weeks after he assaulted Melissa Morse, and while Billy was deployed at sea for a week aboard the USS *Simpson,* Omar Ballard stopped by the Bosko apartment for another visit. It was around midnight, July 7, 1997. By his own admission he was drunk, stoned, and looking for sex. He knocked on the door and said he needed to use the phone. Michelle, wearing only a T-shirt and underwear, let him in, offered the phone, and said there was beer in the refrigerator. It was late and she was going to bed. Omar followed her, attacked her, choked her, and when she was subdued, he raped her. He ejaculated and wiped his penis on a blanket. Then something snapped and Omar realized he was in serious trouble. To keep her quiet, he decided to kill her. He found a steak knife in the kitchen, and as he was returning to the bedroom, Michelle was regaining consciousness. He stabbed her three times in the chest, then left her on the floor to die. He washed his hands in the bathroom, rubbed the doorknobs with his shirt to remove fingerprints, placed the knife by her body, and on the way out went through her purse on the kitchen table and took the cash.

Most of the small, 700-square-foot apartment was undisturbed during the attack. Michelle, who was working at a McDonald's, had been a meticulous housekeeper. Billy was expected home the next day and everything was in order. When he found her body around 5:00 P.M. the following afternoon, their apartment was as neat and tidy as always.

A thorough analysis of the crime scene was undertaken and all evidence, including the victim's vaginal injuries, pointed to a sole assailant who had entered the apartment without force. There were no fingerprints other than a few from Billy and Michelle. Investigators spent more than nine hours in the Bosko apartment after the body was found and before it was removed. They inspected every inch, took videos and dozens of still photographs, collected every piece of possible evidence, even went so far as to build a tent over the body for a cyanoacrylate (superglue) fuming and powder test—an attempt to identify latent fingerprints on her skin. The investigation was exhaustive and left no doubt that Michelle's murderer had acted alone.

Almost two years after the rape and murder, the state crime lab finally tested Omar Ballard's DNA. The semen found on the blanket was 21 billion times more likely to have originated with Ballard than with any white man, and 4.6 billion times more likely than with any black man. The semen collected from the victim's vagina was 23 million times more likely to be Ballard's than any white man's, and 20 million times more likely than any other black man's. The blood found under Michelle's fingernails matched Ballard's DNA.

The only DNA samples recovered at the scene were from Michelle and her killer, Omar Ballard.

His third known sexual assault occurred ten days after he murdered Michelle. The third victim was able to identify Ballard and he was eventually convicted and sent to prison. He was not, however, suspected in the rape and murder of Michelle Bosko. His crime spree—at least two other sexual assaults against white women in less than a month, and in the same part of town—did not raise suspicions among the Norfolk police working the Bosko case.

Almost two years would pass before the detectives learned that Ballard was involved, and then he came to their attention only after he confessed from prison. Only then was his DNA tested.

To overlook such an obvious suspect was inexcusable, but the Norfolk police were far too busy to worry about Omar Ballard. They were working feverishly to pin the Bosko murder on an entire boatload of innocent men. What should have been a clear-cut DNA case quickly became a knee-jerk investigation so riddled with incompetence as to seem, at times, unbelievable. The Bosko case ranks as one of the greatest train wrecks in the history of American criminal justice. While breathtaking in its arrogance and incompetence, it is far more heartbreaking in its outcome.

When the state crime lab got a hit on Omar Ballard's DNA on March 3, 1999, twenty months after the murder, the Norfolk police and prosecutors had a total of *seven* current or former U.S. sailors in jail, all charged with the capital rape and murder of Michelle Bosko. All seven had been excluded by DNA evidence. All seven had been excluded by the physical evidence. And with the exception of a DUI, none of the sailors had criminal records.

Like many police investigations that go wrong, this one began with a hunch. Often, a homicide detective will scan the crime scene, form a half-baked opinion based on a gut reaction and clouded by the tension of the moment, maybe even pick out a suspect, and before long the police are marching off in the wrong direction.

In the case of Michelle Bosko, the misguided hunch was made while the body was still being photographed. An officer by the name of Judy Gray was the first homicide detective on the scene. She quickly determined that, since there was obviously no break-in, the murderer was someone known to Michelle. She and her part-ner secured the area. When the crime scene investigators arrived, neighbors gathered nearby and watched in disbelief. Gray stepped outside and began the usual routine of fishing for leads. She talked at length with Tamika Taylor, Ballard's friend, and asked Tamika if she had any idea who could have murdered Michelle. Tamika was reluctant to venture a guess, but Gray pressed her.

"You see that guy over there," Tamika said, nodding at a sailor named Dan Williams (#1), also a neighbor. "I think he did it."

"Why?" Gray asked.

"Well, he's kind of obsessed with her."

And with that, Dan Williams became the prime suspect in the murder of Michelle Bosko. Tamika backtracked and said she wasn't sure. There are a lot of crazy people out there, and so on, and she also mentioned Omar Ballard as someone the police should check out. For some reason, they chose not to do so.

Dan Williams and his wife, Nicole, lived in a small apartment next door to the Boskos. Billy, after finding his wife's body, ran screaming and banged on the Williamses' door. Dan called 911 and went to find Michelle. The two couples were friendly, both navy, both childless. Nicole was dying of ovarian cancer. When Michelle was murdered, Dan was in bed asleep with his wife.

Detective Gray approached Dan and asked if he would mind driving down to the police station and answering some routine questions. Gray had a hunch that he was the killer, regardless of any evidence, motive, or anything other than Tamika's wariness of him. When he readily agreed to be interviewed, Gray was even more sus-picious. By the time Dan Williams arrived at the police station, the police were convinced they'd found their man.

Inside the apartment, the investigators were meticulously gathering evidence that would eventually, hopefully, lead them to the killer. Outside, the homicide team was setting in motion a disastrous chain of events that would lead them far away from the wide trail left by Omar Ballard.

The next blunder in a wrongful conviction is often tunnel vision, which usually occurs just after the hunch. Police grab a suspect, convince themselves they've got the right guy, congratulate themselves for being so clever, then ignore conflicting evidence while embracing anything that will support their hunch. If they can verbally beat a confession out of their suspect, then their case is much stronger and they can avoid a lengthy investigation. Interrogation is often the lazy cop's way of solving a case. If evidence undermining their theory surfaces, they simply discount it. If clear evidence of innocence (DNA) is presented after their man is convicted, they refuse to believe it and stubbornly maintain his guilt.

Dan Williams entered the Norfolk police building around 6:30 on the evening of July 7, less than two hours after the body had been discovered and long before the crime scene work was finished. He had no idea he was a suspect. He was twenty-five years old, a high school graduate, a former Boy Scout who'd been raised by strict parents and taught to obey and respect those in authority. He was quiet, easy to lead, the last kid in class to start trouble. He had no criminal record and had never been subjected to a police interrogation. With his passive, unassuming personality, he was thoroughly unprepared for the ambush just around the corner.

The interrogation began at 8:00 P.M., and, not surprisingly, it was not recorded by audio or video. Cameras and recorders were close by, as in every police department, and they would be used when the time was right. But not yet; some parts of the interrogation should not be seen. Williams waived his Miranda rights, a careless mistake made by between 80 and 90 percent of all innocent people. Guilty criminals are far more likely to clam up or demand a lawyer.

Williams began answering preliminary questions from Detective Gray, while Detective Jack Horton took notes. No one else was in the room. Before long, Williams realized that the police suspected him, and he couldn't believe it. The detectives asked if he would voluntarily supply samples of his blood, pubic hair, and scalp hair, and hand over his underwear. Williams readily agreed. He had nothing to hide. He agreed to a polygraph test, another mistake. Innocent people often say yes to this test because they are eager to prove their innocence. They trust the police. Remarkably, the law allows the police to lie about the results of the polygraph test, which happens frequently. Indeed, the law allows the police to lie at will during interrogations of suspects. The polygraph ruse is a favorite.

At 9:45, Williams was strapped in and answered questions from the examiner. The questions centered on his activities of the day before, and whether he had been in the Bosko apartment recently. Williams answered truthfully and passed the polygraph test. As usual, though, he was told he had flunked the test, and the cops now had proof that he was lying. By midnight, both detectives were unloading accusations faster than Williams could deny them. The language deteriorated. Tempers erupted. Williams insisted he knew nothing about the murder, that he had been next door in bed with his wife when it happened. Gray lied and said they had a witness who had seen him in the Bosko apartment. The police insisted he was obsessed with Michelle and they had witnesses to prove it. Williams had been taught by his parents to respect the police, and he was stunned to have them throwing accusations at him. They really believed he did it! He became confused and found it hard to think clearly.

Williams's wife, Nicole, grew more and more concerned as the night wore on. She called the police station and tried to find out what was happening, what was wrong. When she couldn't get an answer, she went to the police station. Early in the interrogation,

Detective Gray stepped out of the room and talked to Nicole. She asked her what the couple had done the night before. The cops thought that perhaps Dan had sneaked out of their apartment during the night and pulled off the murder, but Nicole assured Gray that her husband had slept all night and never left. At that point, the police knew that Dan had a solid alibi. But it didn't matter.

At 12:30, Detective Gray left the room and Horton, talking man-to-man now, tried to induce Williams into admitting everything. *Just get it off your chest. Do it now because it will look better than if you wait six weeks for the DNA results to come back.* Williams held firm and said he was tired and wanted to go home. At 12:55, according to Horton's notes, Williams admitted that he thought Michelle was attractive. This led to a relentless barrage of insinuations that he was infatuated with her and wanted to have sex.

Finally, the interrogation was getting somewhere. Gray returned to the room and both detectives hammered away at Williams's "obsession" with the victim. They said they could prove he had been in the Bosko apartment the night before Michelle was murdered. Williams was confused, exhausted, and needed sleep. He continually laid his head on the table, and each time the detectives instructed him to lift it back up. Williams, punch-drunk and on the ropes, clung to the truth and denied knowing anything about the murder. The detectives began to question his memory, and suggested amnesia and blacking out. Maybe he'd been sleepwalking when he committed the crime.

This tactic is not unusual in protracted interrogations. Police often suggest amnesia, or blacking out, or sleepwalking, all ploys designed to put doubt in a suspect's mind. Then the police posture themselves as the good guys who are there to help straighten things out.

Finally, it worked. By 3:00 A.M., with the detectives still hammering away, Williams began to question his own memory. Maybe he had blacked out. Maybe he had been sleepwalking. The detectives pressed on, back and forth, with more suggestions following more accusations.

At 4:35, Horton left the room, and Gray began to appeal to Williams's conscience, another tactic. Did he feel any remorse? Michelle is no longer with us. Think of her family. And so on. This worked, too, because Williams suddenly broke down and cried.

At 4:51, the situation changed dramatically when Detective Glenn Ford entered the room. Ford was a veteran cop, a tough character, a hardened interrogator who'd mastered all the tricks. His tactics were harsh, brutal, relentless, and designed to crush the will of any suspect. He had a history of obtaining false confessions.

It was long past time for a confession from Dan Williams, and Glenn Ford was there to get one. With Horton watching and taking notes, Ford placed his chair directly in front of Williams and said he was ready for the truth. He knew Williams was lying and he could prove it. There were witnesses. He badgered Williams nonstop for an hour. He threatened him with a long prison sentence, but promised him leniency if he would come clean and confess. (Ford and Horton later denied this, under oath.) He poked him in the chest repeatedly and cursed him. (Also later denied.)

Williams was terrified and his ability to think clearly was long gone. After nine hours of this ordeal he was ready to crack. The police were convinced he was guilty, and the only way out of the room was to give them what they wanted. He had to cooperate to save himself.

Ford smelled victory, and when they took a break at 5:41 A.M., Ford told Horton, "He's ready to confess." Williams had been under interrogation for almost ten hours, but he was far from finished.

Years later, in prison, he tried to explain why he confessed. "I was confused, upset. I really didn't know right from wrong at that time. I was tired. I wasn't feeling well. I felt helpless and really couldn't take it anymore. So I told them what they wanted to hear. I just made up details. I knew what I was telling Detective Ford was not the truth, but I just wanted the questioning to end."

At 7:00 A.M., eleven hours into the interrogation, the detectives finally turned on the tape recorders. Williams, frightened, drained, and thoroughly confused, gave them what they wanted, and in doing so included many of the details they had suggested throughout the night. His muddled version of the attack also included elements that were obviously not true.

The (first) confession included these details: He had walked across the hall to Michelle's front door. He might have been sleepwalking. He was barefoot, though no bare footprints were found. She let him in. He attacked her. She was screaming, though no one heard screams. He did not ejaculate, though semen was found in the victim and on the blanket. When he left her, she was still screaming. He did not choke her, though the autopsy would reveal strangulation. He did not stab her, though the autopsy would reveal the three knife wounds, any one of which would have been fatal. There was no blood. He was alone, no one helped him. At first he didn't remember how he killed her, but then remembered maybe hitting her in the head with a shoe, though the autopsy revealed no such injuries. He could not describe the shoe.

Using the shoe was a nice touch. This particular murder weapon had been suggested hours earlier by Detective Gray, who later admitted, "We put a lot of these things in his head. He admitted to things that me and Jack (Detective Horton) basically made up."

At 7:15, the tape recorders were turned off and the detectives left the room. Williams was not allowed to leave, so he stretched out on the floor and went to sleep. Later, Gray peeked in on him. Williams was lying on the floor, laughing hysterically, detached from reality.

The interrogation was not over. In their haste, the police had gotten ahead of themselves and their fresh confession would need to be modified somewhat. With Williams still in the interrogation room, Detective Gray went to check on the autopsy of Michelle Bosko. She noticed some startling discrepancies between the findings of the medical examiner and Williams's confession, most notably the knife wounds and the strangulation. There were no head wounds. Even a moderately observant detective would have realized immediately that Williams had no idea what he was talking about.

The medical examiner would later testify that the autopsy results were consistent with the initial theory that the crime was committed by only one assailant.

At 9:25, Gray and Horton returned to the interrogation room, woke up Williams, who was still on the floor, and asked him to sign his written confession. He did and they left.

At 11:00 A.M., Detective Gray barged into the room in a fit of anger and began demanding the truth again. She informed Williams that she had just left the autopsy and described the knife wounds and the strangulation—a ploy known as "contaminating the witness," which is widely frowned upon. Why hadn't Williams told her about the choking and stabbing? Because Williams wasn't at the crime scene, but Gray would not be denied. She began again with the accusations and Williams finally surrendered. To get her to shut up and leave him alone, Williams started talking. In his second confession he stated that he had not used a shoe to kill Michelle but had in fact choked her and stabbed her in the chest, precisely where Gray had described the wounds.

Fifteen hours after he entered the interrogation room, Dan Williams finally got out. He was taken to jail and charged with capital rape and murder. The police had quickly solved the case. They knew they had their man, and everyone could finally get some sleep. Because the investigation was driven by interrogation and not evidence, the police failed to note that Williams had no scratches on his body, even though he voluntarily gave blood, hair samples, and submitted to a swab of his penis. More astute detectives would have determined that the blood and skin found under Michelle's fingernails were clear evidence of a struggle, and that her assailant would be marked in some manner.

News of the murder made the rounds in Norfolk, especially in the apartments near the naval base. It was followed quickly by the news that Dan Williams had confessed. Omar Ballard was shocked the police weren't looking for him. He was somewhat perplexed by the news but also relieved that the bloodhounds down at Norfolk P.D. had picked up the wrong scent. But Omar didn't exactly lie low. He was already looking for victim number three.

———

After his first night behind bars, Dan Williams woke up confused and not sure what he had actually done. When reality set in, he recanted the confession and began to repudiate it. His protests, though, went unheard.

When his court-appointed lawyers read his confession, they knew he was in serious trouble. Regardless of how it was obtained or how it conflicted with the physical evidence, it would likely be presented to a trial jury. Judges rarely suppress confessions, and jurors are quick to believe them. The brutal and overwhelming interrogation methods used by the police never make it to open court. The police simply deny them, and jurors do not believe that anyone, under any circumstances, would confess to a crime he or she did not commit.

The truth, however, is quite different. In almost 25 percent of DNA exonerations to date, false confessions were extracted by the authorities. In 1997, only six states required the police to record, either by audio or video, the *entire* interrogation. Virginia was not one of the six, though now, in the aftermath of the Bosko case, the Norfolk Police Department requires the recording of interrogations.

Williams's lawyers knew the confession would stand. They also knew that a death penalty was likely. They immediately began weighing the possibility of a plea agreement to save their client's life, but Williams would have none of it. He said repeatedly, to his lawyers and his parents and to anyone else who would listen, that he did not kill Michelle. He had been verbally abused by the police, beaten down, and coerced into signing a bogus confession.

The killer struck again ten days after the Bosko murder. Omar Ballard beat and raped a fourteen-year-old girl, who later identified him. He was arrested and eventually pled guilty. But this was of little interest to the homicide detectives. They had Michelle's killer and their investigation had practically shut down. The police were so indifferent that they failed to conduct a routine search of Williams's apartment. The results of the DNA tests would take weeks, maybe months, but there was no doubt in their minds that their solid police work would be proven correct.

In November, four months after the murder, the prosecutors offered Williams a deal. If he pled guilty to the rape and murder, the Commonwealth of Virginia would not pursue the death penalty. Williams would get a life sentence with no chance of parole. His lawyers leaned on him, but he maintained his innocence.

Also in November, Nicole Williams died of ovarian cancer. Dan was not permitted to attend his wife's funeral. She had not been interviewed by Dan's lawyers.

In December, five months after the murder, the crime lab finished the DNA testing of Williams's samples of blood, sperm, and other genetic material. The police and prosecutors were shocked— there was no match. Williams had been cleared, though neither he nor his lawyer were told of the test results until the following April. In January, though, while sitting on the crucial information, the prosecution offered Williams a plea bargain in which he would plead guilty in return for a life sentence. He refused.

In most jurisdictions, the police and prosecutors would acknowledge the obvious—they had the wrong man. But in Norfolk, they were unwilling to admit a mistake. They suddenly had new theories. The DNA results could be explained because: (1) Williams was involved but used a condom, or (2) Williams was involved but did not ejaculate, or (3) Williams had raped and stabbed Michelle but an accomplice left behind the sperm, and so on. The possibility that Williams wasn't present during the murder was rejected.

The goose chase resumed in earnest when the police settled on a new theory that revolved around an accomplice. The obvious suspect was a sailor named Joe Dick (#2). Dick rented an extra bedroom from Dan and Nicole Williams, and since he'd been that close to the murderer and the crime scene, then Dick had to be involved. On January 12, 1998, Dick walked off the USS *Saipan* to meet with the police. He had no idea he was a suspect, and had not the slightest clue that he was headed for prison.

Detective Ford was waiting, and Joe Dick had no chance.

Dick was introverted, withdrawn, easily manipulated, socially awkward, and quick to yield to authority figures. He was an odd young man with few friends. He was thoroughly ill-equipped to handle the confrontation awaiting him.

Around 10:10 A.M., Dick was placed in an interrogation room. Like Williams, he had no criminal record and had never been interrogated. He was extremely nervous. Ford and Detective Don Brenner entered and quickly convinced Dick to waive his Miranda rights, a terrible mistake that would lead to his conviction.

Within minutes, Ford was asking questions about Michelle Bosko, Dan Williams, and the murder, and Dick said he knew nothing more than he'd read in the paper or heard on the street. He claimed to have been on board his ship on the night of the murder. Ford claimed he had proof that Dick had not been on board; therefore he, Ford, knew Dick was lying. Before long, Ford was yelling and accusing Dick of being involved in the murder. Dick maintained his innocence. They went back and forth with accusations and denials. Ford said they had a confession from Dan Williams and implied that it implicated Dick. It did not. The Williams confession mentioned no accomplice. Ford said that the police had DNA evidence proving his guilt. (Detective Brenner would later admit that this was not true.) But, again, unchecked lying by the police is permitted during an interrogation.

Ford finally got around to the polygraph. Dick did not hesitate, though he was worried because he was so nervous and not thinking clearly. He passed the exam, but the game was rigged. Ford gravely informed Dick that he had flunked it, but refused to show Dick the results. Dick, naive enough to still trust the police, was stunned when he heard this. He began to question himself.

Ford followed the usual playbook: Fabricate and then exaggerate purported evidence; express absolute certainty in the suspect's guilt; refuse to take no for an answer; give the clear impression that the suspect will not leave the room until he confesses, regardless of how long it takes; dismiss outright any offering of an alibi; continually remind the suspect that he is in serious trouble; and suggest amnesia or blacking out or sleepwalking or dreaming or anything that will place doubt in the suspect's mind.

Then they used the good-cop-bad-cop routine. Around 2:30 P.M., Ford left the room, and Detective Brenner became downright friendly, imploring Dick to just tell us the truth, get it off your chest, clear your conscience, you'll feel better, think about Michelle's family, and so on. He assured Dick that they had all the evidence they needed, and now it was up to him to admit everything.

Dick proved easier to crack than Dan Williams, but then he was not as strong mentally or emotionally. After four hours of nonstop interrogation, Dick was completely overwhelmed. He gave up and began a tortuous effort to admit to a crime he knew nothing about. Years later, he tried to explain why: "I figured that he [Ford] would shut up if I told him anything he wanted to hear. I was tired and frustrated and just wanted him off my back. I just gave in because I knew DNA would clear me."

Since he did not know the facts surrounding his crime, Dick began by telling a story so preposterous the detectives didn't believe it. No problem—they suggested facts here and there, and even showed Dick a photo of Michelle at the crime scene. For three painful hours they crafted the story, then convinced Dick to adopt their version. Even with such skillful manipulation, Dick's confession was a bizarre account that varied wildly from the crime scene evidence and from the statements made by his now fellow rapist and murderer Dan Williams.

But Glenn Ford was pleased. He had once again nailed his defendant and solved the crime. It took only six hours of abusive interrogation tactics to break the second one. Joe Dick was jailed, charged with capital rape and murder, and held without bail.

After his arrest, his supervisor on the USS *Saipan,* Petty Officer Michael Ziegler, suspected that Dick had been railroaded by the police. He knew Dick well and knew it would not be difficult to coerce him into confessing to a crime he did not commit. Officer Ziegler checked the ship's records and determined that Dick had in fact been on the ship during the time Michelle was murdered. Officer Ziegler went to his commanding officer and was told to cooperate fully with the civilian authorities, the prosecutors, and the defense lawyers. He waited and waited, but no one contacted him to verify Dick's alibi. He later told *The New York Times* that he had "no doubt" Dick was on duty the night of the murder. The ship logs and attendance records were never reviewed by the police.

Joe Dick's parents hired a Norfolk lawyer, Mike Fasanaro, who obtained a copy of the confession and quickly concluded that his new client was guilty. He told the parents that, "without a doubt, Joe was involved in every aspect of the case." A few months earlier, Fasanaro had suffered through the dreadful experience of having a client executed by lethal injection, and that client was very much on his mind. He began to work on a plea agreement that would keep Joe Dick off death row.

Two months after Dick's confession, the state crime lab had more bad news for the police and prosecutors. Joe Dick's DNA did not match the blood, sperm, or other genetic material found at the crime scene.

The police and prosecutors suddenly had a new theory: Three men were involved! And the third guy was still out there.

By this time, Omar Ballard was in prison for his second known rape. A DNA test of his blood would have solved the crime, but Detective Ford and his crack team were too busy for that. Instead of looking at credible suspects, they were now determined to find #3, but they had no clue. The crime scene evidence was of no use because they chose to ignore it. Undaunted, Ford resorted to another dirty trick. He paid cash to a jailhouse snitch to rat on Joe Dick.

Lying snitches continue to plague the American criminal system because police and prosecutors continue to use them. In 25 percent of the DNA exonerations to date, jailhouse snitches were used at trial to obtain the wrongful conviction.

The snitch, who'd been placed in a cell with Dick, chatted with him long enough to hear of an acquaintance known only as Eric—no last name, yet. There was no suggestion at all that this Eric was in any way involved in the murder of Michelle Bosko, but such trivial matters were of little concern to the police. They had to find the third killer. The snitch passed along the name, and Glenn Ford was back in business. He tracked down a sailor by the name of Eric Wilson (#3) and asked him to stop by the police department to answer some questions. Eric knew Dan Williams and had heard rumors about the case. He figured it was his turn to stop by and tell what he knew, which was nothing new.

Eric Wilson had never been interrogated by the police and had nothing, not even a speeding ticket, on his record. He was raised in a small town in South Texas, in a strict Southern Baptist home, by parents who were very close. An average student, he'd joined the navy out of high school and was serious about his military service.

At 10:10 A.M., he was led to an interrogation room, where he would remain for the next nine hours. The interrogation by Detective Ford was his standard act: a quick disposing of the Miranda rights; routine questions that became more pointed, more suspicious; a polygraph exam, "flunked" of course, though in Wilson's case the results were inconclusive; then the heavy artillery. Eric was stunned when told he'd flunked the test, then shocked at Ford's behavior. He would testify later that Ford was "very aggressive, very threatening, very angry, very loud." Ford tapped him on the forehead with his fingers, stopping only when he accidentally poked him in the eye. Ford denies this. His sidekick, Detective Jason Trezevant, recalled it as "probably one of the most relaxed interviews I've been involved in in eighteen years."

And it probably was.

Ford cranked up the pressure, but Eric managed to hang on and deny any involvement. Ford claimed to have plenty of evidence, his usual assertion. He did not, however, divulge any of this evidence to the suspect. There was certainly no physical evidence, and Eric Wilson's name had not been mentioned in the absurd confessions of Dan Williams and Joe Dick. A paid snitch had delivered only the name of "Eric." Detective Ford had somehow connected the dots, and now young Eric Wilson was being pounded with accusations that he had raped and killed a pretty young woman he'd never met. Ford showed Eric before-and-after photos of Michelle.

Police interrogations are based on the presumption of guilt, and Ford was not about to accept any denials. After four hours, he stormed out of the room in disgust. Detective Trezevant took over as the good cop, and the two chatted about things other than why they were there. The conversation drifted, then Eric made the mistake of mentioning a dream he'd had. In the dream a young woman was in distress, something bad was happening to her, though he wasn't sure what it was. Eric couldn't identify the woman, so Trezevant helpfully picked up a photo of Michelle eating a pretzel and suggested that she was the woman in the dream. Eric said he thought so, perhaps.

The gates were now open. Ford was back in the room, chasing the dream. He wanted details—who was in the dream, what was happening to Michelle, where did it take place, and on and on. Eric tried to fill in the blanks, and when he couldn't he got plenty of help from the detectives. Slowly, after several hours, the dream took shape. Eric, Dan Williams, and Joe Dick were attacking Michelle in her apartment, holding her down and raping her. At one point, Ford got tired of all the dreaming and demanded that Eric cut the dream shit and tell them what really happened. Eric was horrified by the thought that maybe he had not been dreaming. Maybe he had really been there, and if so then everything would make sense—the polygraph test, the evidence the police said they had, the constant assertions by Ford and his certainty of Eric's involvement. Confused, frightened, and with his resistance finally broken, he confessed to the rape but not the murder.

Later, Eric would say: "Eventually, it just grates on you. And you finally say, 'Well, these guys are supposed to be the good guys. Maybe they're right. Maybe I did do it. Maybe there's something wrong with me, so that I don't remember doing it.' And at that point you just start to tell them what they want to hear. I would have done anything—anything at all—to get Detective Ford out of my face."

He was placed in a small cell at the police station, and there, alone and frightened, the reality of what he'd just done began to settle in.

Two months later, the state crime lab reported that Eric's DNA did not match the blood, sperm, and other genetic material found at the crime scene.

The police suddenly had a new theory: There were *four* men in the gang! With no hesitation, the detectives scrambled to find the fourth suspect. Again, instead of relying on the physical evidence, they chose to interrogate one of the first three. Since Joe Dick was the most vulnerable, and since his lawyer was the most anxious to cut a deal, Glenn Ford went after Dick. Under intense pressure to save his "deal," and thus his life, Dick finally admitted that three more men had been involved in the attack, for a total of six. He didn't know the other three names, but was sure that one was a George. The fact that Dick didn't know the names of the members of a gang that somehow got itself organized enough to rape and kill a young woman should have been a red flag, but the police were too desperate to slow down. By this time, the young sailor had convinced himself that he was guilty and was willing to say anything.

Somehow, in the frantic world of Glenn Ford's investigation, George morphed into a former sailor named Derek Tice (#4). Tice had been honorably discharged from the navy, left Norfolk, and was living in Florida. His only connection to the Bosko case was through the muddled mind of Joe Dick. He was snatched by yet another heroic SWAT team, charged with rape and murder, and extradited to Virginia. By the time he arrived in Norfolk to have a chat with Detective Ford, he was a nervous wreck.

His questioning began at 2:15 P.M., according to notes taken by Detective Don Brenner. Glenn Ford went through the preliminaries and had Tice sign away his Miranda rights as if they were of little consequence. A few more questions, then Ford asked Tice to tell them everything he knew about the rape and murder of Michelle Bosko. Tice said he knew only what he'd heard, and that he'd been surprised when Dan Williams (#1) had been arrested. Ford suddenly jumped to his feet, knocked over his chair, and began yelling at Tice to stop his lying. Tice, stunned and afraid he might get hit, repeated his story. Ford accused him of lying. Ford then lied himself when he said: (1) that the other three defendants planned to testify against Tice and even claim that the attack had been his idea; (2) that the police had evidence linking Tice to the crime; and (3) that there was a secret witness who would come forward and place Tice at the scene.

Years later, Ford admitted that he might have raised his voice. He also denied that he threatened Tice with death by lethal injection, but Tice recalled things differently. He later said: "Every time that I would say I wasn't there and everything, he would call me a liar and tell me that I was there, that he knew I was there, and that if I kept telling lies I would go to trial and get the needle. Ford said, 'You're going to die. You're going to get the needle. We're going to make sure of it.'"

Hours passed as the grueling interrogation went on and on. Derek Tice began to wonder if everyone was conspiring against him. Dan Williams, Joe Dick, Eric Wilson, the police, the secret witnesses. He began to doubt himself, and began to lose his sense of reality. Nothing was clear anymore. And Ford was hammering away.

Five hours passed, and Tice still denied any involvement. Though he was exhausted, he had no way of knowing that Ford was willing to go much longer, until there was a confession.

At 4:00 P.M., Tice was taken to the fateful polygraph room, wired to the machine, and questioned by Detective Will Sayre, the "expert" at Norfolk P.D. Sayre had also tested defendants Williams, Dick, and Wilson. Without Ford and Brenner present, Sayre performed the exam, and at 5:30 informed Tice that he had flunked it. The polygraph clearly showed that he had been in the Bosko apartment and had taken part in the rape and murder.

According to Tice, Sayre assured him he would get the needle, and that he, Sayre, would be there to watch the execution. (This was later denied by Sayre.)

Sayre went on to say he knew that Ford could be a "little overbearing," and that if Tice wanted to confess, he, Sayre, would be more than willing to take his statement.

At that point, Tice invoked his right of silence. He said to Sayre that he wanted to get a lawyer, and Sayre said that it might be advisable. According to Sayre's notes, Tice said he was not saying anything else until he talked to a lawyer.

For some reason, the business about the lawyer was ignored. At 7:30 P.M., Tice was taken back to the interrogation room. Ford and Brenner walked in and the browbeating began anew. Accusations, denials, threats. Lots of yelling and cursing. Ford had a photo of Michelle. He shoved it in Tice's face and asked him how it would feel if that had been his daughter (Tice had a four-year-old). Tice thought of her, and how traumatic it would be if her father were executed. He started crying. After ten hours, he'd finally cracked.

Years later, he remembered it this way: "Scared, alone, sick to my stomach. I had a headache, thought Ford was telling the truth about all three of them going to testify against me, thought the polygraph could be used as evidence. I was afraid Ford was going to hit me if I didn't make a statement. I wanted out of that room by hook or crook, felt trapped and that the only way out was to make a false statement . . . Now, I just feel stupid."

Tice's confession began with the basic facts, as fed to him by Ford during the early hours of the interrogation. Ford insisted that there were others, more than just four, who were involved, and demanded names from Tice. He mentioned a friend, Geoffrey Farris (#5), but Ford claimed the police already knew about Farris. Who else? Pulling names from the air in much the same fashion as he was pulling facts, Tice mentioned another friend, Rick Pauley (#6).

Like the other three false confessions, Tice's was riddled with inconsistencies. One of the more glaring was his description of the use of a claw hammer to gain entry into the Bosko apartment. No such entry marks had been found, and Ford knew it. Tice also said he ejaculated during the rape.

At 1:30 A.M., fifteen hours after the interrogation began, Derek Tice signed his confession and was taken to jail. Three days later, the local newspaper reported that Williams, Dick, Wilson, and Tice had knocked on Michelle's door, then stabbed and strangled her after a gang rape. Prosecutors said it was one of the saddest cases they'd ever seen.

Ford would later deny that he had "coached" Tice during the confession.

In the Norfolk jail, Tice was placed in the same unit as Omar Ballard, a man he'd never met. In the coming months, the ever-changing theories of guilt would include yet another new one: Tice and Ballard, along with six others, had formed an impromptu gang, primarily of strangers, that got itself organized only long enough to pull off the rape and murder.

Rick Pauley was a former sailor who lived with his parents in Norfolk. He was arrested soon after Tice's confession and taken to an interrogation room. There, Detectives Bobby Backman and Don Brenner repeatedly accused him of the crimes, refused to believe his denials, lied about evidence linking him to the scene, threatened him with death if he didn't cooperate, promised him leniency if he did, announced that he'd flunked his polygraph exam, and ignored his right of silence after he demanded an attorney. After five hours, Pauley was on the verge of cracking and telling the police anything, just to end the interrogation. He later told his mother that they'd almost convinced him he was guilty.

But Pauley refused to confess, and the police eventually gave up. He was lucky, because Glenn Ford was on vacation. His lawyer speculated that if Ford had been on duty, then Pauley would have confessed.

Though he did not, and there was no evidence placing him at the scene, Pauley was charged with capital murder and rape, and thrown in the Norfolk jail where he would spend the next ten months.

The police then rounded up Geoffrey Farris, another former

sailor who lived in the area. Farris was not under arrest when he entered the interrogation room, but that would soon change. Glenn Ford, back from vacation, went through the preliminaries, which of course meant breezing through the Miranda rights. After two hours of accusations, and the obligatory failed polygraph exam, Farris demanded an attorney and stopped talking. Ford told him he was under arrest for the rape and murder, and Farris went to jail where he would stay for the next ten months.

In late August 1998, the state crime lab delivered more bad news to the police and prosecutors. The DNA recovered from the crime scene did not match that of Derek Tice, Rick Pauley, and Geoffrey Farris. Six men in jail, all cleared by DNA.

The Norfolk police suddenly had a new theory: There had been *seven* men in the gang! And the seventh killer was still at large.

Since Derek Tice had been the source of the last two random names—Rick Pauley and Geoffrey Farris—it seemed logical that he might have another up his sleeve. Good police work dictated that Tice be squeezed again.

And it worked. On October 27, during another marathon work-out at the hands of Glenn Ford, Tice coughed up the name of John Danser (#7), and the Keystone Kops took off once again in search of their elusive sperm supplier.

John Danser was a former sailor who knew Williams (#1) and Tice (#4), but none of the others. He had served in the military police and was not easily intimidated. He was arrested at his home north of Philadelphia and extradited back to Norfolk. He was interrogated by Ford, who went through his usual routine. Danser agreed to a polygraph, and when he was told he flunked it he asked for a lawyer. But the interrogation continued. At one point, Ford showed Danser a photo of Michelle at the crime scene and asked if that was the way he remembered her after he'd raped and stabbed her. Danser stuck to his denials. He had an airtight alibi—he'd been at home in Pennsylvania at the time of the murder—and he refused to yield an inch. Ford claimed to have proof that Danser had been in Norfolk at the time of the crime, but, as always, he did not indicate the nature of this evidence. Ford finally gave up and Danser was thrown in jail and charged with rape and murder.

Two months later, he was eliminated as a source of the DNA found at the crime scene.

February 1999. The Norfolk authorities had the seven sailors in jail, and not one shred of physical evidence with which to convict them. This, however, did not deter the prosecutors. They had four bogus confessions and they were determined to use them.

One month earlier, Dan Williams (#1) had finally succumbed to the pressure and agreed to plead guilty in return for two life sentences with no parole. He had repeatedly turned down similar offers, but finally gave in on the eve of his death penalty trial. His alibi witness, Nicole, was dead. His lawyers had conducted no investigation, and they were convinced he would get the needle because no jury would believe his false confession claim. His deal would spare his life, and he felt he had no choice.

Joe Dick (#2) had also agreed to a similar plea bargain. Eric Wilson (#3) refused and continued to recant his confession. He insisted on going to trial. Derek Tice (#4) was also having second thoughts, but eventually refused to plead guilty.

Before the police could hatch a new theory and start looking for Number 8, Omar Ballard finally entered the picture, and things changed, somewhat. From prison, he wrote a letter to a friend and confessed to killing Michelle. The letter was given to the police, who gave it to the prosecutors, who tried to keep it quiet. They eventually gave it to the defense attorneys, but only after a court ordered them to do so.

A quick DNA test nailed Ballard. The police finally had a match! Glenn Ford hustled off to prison to interview his latest suspect. It would be a short interrogation by Ford's standards. No threats, no bogus polygraph test, none of the usual tactics. Ballard admitted everything within minutes. He committed the crime, did it alone, and felt remorse. He described the crime scene and the apartment in detail, and was the first and only confessor to accurately describe the murder weapon, the serrated steak knife. Ford suggested that others were involved, but Ballard said no. Ford pressed this repeatedly, and Ballard grew angry at Ford's tactics. He insisted that he acted alone, but Ford didn't believe him. At the end of the taped statement, Ford asked Ballard if he wanted to add anything. He said: "No, just them four people that opened their mouths is stupid."

In an affidavit signed later, Ballard said: "Ford asked me a series of leading questions in an attempt to get the version of the crime he wanted. For example, Ford would tell me some detail about the killing of Michelle then ask me a question, encouraging me to use the detail he had just provided in my answer. I repeatedly told Ford that I committed the crime alone, but Ford wanted me to say that the other defendants had been involved." Ballard later told a television producer, "Detective Ford is scum. He puts words in people's mouths and won't stop until you agree. And that's what those four white guys are guilty of, 'agreeing.'"

Rather than step back and admit the obvious, rather than reexamining their case and exploring the possibility that perhaps they'd been wrong, the police and prosecutors marched on. They had far too much invested in their fraudulent investigation.

They had a new theory. There were now eight men involved in the crime, with Omar as the leader. Never mind that none of the first four confessions mentioned a gang of eight or the presence of a black man, and never mind that the fifth confession, Omar's, expressly denied the involvement of others.

The Eight Man Gang theory went something like this: Seven white sailors were having a party at Dan's apartment, even though his wife, Nicole, had just returned from the hospital after cancer surgery. They decided to go next door and rape Michelle, since Billy was at sea. She wouldn't open the door. They hung around outside in the parking lot when Omar Ballard appeared. They did not know him, but they nevertheless told him of their plan to gang-rape Michelle. Omar said he could get the door open because he knew Michelle. They followed Omar inside once he convinced Michelle to open the door. They took turns raping her, though it's unclear in what order. Ballard was the only one who ejaculated. They took turns stabbing her, though it's unclear who went first or last. The attack may have happened in the den, or maybe in the bedroom. Such a wild scene in the tiny apartment surely caused a mess, but the gang was thoughtful enough to tidy up behind itself and, of course, wipe away every single fingerprint.

To believe this ridiculous scenario, one also has to believe a long list of other insane notions, such as: Joe Dick (#2) managed to dodge security on the USS *Saipan,* sprint to the apartment, join up with the others, some of whom he'd never met, commit the crime, then sprint back to the ship, dodging security again; that John Danser (#7) made the seven-hour drive from his home in Pennsylvania in five hours, joined the gang, only two of whom he'd ever met, committed the crime, then raced back home; that Geoffrey Farris (#5), who had records to prove he was on the phone with his girlfriend in Australia when the murder took place, actually put down the phone, ran from his home in Norfolk, joined the gang, then raced back to finish the conversation with his girlfriend; and, that the various attackers who stabbed Michelle managed to inflict near-identical wounds of the same depth. Perhaps the most fantastic part of this tale is that a savvy street thug like Omar Ballard would commit such a heinous crime with a bunch of white boys he'd never met.

Not surprisingly, the Eight Man Gang theory collapsed under the weight of its own lunacy. Derek Tice (#4) recanted and wouldn't testify against the three men he'd named, so the prosecutors were forced to drop the charges against Geoffrey Farris (#5), Rick Pauley (#6), and John Danser (#7). They walked out after spending months in a tough jail. There were no apologies, no compensation, no explanations, nothing. And they were the lucky ones.

Dan Williams (#1) tried to withdraw his guilty plea in light of Ballard's admissions, but the judge refused. Joe Dick (#2) had convinced himself he was guilty and even wrote a letter of apology to Michelle's family. Eric Wilson (#3) went to trial and was found guilty of rape. His confession was read to the jury and sunk him. He served seven and a half years in prison and was released in 2005. Derek Tice (#4) was convicted in two separate trials and given life without parole. In the Wilson and Tice trials, Joe Dick testified for the prosecution, but was not believable. The juries, however, were riveted by the taped confessions.

Williams, Dick, and Tice were sentenced to life without parole. Remarkably, in a jurisdiction where the death penalty is frequently used, Omar Ballard was offered a deal that would keep him off death row. A hardened criminal with a violent record, the self-confessed murderer of Michelle Bosko. In any other setting, the authorities would have been itching for a sensational trial. Why was Ballard given a break? The only plausible explanation is that the police and prosecutors were afraid of a full-blown capital murder trial in which Ballard's lawyers would be allowed to ask the jurors the obvious question: *How can you convict this man when four others have confessed to the crime?* Such a trial was far too risky for the police and prosecutors. They quickly cut a deal with Ballard and sent him off to prison for life.

The final outcome of the Bosko case was determined not by the truth, but by lies. So many lies were told by so many people, at so many levels, in so many ways, and for so many reasons, that the truth became irrelevant. But the hard facts gleaned from the crime scene never changed, though they were willfully ignored by the police and prosecutors. There was one assailant, one DNA match. Omar Ballard, by his own admission, acted alone.

———

In 2004, Peter Neufeld, the cofounder of the Innocence Project in New York, was asked to take a look at the wrongful convictions of the Norfolk Four. Neufeld knew of the case; it was legendary in the growing circles of innocence work. He knew of no other case in the country where DNA had excluded so many defendants who were still prosecuted. In the vast majority of cases where DNA excludes a defendant, prosecutors do what should be done. They admit they have the wrong suspect. "DNA trumps the confession," Neufeld said. "The way the prosecutors and police conducted themselves in the Bosko case is so off-the-wall, so unconscionable, and unfathomable, that there really is no precedent for it."

But the case was too big for the Innocence Project. Neufeld turned to a noted capital defense lawyer named George Kendall and asked for help. Kendall was at first skeptical because of all the confessions, but after some research became intrigued by the case. He signed on and convinced three mega law firms to join forces. His firm, Holland & Knight, assumed the representation of Joe Dick. Skadden Arps, with a thousand lawyers and a commitment to pro bono work, agreed to represent Dan Williams. Don Salzman, a lawyer with a passion for pro bono innocence work, took the case. At Hogan & Hartson, Des Hogan signed on to represent Derek Tice. Eric Wilson's lawyer, Greg McCormack, had filed a clemency petition and continued to represent him well.

The firms decided to work together to pursue absolute pardons from the governor of Virginia. They sought out the best experts in the country and asked them to work thoroughly and independently. Highly skilled and objective authorities on crime scene analysis, DNA testing, interrogations, false confessions, and violent crime were consulted and put to work. The three law firms were deep off the bench and threw their considerable talent and resources into the project.

With each expert, the opinion was the same: Omar Ballard acted alone, and the confessions of the Norfolk Four were coerced and unreliable. The four sailors had nothing to do with the crime.

The lawyers assembled an incredible cast of supporters. Four former attorneys general of Virginia, three Democrats and a Republican, urged the governor to fully pardon the four sailors, as did fifteen former judges and prosecutors. Thirteen jurors from the Wilson and Tice trials signed affidavits in which they admitted they had been wrong. They felt as though they had been misled during the trials when they weren't told of Ballard's history of sexual assaults or Detective Ford's history of coercing false confessions. On January 6, 2006, *The Virginian-Pilot,* the largest newspaper in the Norfolk area, editorialized: "If prosecutors or police can provide one piece of solid evidence implicating any of the convicted four, other than their confessions, then the convictions should stand. If not, [the governor] should free them."

Editorials in both *The New York Times* and *The Washington Post* called for pardons.

At the request of the lawyers for the Norfolk Four, twenty-six former special agents of the FBI thoroughly reviewed the case and reached the same conclusion: Ballard acted alone and the four confessions were bogus. FBI agents rarely comment on such cases, and it's even more unusual when they agree that someone has been wrongfully convicted. In this case, the agents were so convinced that they went public. On November 10, 2008, at a press conference in Richmond, Jay Cochran, a former assistant director of the agency, said: "After careful review of evidence, we have arrived at one unequivocal conclusion: the Norfolk Four are innocent. We believe a tragic mistake has occurred in the case of these four navy men, and we are calling on Governor Tim Kaine to grant them immediate pardons."

On August 6, 2009, Governor Kaine granted *conditional pardons* to Dan Williams, Joe Dick, and Derek Tice. Since Eric Wilson had been released four years earlier, no such pardon was necessary, at least in Kaine's opinion. He basically commuted their sentences to time served. After more than a decade in prison, the men were released, though they were still considered felons and sex offenders.

The half-pardons were bittersweet for the men and their supporters. Absolute pardons would repudiate the prosecutions, void the convictions, and show the rare courage of admitting that the legal and judicial systems of Virginia failed the sailors. Absolute pardons would declare them officially innocent and allow them to begin their new lives with a clean slate.

———

Justice slowly emerged from unexpected quarters. In 2010, Detective Glenn Ford was convicted of federal extortion charges and sentenced to twelve years in prison. Ford's scam was both crude and brilliant. He preyed on drug dealers facing long sentences with promises of having considerable clout with the government. For $1,000 or so in cash, he promised to quietly lean on the prosecutors and inform them that leniency was in order because the drug dealer had given valuable assistance to Ford in other cases. However, if the defendant refused to pay the bribe, Ford promised to make things worse. It was nothing less than hardball extortion.

During his trial, the prosecutor proved that Ford's racket had worked for over fifteen years. Thus, while serving as Norfolk's top homicide detective and responsible for numerous false confessions and wrongful convictions, he also netted at least $80,000 in cash.

Ford had other problems. Over the years, as the Norfolk Four case became well known, other victims and their lawyers came forth.

———

The defense teams were frustrated with the conditional pardons but even more determined to exonerate and clear their clients. They filed motions by the truckload as their investigators dug for new evidence.

In 2016, U.S. District Court Judge John A. Gibney vacated the convictions of Dan Williams and Joe Dick and exonerated them. In a rather pointed opinion, Judge Gibney said, "By any measure, the evidence showed that Danial Williams and Joseph Dick did not commit the rape and murder to which they each pleaded guilty, and no sane human being could convict them by the available evidence."

In February 2017, the lawyers for the four filed petitions seeking absolute pardons. One month later, Governor Terry McAuliffe granted the pardons. In doing so, a spokesman for him said, "These pardons close the final chapter on a grave injustice that has plagued these four innocent men for nearly twenty years."

Their criminal records were forgotten and their names were removed from the registers of felons and sex offenders. They were declared *Innocent!*

The Four, though, had one more chapter in mind. With their impressive legal teams, they threatened civil lawsuits against the City of Norfolk and the Commonwealth of Virginia. Neither entity had any desire to go near a courtroom. In December 2018, both settled for a combined $8.4 million.

———

It is twenty-five years after the murder.

Danial Williams lives in central Michigan, near his hometown. When his wife, Nicole, died he was in a Norfolk jail charged with rape and murder. He has never remarried, has no children, and is building a new home for himself. Twelve years of his life were wasted in various Virginia jails and prisons. His greatest anger is aimed at the police and their shameful treatment of the Four.

He says, "These were people I was taught to respect."

He hates to hear the name Glenn Ford and says only, "I wish he'd served a lot more time in prison."

Joe Dick lives near his parents in Maryland. He has tried several jobs and struggles to keep one. He is scarred by what happened and plagued by traumatic stress. Over the years he has sought treatment from a number of therapists, with limited improvement. Of the four men, he has suffered the most. He was the easiest for Glenn Ford to crack. The first to plead guilty. The first to testify against the others. Joe was an easy target in prison and is still haunted by its memories.

Eric Wilson lives in a small town in Texas with his wife and family. He served seven and a half years in prison and tries to live each day without thoughts of what happened. It is impossible. The nightmare is triggered in many ways: the sight of a police car; a television show in which the cops kick in a door, or a prosecutor harangues a witness; the suspicious look from a neighbor he's known for years. He thinks of the years lost in prison and the naval career he once dreamed of. He relishes the conviction and prison sentence of Glenn Ford, but the mere thought of his name evokes the same emotion: hatred.

Derek Tice lives in a small town in North Carolina with his wife and family. He served eleven years, two months, and one day for no reason. He has a good job and is at peace with the world, but has accepted the fact that what happened in Norfolk can never be forgotten. He says, "Twenty years from now I know I'll still have flashbacks."

————

And Omar Ballard has been in prison for twenty-five years with no chance of parole; not that he dreams of getting out. In various interviews over the years, he has repeatedly taken full, sole responsibility for the rape and murder of Michelle Bosko. He acted alone and has declared numerous times that the Norfolk Four are innocent.

GUILTY UNTIL PROVEN INNOCENT

JIM McCLOSKEY

C larence Lee Brandley had run out of options.

Even though he had the best of lawyers, including Houston's celebrated criminal defense lawyer Percy Foreman, he had exhausted his appeals. All of them had been denied, up and down the Texas state judicial line. There was no place to go. For the last six and a half years, he and his dedicated attorneys had suffered through two capital trials and a two-day evidentiary hearing at the courthouse in Conroe. They had presented evidence of what they believed was proof positive, not only of his innocence but also of the racism, corruption, and shenanigans in the courthouse that had put him on Texas's death row.

But now, time was up. This day, February 6, 1987, Judge Lynn Coker would set a date for Clarence's execution.

As the judge took the bench, Clarence sat in chains at the defense table next to his lead attorney, Foreman's legal partner Mike DeGeurin, and his young associate Paul Nugent. As always, Clarence remained outwardly stoic. His demeanor betrayed none of the turmoil and fear roiling inside him. He refused to give his adversaries the satisfaction of seeing him scared. But he knew that this was the end of the line. His elderly mother, Minnie Ola, sat quietly behind him, sobbing. Among observers in the courtroom were Judge Coker's teenage son, there to see his father in action, and the few blacks allowed in by the sheriff's deputy. Most blacks had been refused entry.

Judge Coker asked Clarence if he had anything to say before he set the date. Clarence looked straight at the judge, paused for what seemed like an eternity, and replied in a clear, deliberate voice, "Your Honor, I'm innocent." In response, Coker announced in a flat, matter-of-fact tone, as if he were reading a weather report, that Clarence would be put to death on March 26, 1987.

The hearing had taken all of two minutes. Immediately afterward, Clarence was led out of the courtroom, still in chains, and transported back to death row at the Texas State Penitentiary at Huntsville, thirty miles north on Interstate 45, an imposing fortresslike brick structure completed in 1849 as the first prison in Texas. Here he would await his fate, now just six weeks away.

The city of Conroe is the seat of Montgomery County in South Texas. In the 1980s it was a small town, with around 18,000 inhabitants, and a microcosm of the South's worst racism. Blacks were confined to a neglected pocket of land, a mostly impoverished community consisting of nondescript small houses and flimsy shacks in an area called Dugan, originally settled by freed slaves. The community was small in number and submissive in attitude. They had to be. White men ran things in Conroe, a town with a horrific history of brutal violence toward black men falsely accused of sexually assaulting white women.

Everyone in Dugan knew about Bob White, a black man, who stood wrongfully accused of raping a white woman in her home when her husband was away. While White sat at the defense table in a crowded Conroe courtroom on June 11, 1941, the husband calmly walked up and shot him dead in the back of the head with a .38 caliber pistol. One week later the husband stood trial for White's murder. At the urging of the DA, the jury acquitted him in less than two minutes. Dugan residents also knew what happened to Joe Winters in front of the old Conroe courthouse on May 20, 1922. Winters had been falsely accused of raping a white fourteen-year-old girl who cried "rape" when a passerby spotted her and Winters together. Chained to an iron post and splashed all over with kerosene, he was burned alive in front of the townspeople with sheriff's deputies looking on. Brandley's own grandfather, Dennis "Putt" Brandley, was shot dead in broad daylight for no reason at all by the town bully. As Putt lay groaning on the ground from the first shot, the townspeople watched as the man pumped two more bullets into his body to finish him off. The shooter was never even arrested.

Growing up in Conroe in the 1950s and 1960s, Clarence experienced life in the segregated South. At the Crighton Theatre downtown, all blacks were required to sit in the balcony while watching a movie. On the rare occasions when Clarence's dad could splurge and buy food for his family from a "whites only" restaurant, he would have to order at the kitchen door behind the restaurant and wait outside until it was ready.

———

Brandley's own nightmare in Conroe began on Saturday morning, August 23, 1980, when a regional women's high school volleyball tournament was held at Conroe High School, where he worked as a janitor. That morning, a little after 9:00 A.M., the girls' team from Bellville, about an hour's drive away, had arrived. Cheryl Dee Fergeson, a pretty sixteen-year-old with blond hair and blue eyes, was the team's manager. Her mother had died of cancer a year before, so she lived alone with her father on a ranch outside of Bellville. She and her boyfriend, Frank Rodriguez, planned to marry when they graduated. At 9:15 or so, Fergeson wandered off looking for a restroom. According to the initial accounts of three white school janitors, she was last seen heading up a stairway onto a landing and entering a girls' restroom. At the time, the janitors said, they'd been standing at the foot of the steps waiting for their supervisor, Clarence Brandley, to arrive and issue them new instructions. They had just finished setting up tables and chairs in the nearby cafeteria.

When Fergeson failed to return to the gym, her team became concerned, and started to look for her. The tournament was suspended at 10:40 and everyone joined in the search. An hour later, Brandley and another janitor, Henry "Icky" Peace, found her body in a storage loft above the stage in the school auditorium, hidden underneath plywood boards. She was lying on a yellow gymnastic mat on her back, completely nude except for white tube socks. The double doors that led to the stage were only a few paces from the restroom. Someone had carried her from the restroom through these doors to the stage, and then up a flight of stairs to the loft, where they deposited her body. Her clothes were found two days later by police in a trash bag in the school's dumpster.

An autopsy was performed the next day. Harris County medical examiner Joseph Jachimczyk determined that Cheryl had been raped and killed by ligature strangulation—by something wrapped around her neck. There was a mark on the front of her neck four and a half inches long and one and a quarter-inch wide. Her fingernails were clean and unbroken and her triceps were bruised, suggesting that she'd been tightly held by one assailant while the other forcibly removed her clothes. Vaginal swabs revealed the presence of semen, but Jachimczyk failed to test it for blood type. After thirty days, he later testified, he threw the swabs out when no one from Conroe asked for them. At the time, DNA technology had not yet been developed, but it was possible to scientifically determine blood type not only from blood but also from bodily fluids such as sweat and semen. Thus, any credible lab could have analyzed the swabs for blood type and compared the result to any suspects—if the swabs had not been thrown away.

Police immediately considered Clarence and Icky suspects because they had found the body, which begged the question: Why would they have led the police to the body after taking pains to hide it? Besides that, it would have been almost impossible for Icky to physically overpower and subdue Fergeson. He was 4'10", very fat, and wore thick glasses. Nevertheless, later that day both were taken downtown to the police station for statements, then to the hospital for blood and hair specimens. When they were dropped off back at the high school by a Conroe police officer, he said to them, "One of you two is gonna hang for this."

Then he turned to Clarence and said, "Since you're the nigger, you're elected."

———

One of ten children, Clarence Brandley had grown up in Dugan, graduating from Booker T. Washington High School before being drafted into the army. Once out of the service he had married twice and had five children. For the first time since the army, he'd gotten a steady job as a janitor at Conroe High, where after a few months he was promoted to janitorial supervisor. Things were starting to look up as he began to settle down.

Now everything was about to change. Clarence sensed immediately that he was to be the focus of this investigation. None of the three janitors who saw Cheryl go into the bathroom was asked to give hair and blood samples. Only Clarence was fingerprinted. On Monday he and Icky were polygraphed in Houston. Both were told that they'd passed. But Clarence knew things weren't right. He was twenty-eight, old enough to know all about the racism that motivated both local law enforcement and white, bigoted, and ignorant civilians to go after innocent black men. And it was obvious that the investigators needed to find a killer, fast. School was to start in another week. Hysterical parents, fearing for the safety of their children, flooded the school and the police with calls threatening to keep their kids out of school until the killer was arrested.

The county prosecutor, Jim Keeshan, was not happy with the pace of the police investigation. He couldn't believe that the chief of detectives, Monty Koerner, had given his men Sunday off, the day after the killing. Keeshan was forty and had been DA for five years. He was the man in charge of law and order in the county and decided it was time to bring in the Texas Rangers to run the investigation. On Thursday night, August 28, fifty-five-year-old Texas Ranger John Wesley Styles arrived in Conroe. Because it was his job to assist local law enforcement in three counties, including Montgomery, he was no stranger to Conroe police and prosecutors. They were happy to have him on board. The long-standing Texas Ranger motto is "One riot, one Ranger." A Ranger could make things happen when others could not.

———

Styles had joined the Rangers eleven years earlier, in 1969, after eighteen years as sheriff of Baylor County in North Texas near the Oklahoma border. On Friday morning he reported to Keeshan, attired as always in a large white Stetson hat and big leather boots, a Colt .45 on his hip. He was a heavyset white man, more than six feet tall with a belly that hung well over his Ranger belt. Coupled with his size, his deep authoritative voice made him an intimidating presence when interviewing witnesses.

Styles spent the day in discussions with Keeshan and his colleagues. Around 4:00 P.M. he left their offices and went to Conroe High with several Conroe police officers. Here, before he'd even opened his investigation, he called Clarence into the principal's office and arrested him for the capital murder of Fergeson. The next day's *Conroe Courier* page-one headline blared in large black letters, SCHOOL JANITOR CHARGED WITH MURDER. With it was a full-length frontal photo of Clarence being escorted into the courthouse by a police officer with hands cuffed behind his back, a somber look on his face. No doubt this calmed the nerves of Conroe's citizens, especially the parents of students.

Now Styles needed to find evidence to back up his arrest. On Saturday morning, August 30, one week after the murder, he called a meeting of the police investigative team with janitors John Sessum, Gary Acreman, and Sam Martinez at Conroe High for a "walk-through" of what had happened the day of Fergeson's murder. Intimidated and confused, the three nervous janitors were helped along by Styles and the other lawmen to come up with an account of the day's events that would eventually put Clarence Brandley on death row. Once the walk-through was finished, the three men agreed to statements prepared by the police. These were typed up for them to sign several days later. The finished witness statements mirrored one another and became the basis for the men's trial testimony three months later. The story they presented at trial went like this:

All three began the day shortly before 8:00 A.M. As instructed by Clarence, their first job was to set up the cafeteria chairs and tables. This took about one and a half hours and was finished by 9:30. A few minutes later, while waiting for Clarence to return and give them their next assignment, a young white female with blond hair walked up a set of stairs nearby and went into the women's restroom. The janitors were very close to these stairs. Martinez said the girl wore a pair of blue jeans with a wide leather belt that had some kind of carving, maybe a name, on it.

No sooner had she entered the ladies' room, their story went, than Clarence appeared right behind her, carrying several rolls of toilet paper. As Clarence was walking up the stairs toward the rest-room landing, Acreman told him that a girl was in the restroom. Clarence replied that he had no intention of going into the ladies' room. Clarence then told the men to go across the street to the voca-tional building for their next assignment and wait for him there. On the way over they ran into Icky Peace, who joined them in front of the building, waiting for Clarence to come over and unlock the door so they could set up chairs and tables there.

According to their statements, about forty-five minutes later, close to 10:30, Clarence emerged from the main building and motioned for Icky to come and get the keys so the men could do their work and go home. About an hour later, at 11:30 or so, Clar-ence arrived at the vocational building, inspected the work they had done, and told Acreman, Sessum, and Martinez they could go home, which they did. He and Icky returned to the main build-ing. Both Acreman and Sessum commented in their sworn witness statements that when Clarence came to the vocational building to check their work, he was acting differently. He seemed nervous and wanted them to hurry up and leave.

––––

The implication of this story was that Clarence did not have an alibi. Once he instructed the three janitors to go over and wait for him at the vocational building, he was alone on the restroom land-ing, and aware that there was a girl in the ladies' room. Meanwhile the janitors were each other's alibi, since they were always together at the critical times during the girl's disappearance.

Testifying to the grand jury and at his first trial, Clarence said that when he first arrived on the landing, Acreman was standing there, right by the restroom. Martinez was at the bottom of the steps. Sessum and Icky were somewhere in-between. As Clarence had walked up the steps onto the landing, Acreman told him not to go into the girls' bathroom because a girl was in there. Clarence

replied that he was not going in there. He never went into the girls'
restroom; he always had a female check to see if the room was properly stocked, which he had done earlier that morning. Clarence had
never seen the missing girl until he and Icky discovered her body.

After telling the men to go over to the vocational building and
wait for him there, Clarence testified, he had placed two rolls of
toilet paper in the men's room. He then walked to his office and
listened to his radio and had a smoke. He waited twenty minutes
or so before going outside to give the keys to Icky to unlock the
vocational building for the three white janitors. By this time, it was
about 10:00. The reason he made them wait was to extend their
work time to half a day so that they would get credit for a full day's
wage.

Once he gave Icky the keys, he again went into his office and
waited close to an hour before he went over to check their work.
Satisfied, he released Martinez, Acreman, and Sessum for the day.
Around 11:00, he and Icky went back across the street to the main
building to lock up the cafeteria. While there, three girls arrived
and told them that one of their friends was missing. With that, he
and Icky joined the search. Twenty-five minutes later they found
her lifeless body.

———

Don Brown and George Morris were partners, savvy and experienced lawyers with a specialty in criminal defense. They worked
out of an office overlooking the Conroe courthouse square and had
been following the case closely in the papers. Both were liberal lions
who believed fervently in the constitutional rights of their clients
and fought hard to provide them justice. When the Brandley family came to them for help, they signed on without pay. They were
well aware of the racism that permeated the local criminal justice
system and suspected that this was a classic Conroe case: pinning
the rape and murder of a white girl on a convenient black man.

After they spoke with Clarence at length, they were convinced of his innocence.

Their suspicion that racism was behind this case was soon confirmed. Using their own property as collateral, the attorneys raised the $30,000 bond that had been set on September 5. But when they presented it to the sheriff, he flatly refused to let Clarence out. This led to an in-chambers conference with Judge Lee Alworth, attended by DA Keeshan, Sheriff Gene Reaves, and lawyer Don Brown. Reaves readily conceded that the bond was good. Then why, the judge asked, have you refused to release Brandley? The sheriff replied, "Because that little nigger don't belong on the ground." DA Keeshan agreed, repeating almost exactly the sheriff's words: "That little nigger doesn't belong on the ground." Much to Brown's surprise and satisfaction, the judge went ahead and ordered Clarence's release anyway, slated for the following morning. But that turned out to be a ruse.

Secretly, behind the defense's back and before Clarence was to be released, Keeshan and Judge Alworth conspired to increase the bond to $75,000. The next morning, Keeshan filed a motion requesting the bond be increased, with an authorizing order signed by Judge Alworth. Without a hearing, this was illegal. Shocked and infuriated, Brown immediately filed a motion demanding the judge's recusal. To avoid a hearing on his recusal, Judge Alworth voluntarily stepped down, publicly denouncing Don Brown as "the most obnoxious man I ever met" and blustering that "not even Will Rogers would like Don Brown." Then Alworth got back at Brown by appointing Judge Sam Robertson, Jr., of Houston as his replacement. A former prosecutor for nineteen years, Robertson was notorious for his pro-prosecution zeal. One of the first things Judge Robertson did was uphold the $75,000 bond, an amount too high for the lawyers to raise, assuring that Clarence would be incarcerated for the long months until the trial.

It took one week to pick an all-white jury of nine men and three women, and the trial kicked off on Monday, December 8, 1980. Acreman told the jury what he had said in his sworn witness statement, with two changes. Now he described Clarence following the girl from only ten feet behind when she went up the stairs to the restroom. He himself, he now testified, had been fifty feet away from the bottom of the steps while she was walking up the stairway. Martinez and Sessum repeated the story they had told in their sworn witness statements. What really hurt Clarence was Icky Peace's testimony. Icky claimed that Clarence had told him to go up to the loft on three different occasions during their search until Icky finally found the girl, implying that Clarence knew where the body was because he was her killer.

The jury then learned from both defense and prosecution forensic experts about the hairs and semen found on the victim. They all agreed that hair analysis and comparison to particular suspects could be far from conclusive, and that such was the case when examining the hairs discovered on Fergeson. Two unidentified Caucasian hairs had been found on her inner thigh, one a brown body hair, the other a reddish-brown pubic hair. It was noted that hair samples had been taken from Clarence and Icky, but none had been obtained from the other three white janitors. Keeshan saw no need to do that, he said, as it would be a "needless imposition" on the men. The judge, too, refused the defense's request that specimens be taken from the three men for comparison purposes. A hair found on one of Fergeson's socks was microscopically compared to Clarence's hairs, but neither expert could agree as to whether it was a head or pubic hair.

The case went to the jury on Friday, December 12.

Bill Srack was one of the jury members. He wasn't from Conroe. He'd grown up in Houston and worked there as a construction manager for Shell Oil. In 1971, he and his wife sold their Houston

home and moved into a quiet leafy bedroom community south of
Conroe. Srack was a Republican who had no strong feelings about
civil rights or the racism inherent to the justice system in Conroe.
He had been only vaguely aware of the Brandley case, had hardly
given it a thought, in fact, until he was selected for the jury. This was
his fifth time on a jury. He'd served on four in Houston: two federal
and two Harris County.

Bill Srack caused quite a stir in the jury room during the eleven
hours of deliberation on Friday, followed by more deliberation
on Saturday morning. He wasn't convinced of Clarence's innocence, but he had reasonable doubt and stuck to it throughout. He
explained later that he wasn't all that impressed with the janitors,
especially Acreman, and certainly not with the medical examiner
who'd discarded the vaginal swabs. He didn't think Keeshan had
proved his case, and he made his views known to the other jurors
at the outset. Things got heated quickly. There was shouting, and it
got louder. He was called "nigger lover" several times, especially by
three male jurors who banded together against him. On occasion he
would retreat to the coffee room to sit by himself, hearing the words
"nigger lover" float in from the adjacent jury room. Sequestered at a
hotel with the other jurors on Friday night, he sat alone at breakfast
on Saturday while the others ate together. In the end, he was the
only one of the twelve who voted not guilty.

———

Standing up to the eleven took a lot of courage; it also took a lot out
of him. He wasn't Henry Fonda in *12 Angry Men,* who managed to
bring the others around. This wasn't Hollywood. This, he felt, was
hell. In all his life he had never felt so reviled and lonely. Finally,
Judge Robertson accepted the fact that he had a hung jury, called
them in, and curtly dismissed them. In earshot of all, including the
departing jury, he ordered Clarence to stand up. He then told him
he was denying bail pending a retrial, "in that I find proof is evident

that a dispassionate jury would not only find you guilty of capital murder but would assess punishment of death."

As a devastated and beaten Bill Srack left the courthouse, he heard another juror tell the press, "There goes that son of a bitch." And it wasn't over. His phone rang incessantly from the minute he arrived home that Saturday. The calls went on for months, a steady stream day and night. The callers would either remain silent, call him a "nigger lover," or threaten to "get" him. Eventually the calls became less frequent, but the stress he and his wife endured for months was almost unbearable.

Srack's dissenting vote would also come back to bite him years later. In the late 1980s, he retired from corporate life and applied for a job as purchasing agent for Montgomery County. He was a finalist for the job, and was interviewed by a panel of three judges, one of whom was the Honorable Jim Keeshan, who'd been elevated to a county judgeship in late 1985. Keeshan peppered Srack with questions about his vote at Brandley's trial seven years earlier. Among other blistering comments and questions, Keeshan questioned Srack's rationality and ability to get along with people, since he had stubbornly clung to his lone dissenting vote against the wishes of his fellow jurors. Needless to say, Srack did not get the job. Another bitter pill to swallow for voting his conscience.

Fed up with Judge Robertson's blatant favoritism toward the prosecution, Brown and Morris went after him in a recusal motion. Robertson's prejudice and bias against Clarence was easy to document, they told him in a hearing, and they indicated that they would file the motion in court. To avoid public embarrassment, two days later Robertson stepped down, just as Judge Alworth had in November before the first trial. The next day, newly elected Judge John Martin was appointed to preside over the second trial. Since he was a criminal defense attorney whom Brown and Morris knew well, both men were happy with his selection. They saw it as a good omen for the new year, 1981, as they began to prepare for the new trial.

Little did they know. It didn't take long for Judge Martin to show his true colors. In a pre-trial in-chambers conference he scolded Brown like a child, telling him to "shut your damned mouth so Jim Keeshan can talk."

Then, on the eve of the trial, a crack appeared in the janitors' story. Brown got a telephone call from John Payne, whose brother Ed lived on the same property as his daughter, Cynthia, who was married to janitor Gary Acreman. Ed told John that when Acreman came home from work the day of the Fergeson murder he was very nervous, pacing up and down. He told Ed that a girl had been murdered at the high school and her clothes were thrown in the school dumpster. This was explosive information, because Acreman had always told police and had testified at the first trial that he didn't know a girl had been killed at the school, having been dismissed early by Brandley after he'd finished his work at the vocational center. Acreman said he didn't learn about the murder until he read about it in the Sunday paper. Since police didn't find her clothes in the dumpster until Monday, how did Acreman know they were there?

But by the time Brown got to speak directly to Ed Payne, Payne had reneged on the story, and refused to discuss it further. When Brown told Keeshan about the call from John Payne, Keeshan just smiled and said he felt "comfortable" with his case and saw no need to interview Ed Payne. Janitors Acreman, Martinez, and Peace gave essentially the same version of events that they had in the first trial. Sessum was reluctant to testify, so neither side elected to call him to the stand.

This time, Keeshan produced a new witness for the prosecution, a black teenager named Danny Taylor.

Taylor told the jury that he had worked at the high school for a short while during the summer of 1980. One day he happened to be with Clarence when a group of white high school girls walked by. Once they passed, Taylor said, Clarence had remarked, "If I got one of them alone, ain't no tellin' what I'd do." Judge Martin allowed this testimony over the vociferous objections of the defense, who contended that it was not true, and that even if it were, it would irreparably impair the all-white jury's view of the defendant. Clarence huddled with his attorneys and told them that this surprise witness had been fired for threatening their boss with a butcher knife. Although the judge allowed that information in, the damage had been done.

Ranger Styles testified that the reason he never obtained hair and blood samples from janitors Acreman, Sessum, and Martinez was that "they hadn't been in contact" with the victim, Cheryl Fergeson.

The prosecution hammered home that Brandley must be the killer because he was the only one who had a set of keys to the doors that led from the restroom landing to the auditorium stage. Never mind that the doors were frequently propped open, that others had master keys, or that it had never been determined that the doors were actually locked at the time of the murder. Clarence's attorney Morris brought in David Harris, the supervisor of the custodial staff, who knew of another set of keys in the possession of Clarence Robinson, a white man who was Brandley's predecessor supervising the janitors. Those keys had not been returned to the school. Mr. Robinson's son, James Dexter Robinson, had worked briefly at the school as a janitor until quitting a month before Fergeson's murder. Neither man had been investigated or considered a suspect.

Attorneys Brown and Morris decided it was not in Clarence's interest to testify. His timeline had contradicted the testimony of the other janitors at the first trial, and it was their version that had apparently been accepted by that jury. In their summation, the defense focused on the inept and prejudiced police investigation, the unidentified Caucasian hairs found on the victim's inner thigh, the incongruity of Clarence hiding the body but then wanting Icky to find it, and the likelihood that two people killed Fergeson as suggested by the bruises on her upper arms.

In his summation, Keeshan went so far as to theorize that because Clarence worked part-time at a funeral home, he may have had a fascination with corpses. Keeshan concluded, "We know that whoever did this was not repelled by a dead body. Somebody stayed there and took the clothing off that body. Somebody had intercourse with that body, apparently after she was unconscious or dead." Early on, when Morris saw where Keeshan was going with this preposterous theory, he strongly objected, but Judge Martin allowed Keeshan to proceed.

By the time he finished, Keeshan had painted Clarence not only as a rapist and killer, but also as a necrophiliac who lusted after young white girls and attacked Cheryl Fergeson with the "bestial rage of an animal." The racism in his diatribe was flagrant. Keeshan closed by imploring the jury to "help make your community safe and a good place to live. A place where your children and grandchildren can go to a school function without fear that some monstrous person will commit an offense like this." Shortly after that, the case went to the jury for deliberation. That day, Friday, February 13, 1981, after one hour, the jury reached its verdict: Clarence Lee Brandley was guilty of capital murder.

The next day, the jury was tasked with deciding on a sentence of life imprisonment or death. For this, they heard new testimony. Jo Ellen Parrish, a nineteen-year-old black woman, testified for the prosecution. She said that in March 1979 she was at a club in Dugan called the Doll House. When it closed for the night, Clarence, she claimed, with a sawed-off shotgun stuffed in the back of his pants, forced her to go to his house where he lived by himself.

They were in the back bedroom when her boyfriend angrily and loudly banged on the door looking for her. Clarence had his hands around her neck choking her, she explained, so she couldn't cry out. Her account of what happened once her boyfriend left was confusing and contradictory. She said Clarence tried to force her to have sex, but "nothin' happened." Then he cooked her a meal and "wasn't mean" to her. At some point, she said, she ran out of the house wearing only her underwear and a housecoat that belonged to Clarence, and went to a friend's house. The next day she went home and explained her absence to her boyfriend by accusing Clarence of trying to rape her. He took her to the police and she made a statement.

No charges were ever filed concerning Parrish's allegations, suggesting that the police did not find them credible. But now, in the punishment phase of the trial, her testimony was damaging. In the wake of Parrish's accusation, the police had gone to Clarence's house and retrieved an inoperable rusty old shotgun that his mother had found years before. Clarence pled guilty to possession of a prohibited weapon and was still serving out his sentence of a three-year probation, which did not leave a good impression. For purposes of cross-examination the defense asked the DA to produce Parrish's statement and another one she'd made when Clarence was arrested in August 1980. Keeshan said that his office could not find them, giving the prosecution the last word.

Keeshan concluded by telling the jury that what was done to Fergeson was "an act of a beast."

It took the jury only forty-five minutes to decide on death.

In March 1981, sheriff's deputies transported Clarence to the Ellis Unit Death Row House in Huntsville. He was several months shy of his thirtieth birthday. "Scared" is inadequate to describe how he felt. Being confined in the county jail during the trials is one thing, but death row is quite another.

He was immediately stripped, shorn of all his hair, and issued an all-white set of clothes, the uniform for death row prisoners. The only thing that differentiated him from the others was the number 680 on his clothes, which became his name. His cell, which was nine feet by three feet, had a bed and toilet. The Bible became his constant companion, a refuge from which he drew inspiration and strength. He missed his family terribly, especially his mother, who was heartbroken over her son's fate. He was particularly close with his twin sister, Florence, and his younger brothers Tim and Ozell. The four of them had lived with Minnie Ola when she divorced their father and moved back to Dugan from Houston.

While Clarence was in jail, his lawyers fought on. Don Brown submitted a motion for a new trial, arguing that they had testimony from new witnesses. Although Judge Martin denied most of Brown's proposed witnesses, he did allow—over the strenuous objections of Keeshan—Oscar Johnson, the owner of the funeral home where Clarence had worked. Johnson told the judge that Clarence's work there had nothing to do with dead bodies. He performed menial tasks. Corpses were solely Johnson's province. Brown then argued to the judge that Keeshan knew that, but told the jury the opposite, trying to make Clarence seem like a necrophiliac. Regardless, Brandley's new trial motion was denied, so the next legal step was an appeal to Texas's highest court for criminal matters, the Court of Criminal Appeals, aka the CCA, for a new trial.

The next crack in the prosecution's case emerged in the spring of 1981. The *Houston City Magazine* published a feature story that questioned the conduct of the police and prosecution as well as the soundness of the jury's verdict. Included in the story was an interview with Icky Peace, who offered explosive information. For the first time he revealed that the Conroe police officer, in Icky's presence, told Clarence that since he was "the nigger, he was elected." Icky said he told Keeshan about this, and Keeshan told him to keep his mouth shut because it could jeopardize the case against Brandley. Icky also admitted that he lied at the Brandley trials when he denied that anyone had threatened him into giving incriminating testimony against Brandley. This confirmed what he had originally told a Brandley defense investigator, Lorna Hubbell, shortly after Clarence's arrest.

Icky had told Hubbell that when he gave his affidavit right after the crime, he didn't know what it said because he couldn't read or write. The police scared him into signing it anyway, Ranger Styles choking him with the diabetic chain that hung around his neck to make sure he stayed in line. Despite telling the reporter, though, Icky refused to provide the defense with an affidavit describing the abuse.

As the calendar year 1981 dragged on, court personnel, particularly Peggy Stevens, the district clerk in charge of the court records, stymied Brown and Morris in their attempts to obtain the trial exhibits—the victim's bloodstained clothes, the hairs found on the victim's body, crime scene photographs, and so on—that were required for the appeal to the CCA for a new trial. Toward the end of the year the Brandley family, frustrated with the slow pace of the appeal and not understanding that the delays were no fault of Brown and Morris, decided to seek new attorneys. They succeeded in raising $25,000 to retain Houston attorney Percy Foreman, who had made his name representing high-profile clients such as James Earl Ray, the assassin of Martin Luther King, Jr.

Brown and Morris initially felt sidelined. They had worked hard on Brandley's behalf through two trials on an almost pro bono basis. But their belief in Clarence's innocence was such that they agreed to stay on and work with the Foreman firm, with an assurance from Foreman that he would allocate the fee equitably.

Courthouse insiders knew why Brown had not yet received the trial exhibits, and it deeply disturbed a few of them. One by one, independent of one another, three contacted Brown and secretly met with him to tell him what was happening. They could no longer remain silent, despite their fear that they could lose their jobs if discovered. The first to come forward was Frank Robin, newly working as Jim Keeshan's assistant DA. He nervously told Brown on a confidential basis that the key exhibits had disappeared from court reporter Mary Johnson's office while she was preparing the trial transcripts several weeks earlier. Worse yet, Judge Martin, DA Keeshan, and Peggy Stevens were working together to cover it up and not tell the defense. If the disappearance ever came to light, Keeshan was going to say that a janitor had mistakenly thrown out the exhibit box.

Soon after Brandley was sent to death row, Janet Dial, Judge Martin's secretary, resigned. She didn't like the coziness developing between her boss and Keeshan. Almost every morning of the second Brandley trial, she would see Keeshan go into Judge Martin's office and huddle with him behind closed doors. This didn't sit right with her.

Not long after Brown heard from Assistant District Attorney Robin, he got a phone call from Janet, who told him that court reporter Mary Johnson wanted to meet with him in secret in a remote place near Lake Conroe. She wanted Janet to be there as well. Brown brought his law partner Morris and the four of them talked in Mary's car. The attorneys felt like they were meeting with Deep Throat, the informant of Watergate fame.

A frightened Mary told her story with the stipulation that the lawyers never reveal her to be their source. She said that when she'd arrived for work on Monday morning, January 11, 1982, the exhibit box had disappeared over the weekend. Scared to death that she would get blamed and recognizing the importance of the disappearance, she immediately told her boss, Judge Martin. Much to her surprise he instructed her not to tell a soul, especially the defense, because "they would just make a big deal about it." She said Keeshan had the keys to her office; one night when she was working late she heard the key in the door and in walked Keeshan and his investigator Charlie Ray. Surprised to see her, they made some excuse and hastily retreated.

She also knew that Keeshan was going to blame the disappearance on a janitor if they got caught, which was ridiculous because janitors were forbidden to enter her office. She did her own cleaning.

Once Mary had finished her account, Janet told the attorneys that Judge Martin and DA Keeshan had met before each day's proceedings during the Brandley trial. Mary piped up that she also knew about them; she'd heard them "rehearsing rulings and objections so they could get their way in court."

Brown and Morris had heard enough. Without citing their sources, they dropped the hammer on Judge Martin, just as they had with his predecessors, Judge Alworth and Judge Robertson. They drew up a motion for recusal and presented its contents to him privately in his chambers, primarily focusing on his collusion with Keeshan to cover up the disappearance of the trial exhibits. One week later, Judge Martin announced to the local paper that he was departing the Brandley case because he had "personal knowledge of some missing exhibits." The deeply corrupt affair was thus minimized so that he could avoid public humiliation.

A fourth Conroe judge took over the case, Judge Lynn Coker. The first thing Judge Coker did was deny a defense request for a hearing to determine the truth behind the disappearance of the trial exhibits. This denial protected his fellow jurist John Martin from scrutiny concerning his role in covering up the missing evidence.

In January 1983, Don Brown filed the appeal to the CCA. It detailed ongoing judicial and prosecutorial misconduct as well as the police ineptness that led to the conviction of an innocent man. He filed it alone, as his partner George Morris was ill and soon to die of lung cancer.

Two long years later, in May 1985, the CCA denied the appeal for a new trial. The decision affirmed the correctness of the prosecution of Clarence Brandley and the conduct of Judge Martin and DA Keeshan.

The next legal step for the prosecution was to set an execution date. Even though Judge Martin had been forced off the case three years earlier, he elbowed Judge Coker aside and insisted that he be the one to set the date. This was his revenge; it was payback time. As a way to demonstrate his appreciation for her twenty years of devoted service to courthouse administration, he picked District Court Clerk Peggy Stevens's birthday, June 16, 1986, as the date for Clarence to die. Nonetheless, Clarence got a stay of execution when his defense team developed exculpatory evidence that pointed the finger of guilt at a new suspect. This led to an evidentiary hearing in the summer of 1986, in which Clarence's lawyers presented evidence that they felt sufficient to justify a new trial.

By this time Mike DeGeurin, Percy Foreman's law partner, was Clarence's lead attorney, working with the continued assistance of Don Brown. DeGeurin was smart, talented, likeable, and highly regarded by the legal community. He had great people skills and could convince witnesses to tell him what they knew, both on the stand and in person.

Things had begun to unravel for the prosecution when DeGeurin received a phone call from a Conroe attorney, W. B. Etheridge, informing him that his client, Brenda Medina, had recently told him that her former boyfriend and the father of her child, James Dexter Robinson, had told her on the day of Fergeson's death that he had killed a girl at the high school. He had hidden her body well enough to give him time to get out of town early the next morning and return to his hometown of Greenville, South Carolina.

Etheridge told DeGeurin that he had taken Brenda to see the new DA, Peter Speers (who had succeeded Keeshan), with her story. Speers had failed to inform DeGeurin of this, which legally he was required to do. This was egregious misconduct: Speers had ignored another man's confession to a crime for which someone else was about to die; he had not disclosed this confession to the condemned man's attorney; and he had made no attempt to investigate its veracity. DeGeurin was furious.

Brenda testified at the evidentiary hearing, telling the same story to the presiding Judge Coker. James Robinson testified as well, having been persuaded by Richard Reyna, a defense investigator, to come to Conroe to "clear his name."

Robinson had worked at Conroe High as a janitor until July 29, 1980. He admitted on the witness stand that he had told Brenda he'd killed a girl, but that was months before Fergeson was killed, he said. It was just a story he made up to scare Brenda during an argument. He also claimed on the witness stand that he left Conroe for home on August 6, seventeen days before Fergeson was killed.

He agreed to take a polygraph. The polygrapher testified that when he asked Robinson if he'd killed Fergeson, he remained silent for four and a half minutes before replying, "Well, I could have done it and forgot," before quickly adding, "No, I'm not that kind of person. I'm innocent."

Gary Acreman surprised the defense when he testified that James Robinson did come to the high school the morning of August 23. He said James just popped his head in and told Acreman, "Don't work too hard." Acreman said he had never told anyone this because "it slipped my mind." Ed Payne, testifying through a voice box after losing his larynx to cancer, affirmed what he had told his brother, John, during the Brandley trials. That is, that Acreman came home from school on the day in question, very nervous, and told him that a girl was killed that morning at the high school and that he saw someone throw the girl's clothes in the dumpster.

John Sessum, one of the three janitors working together on the day of the murder, testified for the first time that Acreman had talked to the girl for "a good three or four minutes" before she went into the restroom. Then Acreman had disappeared for thirty to forty minutes after Clarence sent them to the vocational building. Sessum said that Acreman, on the way to the first trial, told him not to say that he had spoken to the girl. Sessum then added that he was afraid of the Texas Ranger, who'd threatened him with jail at the first trial if he changed his story from what was in his affidavit following the walk-through.

Believing that their witnesses had held up well at the evidentiary hearing and feeling cautiously optimistic, the defense was shocked and bitterly disappointed when on December 22, 1986, the CCA again denied a new trial for Clarence. The Court agreed with Judge Coker's findings that the witnesses for the defense were not credible. Case closed. With that, on February 6, 1987, Judge Coker set a new execution date of March 26, 1987.

That was when I got involved. Clarence's brother, Ozell Brandley, saw me on *The Today Show* in November 1986 with Nate Walker, a man Centurion had just exonerated. He asked me to come to Houston and help the defense team free his brother, who was soon to be executed. After I read the record of the case, Ozell introduced me to DeGeurin and a new lawyer at the firm, Paul Nugent. After several hours of discussion in their office, they invited me to join the defense team in its last-ditch effort to save Clarence's life. Nugent put me up in an apartment above his home's garage, and DeGeurin loaned me his mother's old Chevy.

With three weeks to go, investigator Richard Reyna and I went to work, me dressed in black, wearing my priestly white collar, and Richard in neatly pressed jeans and cowboy boots. On March 7 we pulled up to Sessum's trailer on the outskirts of Conroe. We figured if Robinson and Acreman had murdered Cheryl Fergeson, Sessum was an eyewitness, and maybe he would be willing to talk as the execution date loomed. Over the next ten days, in bits and pieces, he did tell us who killed Cheryl and how it happened.

It had been Acreman and Robinson.

Sessum recounted that he and Martinez had been at the bottom of the steps and had heard Cheryl's screams for help as Acreman and Robinson dragged her into the bathroom near the top of the stairs. He had been having nightmares ever since about what he'd witnessed and felt tremendously guilty for not having stopped the attack. "I was the one who caused her death. I could have saved her if I went up there," he lamented. But now he was resolved: "I let one innocent girl go to her death, I'm not gonna let an innocent man go to his. What do you want me to do?" On St. Patrick's Day he told the story in a video statement.

On that same day, Richard and I caught up with Acreman. When we told him that Sessum had implicated him in the murder of Fergeson, he began to shake uncontrollably and agreed to give a video statement as well. In it, he absolved himself of any involvement and placed the blame entirely on Robinson. Both Sessum and Acreman exonerated Clarence, stating that he showed up ten minutes after the girl had been raped and killed.

DeGeurin and Nugent submitted the videos to Judge Coker and on March 20, six days before the scheduled execution, Coker reluctantly ordered its stay. Two weeks later Sessum courageously went on *60 Minutes* and told what he had witnessed to Harry Reasoner and the nation. By that time, Acreman had recanted his video at the urging of the DA's investigators, although he still maintained that he saw Robinson throw the girl's clothes in the dumpster. Ignoring Sessum's statement and Acreman's information, the DA's office refused to admit that they'd been wrong. Speers remained bound and determined to keep Brandley's conviction intact.

For the first time, however, the CCA ruled in Brandley's favor, granting him another evidentiary hearing, and appointed a new judge to hear the case. The new judge was Perry Pickett, retired after thirty years on the bench in West Texas's Midland County and now serving as a CCA visiting judge appointed to hear special cases. Pickett was a tough and courageous judge who had escaped from a Nazi POW camp during World War II and hid behind enemy lines in Italy until the Allies liberated his location. The first thing he did was hold a change-of-venue hearing in the Conroe courthouse. He took testimony from a wide assortment of people, black and white, including the heroic Bill Srack, two prominent and eloquent black Conroe church ministers, and the gutsy Janet Dial. Each told a story of racism and cronyism plaguing the justice system in Conroe, currently and historically.

At the end of the hearing, Judge Pickett announced that "there exists here a volatile and explosive situation not conducive to the fair administration of justice. The ends of justice dictate that this case be transferred to Galveston County." He ordered a new evidentiary hearing to begin in one week, on September 28, 1987. With that, the courtroom erupted in cheers, the African Americans in attendance letting out long-suppressed feelings. They knew that something right and good had just occurred for people of color, maybe for the first time in that courthouse. And Clarence Brandley finally could breathe a little easier as his case departed Conroe and headed for Galveston.

Judge Pickett's evidentiary hearing covered every aspect of the case. For two weeks in a Galveston courthouse he took testimony from forty-six witnesses in order to determine if Brandley had received a fair trial and whether there was sufficient new evidence to give him a new trial.

Sessum told his story describing Acreman and Robinson grabbing the girl and dragging her into the bathroom. Ed and John Payne told of Acreman's suspicious behavior when he returned home the day of the crime. Three new witnesses who worked at the City Cab Company with Acreman told of discussing the high school murder in the office one day, prompting Acreman to suddenly exclaim that Clarence didn't do it and he knew who did. Two others told the judge they saw Robinson in Conroe three days before the murder. It was established that the blood on the victim's shirt was type A, and that both Robinson and Acreman had type A blood. Cheryl Bradford, a volleyball player at the tournament, testified that she saw two white men fitting the description of Acreman and Robinson briskly exit the gym door twenty to thirty minutes after she saw Cheryl in the hallway on her way to the restroom. This same witness got "chills" when she saw the photo of Robinson on *60 Minutes,* believing that he was one of the men she saw hurrying to exit the gym.

On November 19, 1987, Judge Pickett issued his opinion, recommending to the CCA that it grant Clarence a new trial based on his findings of fact. He stated: "The Court became convinced that Clarence Lee Brandley did not receive a fair trial and did not commit the crime for which he now resides on death row." He went on: "The testimony at the evidentiary hearing unequivocally establishes that Gary Acreman and James Dexter Robinson are prime suspects and probably were responsible for the death of Cheryl Dee Fergeson." He lamented the disappearance of the trial exhibits containing the Caucasian hairs found near her vagina—removing the possibility of comparing these to Robinson's and Acreman's hair. Pickett found highly suspect Keeshan's testimony that he didn't order Acreman or the other white janitors to provide hair or blood samples because it would have been a "needless imposition." Nor was he impressed with Ranger Styles's response to the same question: "Let's say I didn't do it, and it wasn't done; and why it wasn't done I don't know."

Citing credible details of testimony by Mary Johnson, Janet Dial, and Frank Robin, Judge Pickett found that Judge Martin and DA

Keeshan had conducted constant secret ex parte discussions prior to Clarence's daily trial proceedings, and conspired to cover up the disappearance of the trial exhibits. He characterized the testimony of Judge Martin and Peggy Stevens, in which they denied this, as "not truthful" and "not credible." Mary Johnson paid a heavy price for her courageous and honest testimony against her boss, Judge Martin. He fired her soon after Judge Pickett's opinion was issued. Additionally, she became persona non grata in the courthouse, where former colleagues considered her to be disloyal to the Conroe judiciary. Her career as a court reporter in Montgomery County was over.

Judge Pickett came down hard on the investigative tactics and mindset of Ranger Styles. Icky Peace and Sessum related Styles's threats and his intimidation of them to get their false testimony. Both testified that they were still afraid of him. Sessum was threatened with jail if he didn't cooperate after the walk-through. Icky spoke of Styles visiting his home one night and taking him to a local police station. Styles kept him there until 1:30 A.M., all the while roughing him up and choking him with the neck chain Icky wore. When Icky had complained to the DA's office, they told him he was "hallucinating" and "imagining things."

———

For his part, Sam Martinez stuck with his testimony, telling Judge Pickett that he, Martinez, had "got it straight" the first time—meaning after the walk-through with Ranger Styles. Martinez never admitted that he saw what Sessum saw, even though he was with Sessum when the girl was assaulted. The reason may have been that Martinez's father was a janitor at the courthouse; Martinez may have wanted to protect his father's job by not going up against the powerful Keeshan.

The judge made it clear that Styles had operated with "blind focus" by arresting Brandley even before he'd begun his investigation. This had led to "the inescapable conclusion that the investigation was conducted not to solve the crime, but to convict the Petitioner." The judge added that "the state of mind that he [Styles] had already gotten his man precluded him from following any leads that might prove his preconception wrong."

The Court also took evidence on the racist climate that pervaded the prosecution of Clarence, including the entire investigation and post-trial proceedings. He referenced the fact that the Montgomery County prosecutor's office recommended in its internal manual that when a black person was on trial, prosecutors were to strike all prospective black jurors during jury selection. Bill Srack described his harrowing experience as a juror and its aftermath. Others described the frequent use of the term "nigger" by police and prosecutors, and the racism rampant in the courthouse.

In conclusion, Judge Pickett stated, "In the thirty years this court has presided over matters in the judicial system, no case has presented a more shocking scenario of the effects of racial prejudice, perjured testimony, witness intimidation, a predetermined investigation, and public officials who, for whatever motives, lost sight of what is right and just." He then recommended to the CCA that it order a new trial for Mr. Brandley.

———

In Texas, only the CCA has the authority to vacate a conviction and order a new trial. It took the CCA two more years before issuing, on December 13, 1989, an opinion that affirmed all of Judge Pickett's findings of fact. It ordered a new trial for Clarence, ruling that the "contrived" investigation resulted in a "subversion of Justice" and that the prosecution presented "false" and "inherently unreliable" testimony by suppressing evidence that favored the defendant. Nevertheless, DA Speers refused to give in and appealed to the U.S. Supreme Court. His appeal was rejected without comment.

With this, Speers decided not to retry Brandley, and all charges were dismissed. On January 23, 1990, Clarence emerged from death row an exonerated and free man.

By that time his case had become a cause célèbre. His freedom was celebrated not only by his mother, children, siblings, and a legion of supporters, both black and white, but also by the print and broadcast media nationwide.

Clarence went on to start up a storefront church and serve as its pastor. When he couldn't sustain a living this way, he tried his hand at a variety of pursuits until finally getting a job as a mechanic with Houston's Metropolitan Transit Authority. There he remained for thirteen years. He eventually moved back to a small Montgomery County town and retired to a quiet life with his longtime devoted companion, Dorothy Moore. On September 2, 2018, three weeks shy of his sixty-seventh birthday, Clarence passed away from pneumonia.

Clarence was never compensated for his wrongful imprisonment on death row. He initiated lawsuits against the authorities responsible for his false conviction, but a judge dismissed them, saying those agencies had sovereign immunity. In 2011 he was denied compensation under the Texas compensation statute for false convictions. The fund claimed that his application was made too late. To add insult to injury, Texas ordered him to pay $25,000 for child support payments in arrears during his nine and a half years of false imprisonment. His weekly wages were garnished for many years.

An interesting footnote to the case is the reappearance of the trial exhibits. When Charlie Ray, the former investigator for DA Keeshan, died in January 2018, his family discovered a box of the Brandley trial exhibits in their garage. Ray had been with Keeshan when they entered Mary Johnson's locked office on the evening she was still at work. The exhibits disappeared from her office on a weekend shortly thereafter. The exhibit box was turned over to current DA Brett Ligon. To this day we do not know what was in the box and what happened to its contents. What we do know is that Ligon called in the Texas Rangers and the Conroe police department—the very agencies responsible for the miscarriage of justice that sent Brandley to death row—to look through that evidence and see if there was anything that could be retested.

I was privileged to be one of the eulogists at Clarence's memorial service. I told the attendees that he was one of the bravest men I had ever known. He never panicked as the clock ticked close to his date of execution with no apparent progress in his case. He stood calm and strong in the face of almost certain death for a crime he did not commit. He came within a week of that fate and accepted it with a quiet dignity and courage that inspired all of us working feverishly to save him. His coolness under fire steadied us all.

Clarence was a good and kind man. A decent man. He was humble and reserved. If he had any hate or anger in his heart for those that did him wrong, I never saw or sensed it. From the beginning to the very end, after all the injustices he suffered during his imprisonment and in the years that followed, he never wore them on his sleeve. He was loved by all of us who came to know him.

———

Acreman and Robinson have never been charged for the rape and murder of Cheryl Fergeson.

AUTOPSY GAMES

JOHN GRISHAM

The first recorded autopsy of note was that of Julius Caesar in 44 B.C. The Roman emperor seriously underestimated the loyalty of his colleagues, and when he brazenly declared himself to be Emperor for Life, they took offense. They also took up knives and attacked him on the Senate Floor. A mob of about sixty flailed away at Caesar, who, in addition to being shocked, was also defenseless. They left him a bloody mess, fled the scene, and, typical for politicians, immediately began denying they were involved or blaming other people.

For reasons that were never clear, someone with authority requested an autopsy, though it was evident what had happened. Autopsies were nothing new; the Greeks had been dissecting corpses for five hundred years.

As a crowd looked on, a distinguished physician, Antistius, went about the gruesome task and soon confirmed the obvious: Caesar died from a massive loss of blood. There were twenty-three stab wounds.

In the 1500s, Leonardo da Vinci, in his never-ending thirst for knowledge, collected cadavers and dissected at least thirty of them, not to solve crimes or study diseases, but to understand and illustrate every part of the human body. His rival, Michelangelo, occasionally put down his chisels and brushes, picked up the scalpel, and conducted his own research.

By the Middle Ages, autopsies were common in Europe and Asia, but they were seldom used in criminal investigations. In the 1800s, as the United States' population soared almost as fast as its murder rate, autopsies became useful tools for criminal investigators. In almost every murder, the best source of evidence is the body. Pathologists in America gained expertise in sifting for clues through the remains of the victims.

Founded in 1936, the American Board of Pathology (ABP) made the first serious effort to regulate the practice by promulgating standard requirements for certification. The field continued to grow, as did the crime rate, and by 1940 it was well accepted in American criminal procedure that the doctor who performed the autopsy had to be "board certified" by the ABP before he or she could testify. As the need grew, forensic pathologists became more involved in solving crimes and the science was modernized. More regulations followed. With time, the National Association of Medical Examiners (NAME) began regulating the certification of pathologists.

NAME also handled complaints against its members, and, as in all fields of medicine, there was never a shortage of bad actors. In 1992, an infamous Texas pathologist named Ralph Erdmann attracted national attention because of the large number of autopsies he claimed to have performed. He worked in rural Texas and handled the work for about forty counties that could not afford to hire their own medical examiners—and Erdmann was eager to help. He even made house calls, driving to the counties and performing wherever necessary. Most of the counties lacked proper facilities, so Erdmann adapted on the fly. He dissected corpses in parking lots, garages, and alleys. He became a darling of the police and prosecutors because he could massage his testimony to support their theories of guilt. He fancied himself the "Quincy of the Texas Panhandle," after the TV character made popular by Jack Klugman. Eventually, his shoddy work caught up with him, as did the complaints from defense lawyers. When Erdmann was finally investigated, it was determined that in at least one-third of his autopsies he had never opened the corpse.

He averaged 300 autopsies a year and claimed to have peaked at 480, an astonishing number.

NAME recommended that a medical examiner do no more than 250 per year. If a doctor exceeded 325, NAME would not certify the lab where he worked.

Given that a typical autopsy takes between two and four hours, followed by the preparation of a report and other paperwork, Erdmann's numbers were extraordinary.

Such numbers, though, were a drop in the bucket for a pathologist who roamed the state of Mississippi in the 1990s. Nicknamed "The Cadaver King," he cornered the market on autopsies and handled 80 percent of the state's homicides during his reign. He once boasted of doing 1,000 autopsies a year. Even 1,500, or more.

At his peak, he claimed to have performed 2,000 autopsies in one year.

———

His name was Dr. Steven Hayne.

He was born in Los Angeles in 1941, finished medical school at Brown University in 1976, and specialized in pathology. He worked for various hospitals around the country for a few years before taking a job as the medical director of a laboratory in Rankin County, Mississippi, in 1985. As a sideline, he began doing autopsies for $400 each.

His timing could not have been better. Because of the low pay and other issues, Mississippi couldn't keep a permanent state medical examiner. If a county coroner suspected foul play in a death, it was his duty to arrange an autopsy. There was no central state morgue or lab to ship the body to, no state agency or clearinghouse to monitor and regulate autopsies. The county coroners, all eighty-two of them, had to call a pathologist and beg for an autopsy. Since virtually all pathologists loathed the work, and the small fees, not to mention the unpleasant prospect of testifying in court, there was a perpetual backlog of corpses in need of examination.

Enter Dr. Hayne. He sniffed out an opportunity and let it be known that he was open for business. To him the math was simple: Good money could be made with an assembly-line approach. He began by doing several autopsies a month, quickly, efficiently, and with the friendly service attitude of a car salesman. Before long he was doing one per day, and just getting started. By word of mouth he advertised his services, and the coroners, police, sheriffs, and prosecutors gladly shipped their corpses to him. He also advertised in police bulletins and newsletters. In 1988 he did 320 autopsies. By 1990, he was doing 1,200 a year.

Not only was Dr. Hayne an incredible workhorse, he was also a marvelous witness for the prosecution. Affable, glib, and smart, he wowed juries for years with an effective combination of folksi-ness and sharp medical knowledge. He used big words and small ones, and he spoke in a clear voice with no accent. He didn't sound like people from Mississippi. He was from California, and Brown University, and other faraway places. Lawyers have known for years that the farther an expert travels to get to the courtroom, the more impressed the local folks will be. With constant practice, Hayne played the role perfectly.

When he wasn't at the autopsy table or in a courtroom, he worked as the director of the Rankin Medical Center lab and directed a kidney care center. On top of that, he consulted in civil cases and performed private autopsies.

When later questioned about his superhuman workload, he explained: "I normally sleep no more than two or three hours a day. I also work seven days a week, not five. I don't take vacations. So I work at a much more efficient level and much harder than most people. I'm blessed with that and cursed with that, but that's what I carry with me, and I work very, very hard. I have an ability to work long hours and I don't make a lot of errors. I think my record speaks for itself."

But there were errors, and plenty of them.

As Hayne cornered the market on autopsies, dead bodies arrived at his small morgue at an astonishing rate. It was not unusual for six or seven to be waiting for the knife, and they were often stacked up like cordwood on the holding ramp. One state official who saw the operation said, "It looked like an autopsy factory. There were no safety precautions." A former state official said, "Hayne was constantly looking for ways to cut corners. Evidence was frequently improperly labeled. Evidence was tainted because it was improperly packaged and preserved. They didn't take safety precautions with chemicals or biological materials." One police officer described the morgue as a "sausage factory." A police chief described seeing five corpses lying side by side, all cut open, in various stages of being examined. He worried about cross-contamination. One state official questioned whether Hayne was doing all the work himself. He said, "I've always found it impossible to believe that Steve did all the autopsies he claimed to have done. He was never in the prime of health. He could not have stood up to the regimen he claimed to have followed."

Whether he actually did the autopsies or not, Dr. Hayne was certainly sending bills for them. Before long he had increased his rate to $1,000 per autopsy, plus $350 an hour to testify in court. He was taking bodies from all over the state and had become its de facto medical examiner. Since he billed each county separately, and since there was no centralized recordkeeping, no one but Hayne knew how many autopsies he was actually doing or how much money he was making. The math, though, was fairly straightforward. He was grossing over a million dollars a year as an uncertified forensic pathologist.

His apologists considered him a real asset to the State. He was doing work few other doctors would. Prosecutors loved him because he was great in court, could convince a jury, and was creative in finding evidence that supported the State's theory of guilt.

To this day, no one knows how many wrongful convictions began with a scalpel in the hands of Dr. Steven Hayne.

———

One of the first began on September 15, 1990, with the abduction and murder of a three-year-old girl named Courtney Smith.

She lived with her mother, grandmother, two sisters, and three uncles in a blue clapboard cottage on an unpaved road on "the other side of the tracks" in the small, dying town of Brooksville, Mississippi. The neighborhood was a grid of gravel roads running between shotgun houses, all built long before 1990. Some were well maintained with fresh paint, flower boxes, and grass lawns. Most were in a perpetual state of disrepair. A few had been abandoned. On some of the lots multiple dwellings had been erected and several generations of a family lived clustered together. Mobile homes were scattered about haphazardly. Though the neighborhood was poor, there was little serious crime. Many of the residents slept with their doors and windows unlocked, if there were locks at all.

On that Saturday evening, Courtney and her sister Ashley, age five, had dinner with their grandmother and great-grandmother, then walked home, a few minutes away. It was still summertime, hot and humid, and the neighbors were outdoors, porch-sitting, cooking on the grill, and playing in the streets. At home, their mother, Sonya Smith, bathed the girls and prepared them for bed. She dressed Courtney in a T-shirt with a duck on the front and the word MISSISSIPPI across the top. When the girls were asleep, Sonya got dressed herself and went out for the night. It was, after all, Saturday, and she enjoyed the bar scene in the local honky-tonks. Her mother, Ruby, said she would babysit the girls. Also in the house was Tony, Sonya's brother, and one of the girls' three uncles who lived with them.

Ruby, the grandmother, got bored and left with some friends. Uncle Tony was fast asleep on the sofa. The girls were asleep in the bedroom. There was nothing unusual about the tag-team approach to the babysitting. Aunts, uncles, grandparents, cousins, and neighbors all pitched in to help with the kids.

Around midnight, a man from the area entered the house through the unlocked front door and walked past the sofa where Tony was asleep. He looked into the first bedroom, saw two little girls sleeping, picked up Courtney without waking her, and walked out. He took her down a short path and away from the houses. Near a pond, he laid her on the ground, uncertain what to do next. When he penetrated her vagina with a finger, she finally woke up and began crying. When she wouldn't stop, he choked her and then tossed her into the pond. She couldn't swim and struggled to stay afloat. When her little head dipped underwater for the last time, the killer walked back to his car and drove away.

Sonya Smith spent Sunday morning looking for her daughter, assuming she was with another family. Initially, there was no panic because children were known to stay with whoever happened to be keeping them. By late afternoon, though, it was apparent Courtney was indeed missing. The police were called around 8:00 P.M., and by then hundreds of people were searching for the girl.

On Monday morning, the town's police chief saw the partially submerged body of a child in the pond. He pulled it out and laid it beside the water. The child, a little girl, was wearing a duck

T-shirt with the word MISSISSIPPI across the top. She had bled from wounds to the groin and head. The chief wrapped the body in another officer's jacket and waited for the sheriff's office.

The first to arrive was Deputy Ernest Eichelberger, who, in spite of his uncommon last name, was a burly African American who had been in law enforcement for only five years. As the deputy chief, he assumed the role of lead investigator. He knew a child was missing and found Courtney's father, who made a positive ID.

Eichelberger then turned the body over to the county coroner, who immediately sent it to Dr. Steven Hayne for an autopsy. He completed it that night and determined that the child had been choked but most likely died by drowning. She had been sexually assaulted, but he found no pubic hair or semen and concluded the killer had not forced intercourse. He found some bruises on her right wrist that he thought might have been caused by human teeth, but wasn't certain. He ran some more tests and decided the bruises were made around the time of death. Some other marks may have been animal bites.

With the human bite mark theory in play, Dr. Hayne and the investigators were in luck. At that time, Mississippi was home to one of the country's leading bite mark experts, the phenomenal Dr. Michael West.

As a small-town dentist in Hattiesburg, Mississippi, Dr. West had somehow become an expert witness and had launched himself onto center stage in some of the most sensational trials in the state. Almost overnight, Dr. West became a forensic expert not only with bite marks, but with ballistics, gunshot reconstruction, wound patterns, bruises, tool mark patterns, arson, glass breakage, and fingernail scratches. In almost every case, his sidekick, Dr. Hayne, performed the autopsy, then called in West to nail down the proof.

When Dr. Hayne finished Courtney's autopsy, he called Dr. West and asked him to come to the morgue as soon as possible.

They had another murder on their hands and the killer, for some reason, had chosen to bite his victim.

Dr. West did not arrive in time. Late Monday night, the mortician who owned the morgue decided to proceed with the embalming without notifying anyone.

The following morning, Dr. West examined the freshly embalmed body, and quickly agreed with his pal that the bite marks on the wrist were from human teeth. He excised some skin around the wounds, studied their marks, and wrote a short report. He billed the county almost $3,000 for his labors and informed the coroner that he was ready to provide further assistance as soon as the sheriff had a suspect.

———

Suspects were plentiful. Deputy Eichelberger's method of investigation was to arrest all of them, throw them in jail, and wait for the truth to come out. The first was Courtney's great-uncle by marriage, a man named Mickens, who was known to drink too much and when drinking often touched women inappropriately. To Eichelberger, that was enough proof that Mickens was somehow involved in the rape and murder of a child. When the suspect appeared on the evening news, handcuffed and bewildered, a reporter breathlessly covered the heinous details of the crime, which now included not only a murder, but a violent rape, a head wound, and a cut on the mouth.

Eichelberger then arrested Courtney's uncles: Tony, Ernest, and William Smith, all on suspicion of murder but without a shred of evidence against them. Uncle Tony had been fast asleep on the sofa when the killer entered the house and left with Courtney. The three men had just lost a niece, one they loved, protected, and shared a home with. Now they were accused of killing her and were sitting in jail.

Eichelberger was just getting started. He arrested William

McCarthy and David Harrison, two men with nothing to do with the crime, but since they were friends of Ruby's, the grandmother, and in the neighborhood that night, they were suspicious enough to be charged and jailed.

He arrested John Hodge, Sonya Smith's boyfriend; Robert Goodwin, a neighbor; and Lee Harris, a friend of Uncle Tony's.

With his tenth arrest, Eichelberger finally got lucky, though he didn't realize it. He stumbled upon the murderer and arrested him. He was Justin Johnson, a thirty-five-year-old local with a reputation of strange behavior, keeping to himself, and getting arrested. More than once, he was accused of breaking into homes late at night and either attacking or threatening women. The cops picked up his trail because several neighbors reported seeing his blue and white 1978 Buick Electra parked near the pond around midnight. His alibi was lame. At the jail, Eichelberger asked him if he had been arrested before and he replied, "Yes, for a similar deal, attempted rape. Not long ago."

An experienced detective, or perhaps even a low-level beat cop, would have concentrated on Johnson, but Eichelberger was distracted by yet another promising suspect: Levon Brooks.

Johnson was eventually released. Eighteen years would pass before another detective questioned him about the murder of Courtney Smith.

————

Levon Brooks became the prime suspect because he occasionally wore an earring. He lived in Macon, a nearby town, and didn't hang around Brooksville. He knew the Smith family well because he and Sonya had dated a few times years earlier and they were still friendly. Levon was friendly with almost everyone. He loved the nightlife, the clubs, the ladies, and he was especially fond of fancy clothes and the latest fashions. The gold earring was something new and added to his reputation as a man ahead of his time. He enjoyed his job at the Santa Barbara, a nightclub not far from his home. He earned good money there, worked decent hours, and met a lot of women. Levon was thirty-two years old, a bachelor, nice-looking, and always played the field. He managed to stay friendly with all his ex-girlfriends.

On the Saturday night Courtney Smith was abducted and murdered, Levon was working at the Santa Barbara, eight miles away from her home in Brooksville. Numerous alibi witnesses would swear on the witness stand that he was there mixing drinks, cooking in the kitchen, watching the dance floor, and, as always, flirting with the ladies.

However, such clear proof would be no match for the bogus scientific testimony cooked up by Drs. Hayne and West and presented to the jury.

The earring theory began its long and tortured journey with the assumption made by the investigators that the only possible witness to Courtney's abduction was her five-year-old sister, Ashley. As the days passed with no clues, a jail full of "suspects," and pressure mounting to solve the crime, the investigators decided to concentrate on Ashley and prod her into remembering something.

Interrogating children, especially those traumatized by violent crime, is a fragile, complicated business that should be handled by qualified forensic professionals with a background in psychiatry. Five days after Courtney's murder, and the day after her funeral, Ashley sat for her first interview. The officer had no background in psychiatry, psychology, or therapy. He was a local cop who had once hosted a kids' show on television; thus he claimed to have a certain talent in dealing with children.

The interview was a disaster and should have made the police realize that Ashley should be left alone. She said things the police knew to be outright fabrications. She said her uncle Tony pulled a knife on the intruders, but later changed it to a gun. Her ramblings were often fantastical and absurd, as when she said the abductor had fled with Courtney in an airplane. In the next interview she tried to identify the abductor or abductors: he was a black man named Shavon; then Travon, who went to college with her mother; Travon then had an accomplice; then he had two, one white, one black; then he was a lone white man named Clay; he had a stocking over his head; then it was a Halloween mask. In another interview, she added more details: the attackers left with Courtney but returned home with potato chips and drinks; one of them taunted her, saying, "Ha, ha, we got your sister"; one also had a bag full of money.

The truth was that Ashley had slept through the entire abduction and didn't realize her sister was missing until she woke up the following morning. From that moment until her first interview five days later she never claimed to have seen the abductor. Only when the police began suggesting details did her vulnerable imagination take over.

Wearing a quarter in one's ear was a fad that came and went in some black communities. When the interviewer asked Ashley about a quarter in the abductor's ear, she took it and ran. Yes, the man did indeed have a quarter in his ear.

The shrewd detectives surmised that perhaps the quarter was really an earring. Levon Brooks was one of very few local black men wearing earrings in 1990.

Finally, the cops had a real suspect. They showed Ashley a series of photos of black men and manipulated the lineup to cast more suspicion on Brooks. She identified him and added that he had blindfolded Courtney with a stocking—two details that were first suggested by the police and not Ashley.

Tenuous as it was, the earring was the only possible evidence linking Brooks to the crime. He had not been in the area at the time of the crime; indeed, he had never been to the current home of Sonya Smith. He had never met Courtney or Ashley. He had no history of sex crimes and had never been accused or suspected of abusing children.

————

Even as the investigation began to focus on Levon Brooks, the investigators were busy elsewhere.

On September 23, Dr. West arrived in town with his tool kit and a sack of plaster. He began with the ten men in jail, none of whom had lawyers, and convinced them to provide dental molds of their teeth. No lawyer worth his salt would allow such a procedure without a warrant or a hearing, but due process and legal protections were of little significance. The "suspects" felt as though they had no choice but to cooperate.

Oddly enough, Dr. West also shoved a tray filled with plaster into the mouth of Sonya Smith, the victim's mother, and made a dental mold from it. No one had even remotely suggested that Sonya was involved in the murder, nor did anyone have a clue as to why she would be suspected of biting her daughter's wrists.

A total of ten "suspects" consented to the dental molds, including the killer, Justin Johnson. The next day, Dr. West informed the authorities that he had completed his examination and all ten had been excluded as the source of the bite marks.

————

With the first batch of suspects cleared, Eichelberger concentrated on Levon Brooks. He arrested him for murder and informed Dr. West that he had a prime suspect. He and another deputy drove Brooks two hours to Hattiesburg, to the West Dental Clinic, where the twelfth mold was taken.

The next morning, Dr. West called the investigators with the news they were counting on. In his opinion, Levon Brooks was the only person in the world who could have left the bite marks on the victim. He wrote: "The dental structures of one Levon Brooks did indeed and without a doubt inflict the bite marks found on the body of Courtney Smith."

Indeed and without a doubt. This was a brand-new standard in forensic science and courtroom testimony, one obviously created by Dr. West and one he would use repeatedly in years to come. Defense lawyers sometimes, but certainly not always, objected to the near-lethal phrase. Judges—few of whom had any grasp of basic scientific principles, and most with little desire to educate themselves—overruled the objections and let West run with his new standard. Jurors didn't know the difference. On appeal, the Mississippi Supreme Court almost always found a reason to allow it.

Before West, experts at trials were constrained to define their conclusions as within "a reasonable degree" of medical or scientific certainty. West was allowed to blatantly opine that there was no doubt about his findings.

The State then had all it needed to indict Levon Brooks for capital murder: (1) the confused and often sensational meanderings of a traumatized five-year-old sister of the victim; (2) a manipulated photo lineup presented to the same child; (3) a polygraph exam Brooks allegedly flunked; and (4) the unequivocal bite mark opinion of Dr. West.

The trial began on January 13, 1992, some sixteen months after the murder. The prosecution was led by Forrest Allgood, the elected district attorney and a staunch believer in the death penalty. Though it would be the first time Allgood relied on the tag team of Hayne and West, they would join forces many times in the following years. Few if any other prosecutors used them as often.

In his opening statement to the jury, Allgood laid out his case. Since he had no physical evidence other than the bite marks, he relied heavily upon them. Allgood told the jury: "He left his mark in the form of some teeth marks embedded in her arm. The State of Mississippi, ladies and gentlemen, is simply going to prove to you that that man is Levon Brooks."

The State's first witness was Ashley Smith, now seven years old. She was as frightened as any child would have been, and the judge didn't help matters. He quizzed her first and warned her that if she didn't tell the truth, she would "go to the devil."

Scaring the hell out of the child seemed an odd way to begin.

Allgood's questions were concise, easy to understand and follow, and elicited well-rehearsed answers from Ashley. Her prior fantasies, inconsistencies, and conflicting stories vanished. However, on cross-examination, the defense attorney began asking about her initial stories. What about the different men, black and white, who abducted her sister? What about the getaway in an airplane? And Uncle Tony giving chase with a knife, or was it a gun? And bad men who returned to the house with potato chips, or a sack full of money?

As in her initial interviews, she became confused and quickly lost credibility.

None of it mattered to Allgood, because he had what he wanted. During his closing argument four days later, he brazenly told the jury: "From start to finish, the little girl has never identified anybody else as being the man who came into her bedroom and took her sister away except the defendant. Nobody else."

Dr. Hayne testified that Courtney probably died of freshwater drowning but had bruises to her head and cuts on the inside of her vagina. No semen was found. He told the jury that the marks on her wrist were probably made by human teeth, and explained that he had consulted Dr. Michael West, who agreed. Hayne then testified that the bite marks were inflicted at the time of death or shortly thereafter. Thus, the person who bit her was the person who killed her.

Experts who later reviewed the case agreed that the testimony was terribly flawed. It was virtually impossible to determine (1) the origin of bite marks on a body submerged in water as long as Courtney's and (2) whether the marks were made before or after her death.

Other unfounded and sensational facts were introduced. As Hayne was describing the cuts on the victim's vagina, he told the jury they could have been made by a finger or a penis. Out of nowhere, Allgood asked, "What about a broom handle?"

A broom handle?

No one had yet mentioned a broom handle. None had been found at the crime scene. No report mentioned one. There had been no hint of one anywhere in the investigation.

But Allgood pulled one out of thin air and Hayne was quick to agree that, yes, the injuries could have been caused by a broom handle.

The defense objected to the sudden inclusion of such a sensational detail, but the judge allowed it anyway. The jury was left with the horrifying image of Levon Brooks raping the child with a broom handle. Since no semen was found, perhaps he didn't use his penis. Therefore, he had to use something else. Why not a broom handle?

That awful image was solidified when Allgood, in his closing argument, reminded the jury of the totally fictitious broom handle.

Dr. West took the stand on the fourth day of the trial and spent the first thirty minutes convincing the judge and jury that he was one of the country's leading experts in forensic odontology. He described himself as a "senior crime scene analyst" and boasted of an appearance on the Phil Donahue television show. He claimed to have testified as an expert in thirteen states, then clicked off all thirteen to impress everyone. His thick résumé was clear proof of the breadth and depth of his knowledge. It listed dozens of articles he had written and published on bite mark analysis. However, few if any had been peer-reviewed by experts and scientists. West claimed to have close associations with Scotland Yard, the Royal Canadian Mounted Police, and law enforcement agencies all over the world, including "Israeli intelligence." He ran through a list of the places he had lectured, including China, and ending, as always, with the "FBI Academy in Quantico, Virginia."

The defense offered a half-hearted inquiry into his credentials but the judge waved him through. Since Dr. West had been qualified as an expert and allowed to testify in so many other jurisdictions, then certainly he must know his stuff. Surely some other judge back there had taken the time to research his qualifications.

Dr. West was off and running. Allgood began by confronting his biggest problem: The body had been embalmed before West got to it. No problem at all. By the time West finished his explanation, he had convinced the jury that the embalming actually helped preserve the skin and somehow, miraculously, made it easier to match the bite marks to Levon Brooks.

He then wowed the jury with his analysis of Levon's teeth. Using enlarged photographs and plaster molds, he carefully and methodically explained how he made his identification. He used words like *fractures, bevels, cutting edges, L-shaped curves, facets,* and *a scalloped-out area with a sharp edge*. He explained the differences in human skin and how it varies on the body. Different teeth leave different indentions on different skin.

Oddly enough, his plaster molds of Levon's teeth were for some reason insufficient. He needed more detail, so just before the trial he visited Brooks in Noxubee County jail and convinced him to open his mouth. When he did, Dr. West pressed in a wad of Silly Putty—the actual toy. He extracted it, looked it over, and claimed it provided greater detail of Brooks's upper incisors than the plaster molds.

Dr. West explained that the bite marks on Courtney's wrist were tiny, barely noticeable, and could not be seen by the average person. Fortunately, at least for the prosecution, West had an answer. He had developed and pioneered an investigative technique that would save the day. By using a pair of yellow goggles and a certain brand of ultraviolet light, West claimed he could see and find injuries and indentations that were otherwise invisible. He named his procedure the "West Phenomenon." Using it, he could find clues missed by all other investigators.

After describing his work and analysis, and impressing the jury with his expertise, vocabulary, experience, folksiness, and even, at times, humility, West was ready for the knockout punch. He offered the ultimate opinion that the bite marks on Courtney's wrist were "indeed and without a doubt" made by Levon Brooks.

The defense did not object. The judge said nothing.

The State offered no other credible evidence. No one from the crime lab testified because there was no biological evidence linking Brooks to the crime. The jury chose to believe the experts, Hayne and West, over the alibi witnesses who placed Brooks in the night-club where he was working at the time of the abduction. After five days of testimony and arguments by the lawyers, Levon Brooks was found guilty of capital murder.

Two days later the jury sentenced him to life without parole, and he was taken to the State's infamous prison at Parchman.

———

A few months passed and life returned to normal in Brooksville. With the murderer convicted and put away, folks felt safer and began to relax.

But in early May the killer struck again, and in much the same way. The second murder was so similar to Courtney's that someone in law enforcement should have asked serious questions.

The victim was Christine Jackson, another three-year-old child who lived not far from Courtney Smith. She lived with her mother, Gloria, and some siblings in a dilapidated shack on a gravel road in a remote area of the county. Gloria, not exactly a hands-on mother, was often in trouble with social services because of concerns over the health and welfare of her children. They were often unfed and neglected. Boyfriends came and went, but one, Kennedy Brewer, moved in and tried to help with the bills and kids. He was only nineteen years old and looking for steady employment.

On Saturday night, May 2, 1992, Gloria left the kids with Kennedy and went to the clubs with some friends. Her first, and favorite, was the Santa Barbara, now minus its longtime floor man, Levon Brooks, who was only three months into his life sentence. She returned home around 12:30 and found Kennedy and her three children asleep. She rousted her boyfriend and they had sex in another room, then returned to the bedroom and went to sleep.

Justin Johnson was in the area. He was living with his parents, about a mile away, and decided to take a long walk in the dark, with no destination in mind. Years later, when he confessed to both murders, he said he was following voices that led him to a small shack just off the road. The voices told him to open a broken window, lift it up, reach inside, and gently take a child sleeping on the floor. This he did without disturbing Gloria and Kennedy and without waking Christine or her siblings. He carried her into the woods, and when she awoke he put her down and they walked, hand in hand, deeper into the darkness. They stopped near a creek. The voices returned with a vengeance and told him to "sex molest her, hurt her, and dispose of the body." He undressed and raped her, ejaculated, choked her, and then threw her in the creek. He started crying and jumped in to save her, but she had already been swept downstream. Cold and wet, he sat on the edge of the creek for a long time and cried and listened to the voices in his head. At some point he walked back to his parents' home.

As soon as Gloria realized her daughter was missing on Sunday morning, she began frantically calling friends, neighbors, and family members. When a deputy arrived, at least two dozen people were searching for Christine.

Gloria and Kennedy told the deputy their versions of what had happened the night before. They were certain Christine was asleep at the foot of their bed when they fell asleep. She was gone when they woke up. There were no signs of forced entry, though none of the doors had locks.

The road to a bad conviction often begins at the crime scene with a misguided hunch. The deputy evaluated the situation and decided that since no one broke into the house, it had to be an inside job. The only adults inside the house were Gloria and Kennedy.

Deputy Eichelberger joined the brain trust and quickly agreed with the deputy's gut reaction. From that moment forward, Kennedy Brewer was the prime suspect. There was no hint of a motive. No evidence. No dead body at that point. And no clue as to how he could have eased himself out of bed, taken the child, carried her away, raped her, disposed of her body, then returned to his bed and fallen asleep without disturbing Gloria.

As usually happens, the hunch led to tunnel vision, and the investigators focused on Kennedy. They had their man.

The search continued with no success until a police helicopter spotted the body on Wednesday, four days after the murder. It was still in the creek and evidently had just floated to the surface. The county coroner sent the body to Dr. Hayne for an autopsy.

The police acknowledged the similarities in the two murders but did not believe they could be related. And why not? Their rationale was simple. Levon Brooks could not have killed Christine Jackson because he was incarcerated at Parchman.

As in the Brooks case, the police rounded up the usual suspects and hauled them to the hospital to be examined. Six men, including Kennedy Brewer and Justin Johnson, voluntarily gave samples of their blood, saliva, and urine, as well as body, scalp, and pubic hair. Nothing unusual was noticed, except for the scratches all over the arms of Justin Johnson. He told the nurse they were "self-inflicted."

This was not significant because the police were hot on the trail of their only real suspect, Kennedy Brewer, who was adamantly claiming to be innocent.

Dr. Hayne concluded that Christine had been strangled and raped. He collected a sample of semen. He also found numerous abrasions on her arms and legs and suspected they were bite marks. Thus, he needed to consult Dr. West. The tag team worked flawlessly because West was already at the morgue helping with the autopsy. Not surprisingly, he, too, was of the opinion that the wounds were bite marks.

Once again, rapists in Mississippi were on a biting binge.

West returned to his clinic in Hattiesburg and met the sheriff of Noxubee County, who had brought with him a collection of suspects. West took plaster dental imprints from Kennedy Brewer and two other men.

Christine's mother, Gloria Jackson, was along for the trip and also gave a plaster dental mold. No one knew why. As in the first case, there was no suspicion that the mother had taken her daughter from the house, raped, strangled, bit, and killed her, flung her into the creek, then returned to her bed.

Absent from the excursion to West's clinic was the killer, Justin Johnson. The police did not ask him to provide a dental mold. Not that it would have mattered now that Dr. West was practically running the investigation. He knew the police strongly suspected Kennedy Brewer and it was his job to close the case.

A week later he came through. In a letter to the sheriff, he wrote, "The bite marks found on the body of Christine Jackson were indeed and without a doubt inflicted by Kennedy Brewer."

––––––

Since the authorities now had samples of Justin Johnson's blood and saliva, the obvious next step would have been to compare them to the semen taken from Christine's body. This did not happen, not at that time anyway. Sixteen years would pass before the samples were compared. Meanwhile, Kennedy Brewer would come within days of being executed by lethal injection.

By 1992, the science and technology of DNA testing was still evolving. It was being used to solve criminal cases but seldom in Mississippi.

What was available at that time was bite mark analysis, and with it came a long and contentious history. The majority of legitimate scientists and forensic experts believed it was thoroughly unreliable. It was considered "junk science," along with comparisons of hair, boot prints, blood spatter, glass breakage, and other matching "proof." However, since it had been used in trials for decades, the courts allowed it.

———

In a 2001 study, twenty-five well-known bite mark experts were given four identical sets of bite marks and asked to compare them with seven sets of dental molds. The error rate was an astonishing 63.5 percent. Only one-third accurately "matched" the marks with the teeth. Almost all of them continued consulting and testifying in bite mark cases as if the study meant nothing.

The specialty of bite mark analysis is based on three assumptions. The first is that each person's teeth are unique and leave prints that are traceable. The second is that skin, once bitten, has markings that are distinguishable. The third is that trained experts can study the marks and identify who made them.

None of these assumptions are supported by scientific evidence. In 2009, the National Academy of Sciences (NAS) declared that bite mark analysis as a forensic specialty was not based on science. As recently as 2022, the National Institute of Standards and Technology (NIST) found that skin cannot record and preserve the details of a bite, and, further, that analysts do a lousy job of matching teeth marks with whoever did the biting. In many cases, the findings were so conflicted the analysts could not even agree on what was a bite and what was not.

The NIST and NAS reports fall in line with other studies. In 2016, the Texas Forensic Science Commission declared bite mark analysis so unfounded that it should no longer be used in criminal trials. A moratorium was also recommended by the President's Council of Advisors on Science and Technology.

But, science be damned. Bite mark analysis is still allowed in most jurisdictions; sought by prosecutors, presented by experts, approved by judges, believed by jurors, and rubber-stamped by appellate courts.

————

These later studies were, of course, no benefit to Kennedy Brewer in his trial. Dr. West, after having been qualified as an expert and identified as one of the leading forensic odontologists in the country, testified for hours. As in the Brooks trial, he used enlarged photos of the bite marks and molds of Kennedy's teeth and explained in excruciating detail the preciseness of his analysis. He explained his "direct comparison" method of actually taking a mold of the suspect's teeth and pressing it into the child's flesh.

The autopsy was recorded by video, though the judge refused to show it to the jury because he found it too prejudicial. There was music blaring in the background, conversations between Hayne and West and their assistants, and "callous" behavior by the doctors. Years later, another bite mark expert studied the video and described it: "Dr. West placed Kennedy Brewer's dental molds directly onto Christine Jackson's body several times, with sufficient force to create visible marks."

West's "direct comparison" method, a procedure he alone pioneered, actually created the bite marks he was using to nail Kennedy Brewer.

On March 24, 1995, after deliberating for only an hour and a half, the jury returned a verdict of guilty. Two days later, it returned with a sentence of death. The judge set an execution date two months away and ended the farce of a trial by dramatically saying to Kennedy, "May God have mercy on your soul."

By 1995, the Hayne and West team was attracting plenty of attention and not all of it was positive. Defense lawyers were complaining loudly and reporters were digging through their cases. They
were finding plenty of sensational material.

In a 1991 case, Dr. West testified that by using his incredible
ultraviolet light technique, he could match an abrasion on the victim's body with the shoelaces of the defendant. He also matched
an invisible pattern on the defendant's palm with the strap of the
victim's purse. In a rape case, he matched wounds on the victim's
vagina to the defendant's teeth. Then, using the West Phenomenon,
he also found indentions in the defendant's hand that matched a
screwdriver allegedly used to threaten the victim. In another case,
he matched abdominal bruises to a pair of hiking boots. In a sensational case, *State v. Keko,* the victim had been dead, embalmed, and
buried for fourteen months before the body was exhumed. The team
of Hayne and West quickly found a bite mark that they, somehow,
had missed during the autopsy. Using his yellow goggles and special
ultraviolet light, Dr. West declared the bite mark had been inflicted
near the time of death, and had "indeed and without a doubt" been
caused by the teeth of Tony Keko (the defendant). Defense lawyers
successfully argued for a new trial and challenged West's credentials.
At the time, he was under suspension by the American Board of
Pathology. When the trial judge refused to allow him to testify, the
State (Louisiana) dropped the charges and Tony Keko was released.
His wife's murder was never solved.

And then there was the infamous Bologna Sandwich Case. In
1993, an elderly woman named Amy Ware was eating a bologna
sandwich when someone broke into her house, robbed, and murdered her. The police found a half-eaten bologna sandwich and
froze it. Her body was taken to Dr. Hayne for an autopsy. He consulted Dr. West, who, for some reason, didn't examine the sandwich

for several months. When he finally got around to it, he claimed the teeth marks were consistent with the teeth of the prime suspect, Calvin Banks. They were inconsistent with those of Amy Ware, the victim. However, Hayne and West got their stories screwed up and West didn't realize that Hayne, during the autopsy, had found the remains of a half-eaten bologna sandwich in the victim's stomach. If she had eaten half the sandwich—the proof was in her stomach—how could the teeth marks on the uneaten portion not belong to her? Was it plausible that Calvin Banks took a bite or two either before or after he killed her, then left the rest behind? West took photos of the frozen sandwich; then, for some reason, he threw it away.

Forrest Allgood prosecuted Calvin Banks for the murder. West testified and convinced the jury that the teeth marks in the sandwich belonged to Calvin Banks. The jury bought it and convicted him. The Mississippi Supreme Court affirmed the legitimacy of bite mark analysis but tossed the conviction because West threw away the sandwich before the defense could examine it.

In 1992, another elderly woman, Georgia Kemp, was found dead by firefighters in her home. Investigators determined her house had been intentionally set on fire, ostensibly to cover up her murder. Hayne's autopsy revealed knife wounds as the cause of death. He also said she had been raped, though no biological evidence was found. His report made no mention of bite marks. Ms. Kemp's body was embalmed and buried. Suspicion quickly fell upon Eddie Lee Howard, an unemployed man who lived in the general area. He had a sex offense on his record that made him all the more likely to have committed the crime. He was arrested on suspicion of murder, but more evidence was needed. So the body was exhumed and sent back to Dr. Hayne for a more thorough examination. Not surprisingly, he then noticed several bite marks he had somehow missed the first time around. He called in West, who made a dental impression of

Howard's teeth. Voilà! The bite marks were without a doubt made by Howard.

Forrest Allgood prosecuted Eddie Lee Howard for the murder. At trial, Howard insisted on representing himself, with predictable results. He was sentenced to death. The Mississippi Supreme Court again affirmed the use of bite mark analysis but reversed the conviction because Howard had no lawyer. He had one for his second trial but was found guilty anyway.

Eddie Lee Howard spent twenty-six years on death row before being exonerated by DNA testing in 2020. The murder was never solved.

———

In spite of reversing the convictions of Calvin Banks and Eddie Lee Howard, the Mississippi Supreme Court has never shown much sympathy for defendants claiming to be victims of questionable forensics. It affirmed the conviction of Levon Brooks in an 8–1 decision and heartily endorsed bite mark analysis. It held that such evidence is "universally admissible in Mississippi Courts," and said it was as reliable as fingerprints and DNA. The lone dissenting judge called it unreliable, subjective, and not based on science. He also blistered Dr. West with a long and thorough summary of a growing list of outrageous claims.

Kennedy Brewer fared no better with the court. In a unanimous decision, it upheld his conviction and swatted away attacks on West by saying, "The record shows that Dr. West possessed the knowledge, skill, experience, training, and education necessary to qualify as an expert in forensic odontology."

Unfortunately, Mississippi, like most states, elects its judges; all of them. From the lowly justice court judges—untrained jurists not even required to have a high school diploma—to the nine members of its supreme court. Hardball politics and big money often contaminate the elections, with special interests hiding behind the ever-protective shield of law and order. During West's career as an expert witness, the supreme court justices rarely questioned his qualifications and methods. The lone dissenter in the appeal of Levon Brooks faced a well-financed opponent whose slick television ads labeled him as "the only justice who voted to reverse the conviction of the murderer of a three-year-old girl."

The dissenter lost by thirty points.

Again and again, the supreme court endorsed the work of Hayne and West and approved one dubious conviction after another. It seemed oblivious to the growing tide of complaints from defense lawyers, reporters, other experts, and even law enforcement officials.

One outrageous case, though, proved too much for the Mississippi Supreme Court.

In *State v. Tyler Edmonds,* the defendant was a thirteen-year-old boy being tried as an adult for murder. Forrest Allgood was once again prosecuting, and, not surprisingly, was again seeking the death penalty. His star witness was Dr. Hayne, who told the jury that, based on the angle of the bullet's entry into the stomach of the victim, he was of the opinion that not one, but two people had pulled the trigger of the rifle. This testimony fit snugly with Allgood's convoluted theory of the crime. As usual, Hayne was so slick on the witness stand that the unsophisticated jurors bought his testimony and convicted Tyler Edmonds.

In a rare act of judicial bravery, the supreme court reversed on the grounds that Hayne had obviously stepped beyond his field of expertise. During the second trial, and without Hayne's two-hands-on-the-trigger nonsense, the jury acquitted Tyler. He was released after spending five years in jail.

A California lawyer named Christopher Plourd was furious when his innocent client was wrongfully convicted twice for the murder of a cocktail waitress. The client spent ten years in prison and was almost executed. The case against him was built solely on the bite mark testimony of a local dentist. After his client was exonerated, Mr. Plourd decided to expose the quackery. He and a friend named James Rix, who was not involved in the case, devised a sting operation. They used the old photos of the alleged bite marks on the victim's breast, and paid a dentist to make a plaster mold of Rix's teeth. Mr. Plourd looked around the country at the so-called leading forensic odontologists and, by chance, selected Dr. Michael West. He called West, fed him a fictitious story, and hired him to consult. He sent West the photos, the mold of Rix's teeth, and a check for $750. Two months later, West responded with a letter and a twenty-minute video in which he carefully walked the viewer through his thorough analysis. No doubt the teeth (Rix's) caused the bite marks.

Though a complete fabrication as part of a sting, the video is astonishing to watch. West is a confident, polished testifier, and speaks like an expert who's been through many trials and knows how to relate to laymen. He explains his analysis in dental and medical terms, and is believable. It's easy to see how juries could be convinced he knew what he was talking about.

Mr. Plourd publicized the hoax and tried to bring attention to West and his bogus science. For a decade afterward, defense lawyers in Mississippi tried in vain to use it to convince judges to prevent West from testifying.

They were not successful.

In 2001 Brewer's lawyers convinced the Mississippi Supreme Court to allow another DNA test. The results stunned the State. Kennedy Brewer was excluded as the source. The semen had been left behind by another man.

His lawyers ran back to the court and insisted that the charges be dropped and their client immediately released. By then DNA testing was routinely freeing innocent men who had been wrongfully convicted, and in virtually every other case the tests were deemed conclusive of innocence.

Not so in Mississippi. The court refused to believe Brewer was innocent and said, among other absurdities, that "DNA evidence does not prove conclusively that Brewer did not murder the victim," and that there was enough other evidence to indicate Brewer's involvement. The only other physical evidence was the bite mark testimony from Dr. West.

Instead of reopening the case and trying to find the killer—the police had hair, blood, and saliva samples from several suspects, including Justin Johnson—Forrest Allgood announced he would retry Kennedy for the rape and murder. Fifteen years after the crime, and after being cleared by DNA testing, Kennedy would face another trial. He was hauled from death row at Parchman back to the Noxubee County jail, where he languished for almost six years as Forrest Allgood delayed a trial.

In 2007, lawyers from the Innocence Project in New York were allowed to do additional testing. Several boxes of evidence were sent to a lab in California for examination. The analysts used cheek swabs taken from the Brooks case, one of which was from Justin Johnson, and matched it to the semen taken from Chistine's body. Fifteen years after the rape and murder, the crime was finally solved.

The killer was identified as Justin Johnson. He was arrested and soon confessed to the murder of Christine Jackson. He led the investigators to the old house where Kennedy and Gloria once lived with her children, showed them the broken window, said he looked in, saw a man and a woman asleep in the bed, saw two girls asleep on the floor, and described how he lifted Christine through the window without waking her.

The police asked if he was involved in an earlier murder, and he admitted killing Courtney Smith. He remembered driving his car to a pond in the woods, walking to a nearby house, entering through the unlocked front door, walking past a man sleeping on the sofa, finding two little girls asleep in the bedroom, and taking the younger one from the house and into the woods, where he killed her and dumped her body into the pond.

———

Ten days later, Kennedy Brewer entered a packed courtroom and faced the same judge who, thirteen years earlier, had dispatched him to death row with an ominous "May God have mercy on your soul." This time, though, the judge simply said, "You're hereby discharged. You are free to go."

No explanation. No apology.

A month later, Levon Brooks was exonerated in the same courtroom.

Combined, the men spent over thirty years behind bars. The State paid them each $50,000 a year for time served, but capped it at the maximum of $500,000.

———

Four more years passed before the disgraced authorities in Noxubee County could muster the courage to bring Justin Johnson into the courtroom. He pled guilty to two counts of capital murder and was given life without parole. He described how he abducted and killed both girls. He raped Christine but not Courtney.

———

He did not bite either child.

LAST NIGHT OUT

JIM McCLOSKEY

M ark Jones, a native Texan from Corpus Christi, was two
months shy of his twenty-first birthday. He was about to get
married to the love of his life, Dawn Burgett, the pretty twenty-
year-old daughter of a career soldier. Their wedding date was set for
Saturday, February 1, 1992. Jones had worked as a radio operator in
Desert Storm and was now stationed at Fort Stewart in Hinesville,
Georgia. They planned to wed in the base chapel.

This was to be no small affair. Dawn and her mother had invited
150 people. Mark's mother had come in from the Florida Keys; his
father, wheelchair-bound, from Texas. Family and friends had traveled from the Burgetts' home state of Tennessee. Dawn's parents
loved Mark; he was the son they never had.

After the wedding rehearsal at the base chapel on January 31,
sixteen family members and friends arrived at the Golden Corral
restaurant in Hinesville for the rehearsal dinner. Despite a reser-
vation mix-up that didn't get them seated until 8:15, everyone

was in a festive mood and looking forward to the next day's big event.

Among the dinner guests were two of Mark's best buddies from the base, Kenneth Gardiner and Dominic Lucci. A fellow Texan, twenty-one-year-old Kenny had arrived at Fort Stewart five months earlier from assignment in Germany. Before that, he, too, had served in Desert Storm, working as a mechanic on vehicles and tanks. Twenty-two-year-old Dominic, whom everyone called Dino, had been born and raised in Cleveland, Ohio. After a one-year tour in Korea, he had been transferred to Fort Stewart, where he worked as a food specialist. This would be his last billet before discharging from the army.

After dinner a group of the young people drifted out to the Golden Corral's parking lot, trying to decide where to go from there. Kenny and Dino wanted to take Mark to a club for his last night as a bachelor. Mark, a teetotaler, was reluctant and wanted to call it a night. But Dawn urged him to join his friends and even suggested a local club that was having a bikini contest.

At 9:30 everyone went their separate ways. Dawn returned to her parents' house, while the three soldiers headed to the club holding the bikini contest.

Mark was carded at the club and, since he was not yet twenty-one, denied entry. Dino came up with a backup plan: a strip club in Savannah called Tops Lounge that he had been to once. Since Mark and Kenny were not familiar with Savannah, Kenny let Dino drive his new 1992 black, two-door Chevrolet Cavalier, a recent gift from Kenny's father. Off they went, driving the only route Dino knew, forty-eight miles along 95, taking the Route 204/Abercorn Street exit and then heading east onto Victory Drive to Tops Lounge.

As they were driving, thirty-five-year-old Stanley Jackson, a black man, was walking in a dangerous part of Savannah known locally as "Hazard County," the epicenter of the drug trade where buyers and sellers came and went. At 10:05 he was gunned down by a barrage of bullets as he stood at the corner of 33rd and East Broad Street.

James White, also black, was a married thirty-eight-year-old father of eight children, employed as a bus driver and serving as an assistant minister at a small black Baptist church in Savannah. At the moment of the shooting, he was standing at his front door, about to let himself in. Hearing gunshots, he turned in their direction and saw sparks hitting the street. Then he saw a car come out of seemingly nowhere, screeching to a halt in the middle of the intersection.

He told the police when interviewed at the crime scene that two men were leaning out of the car shooting back toward the victim with some kind of rifles. He said that the killer's car remained in the intersection during the shooting for only a few seconds before it sped off, going north on East Broad. A police officer one mile away heard the gunfire and headed in that direction, arriving at the crime scene close to 10:10 P.M. Five shell casings were recovered. Tests later determined that all casings were fired from the same AK-47 assault rifle. Bullet holes riddled a nearby home, though thankfully no one was hit.

Although an autopsy revealed no bullets or bullet fragments in Jackson's body, he had been hit six times by bullets that passed through him. What caused his death were spinal bone fragments that pierced both lungs, causing severe hemorrhaging. Toxicology tests found a "significant level" of cocaine in Jackson's blood, and he'd been carrying a homemade crack pipe. At his death he was on probation for purchasing what he believed to be a rock of cocaine from an undercover agent at a Savannah drug house.

Oblivious to the shooting that had occurred four miles away just ten minutes before, the three young white soldiers arrived at Tops Lounge around 10:15, where Mark got carded again, this time by the Tops Lounge doorman. Listening to the soldiers failing to talk their way in, a taxicab driver and an arriving customer suggested they go to another strip joint, Club Asia. The soldiers got directions and headed for the club, driving north on East Broad until they ran up against the police barricade at the Stanley Jackson crime scene. Here, a police officer gave them new directions and pointed them away from the scene. Still uncertain, they then asked an off-duty cop working as a security guard at a Kroger's for the best route to the club. Finally, they approached a uniformed police officer, Deborah Evans, while she was waiting to cross the street. She directed them to Club Asia, only a few blocks away. Once seated in the club, Kenny and Mark ordered Cokes and Dino ordered a beer and a shot of Soju, a Korean liquor.

Little did they know that their world was about to collapse.

Officer Evans had been waiting to cross the street with James White, the eyewitness to the killing of Stanley Jackson. She was escorting White from the crime scene to Savannah Police headquarters, commonly called "the Barracks," so that detectives could take his statement. It was a few minutes after 10:30, thirty minutes after Jackson had been mowed down.

After the soldiers had driven away, White told Evans that their car "looked like" the killers' car. With that, all hell broke loose. Evans immediately called for backup, dropped White off at the station, and hurried over to Club Asia. Within minutes a swarm of police had escorted the three men out of the club. They were made to stand in front of it so that White, whom they had brought over from the Barracks, could see them more clearly and identify them as the shooters. He could not.

In the parking lot, police searched the car with Kenny's consent and found nothing of evidentiary value—no weapons, no ammunition, no spent shell casings, no dents from ejected shell casings, nothing that connected the car or the soldiers to Jackson's murder or any other crime.

The car was later vacuumed and closely inspected for gunshot residue, with negative results.

Nonetheless, at 10:50 P.M. the soldiers were transported a short distance to the Barracks for questioning. A phalanx of detectives and their bosses reported to the Barracks to lend a hand with the all-night investigation. The lieutenant in charge of the violent crime division, D. Everette Ragan, and Assistant District Attorney David Lock took charge of the investigation.

The police interrogated the young men separately for two hours, trying to extract confessions through pressure and lies. Each of them was falsely told that the other two had confessed, so it would go easier on him if he would also confess.

All three insisted on their innocence and offered consistent accounts of their whereabouts that day and night leading up to their interrogation. Police went to Tops Lounge at 3:00 A.M. and interviewed the doorman who had carded Mark. He affirmed the soldiers' alibi and told the police that all three boys had tried hard to convince him to let them in, that all they wanted to do was help Mark celebrate his wedding the next day. He characterized them as "just three guys wanting to have a good time at a titty bar."

Dino refused to be bullied and threatened to walk out of the station. He was then handcuffed to a chair and stuffed in a closet. When he kicked open the closet door, he was arrested. Mark was worn out and in tears when they told him that he was under arrest for murder.

Meanwhile, James White was in another part of the building giving a detailed statement to rookie homicide detective Harvey Middleton. Twice in the statement he said the Gardiner car "looked like" the shooters' car, but by the conclusion of his statement he had changed this to the soldiers' car being "one and the same" as the killers' car. He also stated first that he thought the shooters were either white or Creole, then later in the statement said they were white.

Middleton got what he wanted—a car identification. But

White's initial description of the car at the crime scene had been markedly different from that of the Gardiner car. White had first told Middleton that the killers' car was an older model, "'85 to '90," with tinted windows, and was "bigger in the back and smaller in the front." The new 1992 Gardiner car was just the opposite— big in the front and small in the back, and it did not have tinted windows.

The three young men were not your everyday suspects. None of them had any prior encounters with either civilian or military police—no arrests, no convictions, no problems whatsoever with law enforcement of any kind. None of the three used drugs, nor did they abuse alcohol. There was no connection between the soldiers and Jackson. The young men had neither motive, means, nor opportunity to commit such a heinous crime.

Nonetheless, with only a car ID, sometime after 2:00 A.M., ADA Lock and Lieutenant Ragan decided to hold the men for murder and ordered them transported to the Chatham County jail.

———

In 1991, more than 40 percent of Savannah's approximately 140,000 residents were black. White men, however, held all the political power, as they always had. There was growing racial tension between the long-tenured all-white city fathers and the politically active black civic and church leadership. Very little room existed in Savannah's calcified city government for racial diversity or mutual understanding.

In recent years, a nationwide crack cocaine epidemic had fueled an explosion of violent crime as drug gangs committed brutal killings in most major cities. In Savannah, the all-black Ricky Jivens gang was particularly murderous. The homicide rate in the city had tripled in two years, from twenty-one dead in 1989 to fifty-nine in 1991. By the time of the murder at 33rd and East Broad in late January 1992, there had been five homicides already in Savannah, predicting an annualized rate of seventy-two. Stanley Jackson's was the sixth.

Black community leaders had become increasingly frustrated with law enforcement, who they saw as failing to invest the same effort in solving cases involving black victims as white ones. The issue had come to a head in mid-September 1991 when a sixteen-year-old runaway and prospective member of the Jivens gang randomly shot to death a man and his dog in the upscale white Savannah neighborhood of Ardsley Park. The affluent residents were outraged and afraid. In response, Mayor John Rousakis and Police Chief David Gellatly called press conferences and personally met with the Ardsley Park residents, assuring them that the killer would be brought to justice. A score of detectives was assigned to the case.

The disparity in how officials reacted to this one white person's murder compared to the thirty-seven black murder victims that year infuriated the city's black leadership. They held press conferences and asked why Savannah city leaders had not visited or shown equal concern for their communities.

In the November election, black voters had a chance to express their anger. Democratic mayor Rousakis suffered a stunning defeat in his bid for a sixth consecutive term, losing to transplanted New Yorker Susan Weiner, the first woman and only the second Republican to win the Savannah mayorship in the city's two-hundred-year history. The *Savannah Morning News,* the city's leading newspaper, credited Weiner's shocking victory to black voters crossing over to the Republican ticket. She had made crime her leading issue; her campaign billboards plastered throughout the city featured no words, only bullet holes.

Stanley Jackson's murder thus unfolded in a Savannah deeply divided along racial fault lines—Jackson was a black man shot by at least two white men, according to a black eyewitness who called himself "Reverend," and now three young white soldiers, by sheer happenstance, had fallen into law enforcement's lap. The authorities believed that if they could find enough evidence to convict the three men, they could demonstrate to the black electorate that black victims were just as important to law enforcement as white victims. Mark, Kenny, and Dominic became perfect scapegoats. The three young soldiers would not receive justice. They would be sacrificed on the altar of politics.

———

The Savannah police quickly figured out how to use TV cameras to their advantage. They alerted the media, and at some time after 2:00 A.M., TV cameras were waiting to film the soldiers as they were led out of the Barracks in handcuffs on their way to the county jail. Even before Jackson's body had been removed, cameras were at the crime scene. By giving the media easy access, the assistant district attorney made the Fourth Estate, formerly an enemy, into his new best friend. (Later, during the trial, cameras were allowed in the courtroom, a rare event in Savannah at that time. The trial was the lead story on all TV channels each night of the proceedings.)

In shock, still unable to comprehend what had just happened to him and his friends, Mark made a collect phone call to Dawn at her parents' house sometime between 2:00 and 3:00 A.M. He asked her not to be angry with him, and then stunned her with the news that they were in the Savannah jail "because they think we murdered someone." In a state of panic, Dawn raced to his mother's hotel, banged on her door, and told her where Mark and his friends were and why.

For the next fifty minutes they drove to downtown Savannah, arriving before dawn. Miraculously they were permitted to visit all three men together through a window. The only thing Dawn remembers from the visit is that someone at the jail gave her Mark's blue jacket.

Later that morning, Dawn wrote a notice and taped it to the

base chapel's door that read, WEDDING OF DAWN BURGETT AND
MARK JONES CANCELED DUE TO FAMILY EMERGENCY.

On February 6, a week after their arrest, a bail hearing was
held for the three men. Dino's grandfather retained local criminal defense attorney Bill Cox for his grandson. He also provided
the funding for Cox to recruit John Watts, Sr., to represent Kenny,
and Watts's son, John Watts, Jr., to represent Mark. Bail was set at
$30,000 for each defendant. In mid-April, when their families came
up with the funds, Kenny and Dino were released and remained
free through the trial. Mark, however, stayed in jail awaiting trial
because his family could not raise the bail.

The preliminary hearing, during which the State was required
to present evidence sufficient for the defendants to be held for trial,
was scheduled for February 26. As the date neared, political pressure mounted. On February 19, more than two hundred people
from the black community, including Stanley Jackson's friends and
family, held a candlelight vigil at the intersection of 33rd and East
Broad. The speakers criticized city officials for not attending and
lamented once again that "when one man died in Ardsley Park,
everybody showed up."

The next day, a thirty-member contingent from the Jackson vigil
attended a city council meeting. Although the group was not on
the agenda, Mayor Weiner, in her second month in office, allowed
its spokesperson, Rev. Leonard Small, to speak. He admonished
Savannah officials for treating cases of black victims differently than
those of white victims, citing the Ardsley Park murder, and called
for an end to Savannah's "institutional racism." He prayed for "racial
unity" and "equal treatment in Savannah."

One week later, at the preliminary hearing, witness White for
the first time claimed that he could positively identify Jackson's
shooters, pointing to Gardiner and Jones. He testified that when
he saw their faces at the bond hearing (during which bail was set),

it suddenly came to him that they were the men who shot Jackson. He added that it was "definitely" them. Needless to say, this greatly strengthened the prosecution's case against the defendants. ADA Lock now had an eyewitness who could identify two of the soldiers as the shooters, and the Gardiner car as the vehicle used by the killers.

The State tried to get Dino to turn against his friends, maintaining that since he'd been the driver and not a shooter, he could get twenty years for voluntary manslaughter in exchange for testimony naming Jones and Gardiner as the shooters. He soundly rejected this.

On the eve of the trial, the State tried again, significantly improving their offer to eighteen months for involuntary manslaughter if he would incriminate his codefendants. Without the slightest hesitation Dino refused, saying years later that there was no way he would "sell out my friends and myself for something none of us did."

The trial opened on November 9, 1992. The jury panel consisted of nine white jurors and three black jurors, together with two black alternate jurors.

The State's case relied heavily on the testimony of James White, who spiced up his eyewitness account by telling the jury that "I saw them good. I was looking right at them." When asked by Lock if he was "positive that the individuals you've identified in court are the ones you saw in the intersection shooting that night," he responded, "I'm positive."

Yet his testimony seemed to undercut his certainty, emphasizing as it did the brevity of his observation and the fear he felt for his life. On the night of the shooting, he testified, he was returning to his home from a church service. As he was fumbling for his keys at his front door, he heard heavy gunfire coming from around the corner of the intersection of 33rd Street and East Broad Street. When he turned to look toward the intersection, he saw sparks hitting the street like "fire." Then a car came into view and stopped in the middle of the intersection. He saw "fire coming from the guns" of what he claimed were two men leaning out of the passenger side window of the car, shooting back toward the victim. He couldn't tell if the fire was coming from one or both guns. Before he knew it, the car sped off, tires screeching.

Clearly traumatized, he thought he was in "a war zone." He observed the shooting for "three to four seconds" at the most. During the shooting he backed up hard against the door and banged three or four times loudly for his wife, Suzette, to let him in. When she finally came to the door he was so "upset and shaken," he had her call the police because he couldn't speak.

Months before the trial, on March 6, 1992, a recently retired E-6 staff sergeant, Sylvia Wallace, had come forward to give Detective Middleton a statement to which she now testified at trial. Her disjointed story was that, on Friday morning, January 31, 1992, she and Mark Jones were chatting in front of the barracks following the conclusion of a major battalion inspection requiring Battle Dress Uniform. When she asked Jones what he was doing that weekend, he replied that he "was going to go into Savannah, that he was going to get married on Saturday, and that he had somebody in Savannah he was going to shoot." When she asked him who, he said, "I got a black guy up there I got to get."

Under cross-examination Wallace admitted that she'd had unspecified "problems" at the time she claimed Jones had made his racist remarks, and that these problems, coupled with stress, had led her to destroy all her army-related possessions except her military dress uniform and to retire after twenty-one years of service. Mark was stunned when she appeared on the witness stand and fabricated this exchange. He barely knew her. They were in the same battalion but different companies. She was twice his age. They had what he considered to be a cordial but very superficial relationship.

Mark's company commander and Mark's roommate both contradicted her testimony, testifying that on the day in question Mark was on leave preparing for his wedding, and that there had been no inspection of any kind.

ADA Lock played the race card again with his next witness. He tried to elicit racially charged testimony from Private First Class Heather Radford, a twenty-one-year-old single mother of a six-month-old. She and Kenny Gardiner had been stationed at the same time in Saudi Arabia and in Germany prior to their September 1991 arrival at Fort Stewart. They were casual friends but nothing more than that.

Among other explosive questions, Lock asked Radford if she remembered telling his two investigators during an interview a month before that Gardiner had told her that he "hated niggers period, he would always say he hated niggers 'cause they wanted to take over the party and the music and the women. He said he would like to dress up in black and kill them." She denied ever telling the investigators this.

Under cross-examination by the defense, she testified that, after her meeting with the two investigators, she met with Lock. During this interview, Lock kept insisting that Gardiner had made that statement, that he hated blacks and wanted to kill them. He pressed her, asking five or six times if Gardiner made that statement. She insisted that Gardiner had never said such a thing.

To rebut her, Lock brought in his two investigators, J. D. Smith and Glen Kessler, who both testified that Radford had told them that Gardiner *had* made these statements. Smith admitted under cross-examination that they had not taped the interview nor drawn up a statement for her to sign.

Since ADA Lock was at a loss to establish a motive for the killing, and knew that there was no connection between the defendants and Stanley Jackson, he decided to accuse the soldiers not only of being racist but also dangerous thrill-seekers. It had been established at trial that the young men loved to play Dungeons & Dragons. Prosecutor Lock tried to convey to the jury that this tabletop role-playing game had helped inspire them to go to Savannah and do what they did. He reminded the jury that the defense expert on D&D had said that the objective of all D&D players was for good to triumph over evil. He postulated that maybe the defendants went to this drug-plagued area of Savannah with the idea that "they were getting rid of evil."

In his summation to the jury, he said, "These guys were obsessed with some kind of thrill. We don't have to prove motive in this case, but we suggest that basically they are thrill-seekers. A sick, demented way of seeking a thrill." Warming to this theme, he went on, "That's the best cover . . . if you wanted to kill somebody for the thrill of it, you might go into an area like that. In fact, I would suggest you would. Maybe because it would get attributed to a drug homicide. Just another drug killing, and so people wouldn't think to look elsewhere." To transform the defendants from role-playing board-game geeks to thrill-seeking killers was a preposterous gambit, one that had absolutely no basis in fact.

When it was the defense's turn, the lawyers drew on strong alibis and an abundance of evidence, both documents and witness testimony, demonstrating that the timing for the murders didn't work and that the defendants were not racist.

A private investigator testified that, if he stayed within the speed limits, it took him fifty-two minutes to drive the forty-eight miles from the Golden Corral, where the rehearsal dinner was held, directly to the Tops Lounge along the same route used by the defendants the night of the crime. This time and distance were not disputed by the prosecution.

Six witnesses, including four dinner guests and two waitresses, claimed that the defendants left the Golden Corral parking lot at

9:30 or very close to it. If they had gone directly to 33rd and East Broad to shoot someone, they couldn't have gotten there before 10:15, and then they'd have to go somewhere to ditch the weapons and ammunition before arriving at Tops Lounge, which was a seven-minute ride from the crime scene. Additionally, they'd have to be pretty cool killers to arrive at Tops Lounge with a demeanor described by the doorman as "just three guys wanting to have a good time at a titty bar." Although Lock refused to accept the word of the witnesses, projecting instead that the soldiers left closer to 9:15, either way it would have been impossible for them to have made it to the crime scene by 10:05.

On the issue of whether the young men were racist vigilantes, the defense had plenty of evidence that they were not.

A U.S. Army colonel, at the request of the base's commanding general, had prepared a profile of Kenny Gardiner a mere three days after his arrest. It stated that Kenny was "a good soldier" and that "no disciplinary action has ever been taken against him . . . and he does what he is told and has never been late or absent for formation." It concluded that "there is no evidence of racism on the part of Gardiner."

The report went on to say that his two roommates were black and, according to them, he never exhibited any racist or prejudicial behavior. One of them, Sullie Kinnie, told the jury that there had never been any racial problems with Kenny, and that Kenny did not like to go out; instead, "reading was his top priority."

Within days of the soldiers' arrest, both Kenny's company commander and Detective Middleton searched Kenny's quarters and the trailer that Kenny shared off-base with Dino. Nothing was found indicating any racial bias, nor anything of evidentiary value: no hate literature or anything related to crime or violent behavior, only comic books and science fiction paperbacks.

The record clearly absolved Mark Jones of even a hint of rac-

ism. First of all, he came from a biracial family. His stepfather was
a black jazz musician. The army report on Mark shortly after his
arrest described him as "a naive, innocent individual . . . who has
a positive attitude and performs his job in an efficient manner." It
goes on to say that "PV2 Jones has never shown any indication of
racial prejudice, and has no significant problems working with Sergeant Davenport, a black American. He has worked diligently by
his side for the past two years."

Sergeant Davenport said that it was "preposterous" to think
Mark would commit a murder. He testified at Mark's bond hearing that he had been Mark's squad leader for more than two years,
including their time together in Saudi Arabia and Iraq, and that
Mark was "not violent nor has he given people any trouble." He visited Mark three times in the county jail before he left for Germany
on assignment.

Mark's black roommate, Aaron McAbee, testified at trial that
Mark had invited him to the wedding, and that he'd never had any
type of racial problem with Mark. It was common for soldiers of
every racial stripe—whites, blacks, and Hispanics—to congregate
in Mark and Aaron's room and watch TV. Mark's black supervisor
who served with him in Desert Storm, Eric Bibbs, told the jury that
Mark "is not a mean or violent person," and that he liked people
regardless of their race or color.

There is not much in the record about Dominic Lucci's racial
attitudes. For whatever reason, the prosecution did not attempt to
paint Dominic as racist. E-7 Special First Class Sergeant Marinaro
supervised Dino soon after he arrived at Fort Stewart in October
1991 from his one-year tour in Korea. When Marinaro was interviewed by the police the week after Dino's arrest, he told them that
he "didn't think Lucci was prejudicial."

The defense also made the point that thorough searches of the
defendants' car and quarters had turned up no evidence against

them. (Neither the police nor prosecution could ever account for where or when or how the soldiers were able to dispose of the weapons or ammunition, or why the car contained no forensic evidence of involvement in a drive-by shooting using assault rifles.) In addition, all three of them had clean records, did not do drugs, did not know the victim, and had no motive, means, or opportunity to kill him.

The defendants did not testify. Their attorneys thought they had presented a strong case, and therefore there was no need to risk Lock confusing and baiting the young defendants on the witness stand.

Just before jury deliberations began, a white juror reported to the judge her concerns that, throughout the two-week trial, another juror, a black female, made no secret of the fact that she knew the victim's father and that she believed the defendants were guilty. She was excused and replaced by a black male alternate who lived two blocks from where Jackson had been shot. This juror admitted to "hearing neighbors talking about how it happened and everything . . . you hear different things all the time." The defense challenged this juror, but Judge Perry Brannen denied his removal.

Jury deliberations began at 3:30 P.M. on November 19, 1992. By 11:51 P.M. they reached their verdict: All three defendants were guilty of malice murder.

As soon as the jury departed the courtroom, Judge Brannen, in a hurry to finish the case, began a brief nine-minute sentencing hearing. No testimony was taken and the attorneys spoke for only a few minutes. At 12:05 A.M. on November 20, a scant fourteen minutes after the guilty verdict, the judge sentenced the three men to life in prison. He later admitted that he secretly had the National Guard on call in case the soldiers had been acquitted. Throughout the trial, the Savannah authorities had feared there might be race riots akin to those in Los Angeles following the April 1992 acquittal of the LAPD officers in the Rodney King assault trial.

The defense attorneys were as appalled as anyone by the verdict and went to work pro bono seeking evidence challenging the conviction. Six jurors provided affidavits stating their belief that the soldiers did not get a fair trial because of abuses during jury deliberations. The jurors described how a fellow juror, Murphy Cooper, a black attorney, intimidated those leaning toward acquittal, accusing them of being racially prejudiced.

He told them that unless they unanimously voted to convict the soldiers, there could be racial disturbances in Savannah similar to those in Los Angeles seven months earlier. Cooper also erroneously told them that anyone who voted to acquit would be identified in open court and could therefore expect racial retaliation.

In 1994, the Georgia Supreme Court denied an appeal of the conviction based on these juror affidavits, ruling that state law disallowed jurors from impeaching their own verdict unless "extraordinary circumstances" beset a particular case, and this case did not rise to that level.

———

The defendants spent the next seventeen years in prison. In 2009, Centurion Ministries, after having spent several years studying the voluminous record of the case, began a field investigation on the soldiers' behalf. Through 2012, Centurion interviewed numerous witnesses in a search for new evidence. It retained new counsel for the soldiers, tapping Seattle attorney Peter Camiel, who had previously served as attorney for other Centurion clients, and Savannah attorney Steve Sparger.

At the top of the witness list was James White, whose testimony had always been questionable. Police had measured the distance between White's front door on East Broad Street and where the car had sat in the middle of the intersection as seventy-two feet. It had been a dark, moonless night with inadequate street lighting.

These factors, along with the short time White had had to

observe the shooting while in a highly traumatized state, fearing for his life, all undercut the reliability of his testimony.

Centurion tracked down White, along with his wife, Suzette, in a room at a Super 8 motel off I-85 just outside Newnan, Georgia, some thirty miles southwest of the Atlanta airport. They were homeless and had all their worldly possessions piled every which way in their room. Over the course of that year, Centurion met with the Whites three times, getting to know them as people and discussing James's testimony and the circumstances surrounding it. Finally, with shame and remorse, the Whites admitted that James had indeed lied at the trial. Ever since, their consciences had been deeply troubling them. This led them to execute sworn affidavits in January 2011, fully recanting White's trial testimony. (Sadly, Suzette died of a heart attack in 2012 at age fifty-one.)

In 2011, Centurion caught up with Heather Radford at her home in central Pennsylvania. By then she was in her eighth year as a state prison corrections officer, and was married to a corrections officer. Initially reluctant, she agreed to speak with us once we explained our purpose and showed her photos of the three men. She said her testimony had weighed heavily on her heart over the last eighteen years, because it hadn't been strong enough to refute the testimony of the prosecutor's investigators in the eyes of the jury. She called the conviction of the three soldiers a "travesty of justice."

She remembered feeling extremely intimidated by the two investigators, recalling that she was a young single mother of a little baby and was essentially alone in the world feeling very vulnerable and scared. Once her testimony concluded, she told us, "I was done. I couldn't deal with the fact that maybe I had something to do with Kenneth's conviction." After speaking with her husband, she gladly executed an affidavit and agreed to testify if we wanted her to. Her 2011 affidavit made clear that Kenny had never made any anti-black comments to her.

When Centurion interviewed Sylvia Wallace at her home in North Carolina, she conceded that she'd told four different stories about what Jones told her and that the testimony of Mark's company commander and Mark's roommate, contradicting hers, was true. Yet she couldn't account for her conflicting stories. Throughout our visit, even when we were not discussing her trial testimony, she would suddenly blurt out things like "I can't take back what I said," or "I cannot change what I said in the courtroom," or "I did not lie and cannot take back what I said." Why she made such statements so wildly out of context is difficult to understand other than indicating her guilty conscience.

Finally, in 2010, after a public records request, Centurion discovered a crucial piece of evidence in police files. Buried within six hundred pages on the case was a one-page Savannah police report referred to as the "Yamacraw report."

It described an incident that occurred at 1:00 A.M. on Saturday morning, February 1, 1992, two hours *after* the three soldiers were in police custody. The incident took place in the Yamacraw Village housing projects. Two white men with military-style haircuts, armed with semiautomatic weapons, driving two vehicles—a white Chevy pickup and a silver two-door 1989–91 Ford Thunderbird—were "threatening to shoot blacks who hung out on street corners." The report had been hidden from the soldiers' defense team for eighteen years.

On behalf of the defendants, attorneys Camiel and Sparger filed a petition in May 2012 that presented the case for the soldiers' "actual innocence" and highlighted the suppression of evidence by law enforcement that pointed to their innocence.

This led to a post-conviction evidentiary hearing held before Judge Sarah Wall of the Wheeler County Superior Court located in McRae, Georgia, in July 2013. McRae, a small town of 5,700 in south central Georgia, is located near the prison that housed the soldiers during the hearing.

This hearing was the first time that the men's parents had reunited since the trial twenty-one years earlier. Kenny's mother and father, Mark's mother, and Dino's father and uncle were in attendance. They all shared the same heartache but now also the same hope: to bring their sons home after all these dark years. Dawn Burgett also attended to show her support for Mark and his codefendants.

At the hearing, Harvey Middleton, once the rookie homicide lead investigator in charge of the case, in 2013 serving as a police officer in Miami Beach, told the judge that "Mr. White's identification was never 100 percent sure. He never gave us a 100 percent positive identification."

Assistant DA Lock also testified that the detectives "were concerned about his [White's] ability to make an ID." This explains why, even though White asked to see a lineup, the police demurred. He was also never asked to identify the soldiers in a photo lineup using the photos taken of the men that night.

Lock's and Middleton's testimony was the first time in the twenty-two-year history of the case that law enforcement revealed this concern. It directly contradicted and undercut White's testimony at trial that he was "positive" Jones and Gardiner were the shooters.

The inability of White to make an identification was a clear violation of the rule established by the U.S. Supreme Court in *Brady v. Maryland* that prosecutors and police are required to disclose to the defense all exculpatory evidence in their possession before trial.

Why had White lied at trial? Here is what he said, in person at the 2013 hearing and in his affidavit:

> *I lied because everybody was pushing me to say it was these guys. The pressure to identify them was overwhelming. To convince me to make these identifications, the police told me that these soldiers*

had been on a rampage killing black people around town, and that they did so because they didn't like blacks. They told me that if I didn't identify them there would be race riots in the city. They told me they knew they were guilty but that they couldn't make a case against them without my identification, and that they would go free unless I identified them. They told me that they needed my help, and that the community needed my help.

My wife and I were getting phone calls from a lot of black folks encouraging me to do "the right thing." I remember in particular Reverend Matthew Brown [a prominent black church pastor in Savannah] telephoning us and telling me the police have the right guys, and that it was time to stand up and come forward. He also told me that the city would have riots and would be in an uproar unless these boys were convicted. Rev. Brown said he would invite me to come speak to his church in the near future. [He never did.]

My wife, Suzette, pleaded with me not to lie on those boys. But I was afraid that if I didn't identify them something bad was going to happen to me and my family. We had eight children at the time, all living at 1703 East Broad Street. Before it was time for me to testify at trial, I told the police and prosecutor that I couldn't make any identifications and that I didn't want to testify. I was told that if I didn't testify at trial the way I did at the preliminary hearing, I would be prosecuted for perjury and be sent to prison.

That freaked me out. I was scared because I didn't want to be away from my family, my wife and kids. So I thought about it and said I gotta keep lying at this point . . . I knew I was lying when I positively identified two of them as the shooters of Stanley Jackson. But much to my regret and shame I did it anyway out of fear . . . Because being a minister of the Gospel I know it says in the Book of Exodus you can't be a false witness. Thou shall not kill, steal or

be a false witness against people. And I did that. And that hurt
me so bad and it's been torturing me for years. For at least 21 and
I'm sorry.

The second *Brady* violation cited in the petition was the suppression of the Yamacraw police report, which stated that other white men had been driving around Savannah housing projects looking to shoot black men on street corners with semiautomatic weapons the same night Jackson had been gunned down. The prosecution was also aware that on October 21, 1991, a few months before Stanley Jackson was killed, two white men driving a small red pickup truck had shot two black men an hour or so after midnight. The first victim was fatally shot in the abdomen while getting out of his car in front of his home. Minutes before, four blocks away, another black man was shot in the left arm while exiting his car outside his home. Witnesses told police that the perpetrators were two white men in their mid-twenties to early thirties. They were described as clean-cut. The cases were never cleared.

Although Lieutenant Ragan's name was written on the top of the Yamacraw report, he, along with Sergeant Stevens, the other officer in charge of the investigation, claimed that they did not remember seeing this report. They did concede at the evidentiary hearing, however, that this document contained information that should have been followed up on by the police.

Lock also conceded in his testimony that in his meetings with Ragan and the detectives the night of the murder, their biggest concern was the need to get more incriminating evidence against the soldiers.

Ronald Holmes, who was black, testified at the hearing on the time and distance it took to get from the Golden Corral restaurant in Hinesville to the crime scene and to Tops Lounge, to underline for the judge how impossible the prosecution's timeline had been.

Holmes had spent fourteen years as a taxicab driver based in Hinesville. He drove from Hinesville to Savannah four to six times a week. He testified that it was forty-one miles from the Golden Corral to the crime scene, and that the quickest time via the shortest route took a minimum of forty-six minutes, going an average of nine miles over the speed limit on the highways. If the three men drove directly to the "Hazard County" area of Savannah, carrying assault weapons and ammunition with intent to randomly shoot someone, they'd have to be careful to keep close to the speed limit so as not to attract the highway patrol on a busy Friday night.

Three former senior sergeants and a twenty-year veteran of the Hinesville police department testified that Sylvia Wallace had told each of them a different story concerning her conversation with Jones, all different from the one she offered at trial.

The defense brought in twenty-two witnesses in all and presented as primary evidence James White's recantation, the testimony of Detective Middleton, and the suppression of the Yamacraw report by the Savannah police. The general staff attorneys representing the State introduced only one witness, trial prosecutor David Lock. Centurion thought its witnesses made a strong case and believed that the hearing went extremely well.

We were wrong.

The soldiers were stunned when Judge Wall issued her opinion in August 2014, one year after the hearing, denying the defendants a new trial. In regard to the Yamacraw report, she ruled that "since Petitioners did not raise this allegation at trial and did not enumerate it as error on direct appeal, this claim is procedurally barred from consideration on the merits by this Court."

This was nonsensical. How could it have been used by the defense at the 1992 trial or in the direct appeal in 1993–94 when it was not known by the defense until 2010? The same objection applied to White's inability to make a positive identification. No one except law enforcement knew that until 2013. By its very nature, a *Brady* violation is typically discovered at some point post-conviction.

The first legal break in the case came in November 2014 when the Georgia Supreme Court, in a 9–0 unanimous vote, quickly remanded it back to Judge Wall, instructing her to rule on the merits and materiality of the suppression of the Yamacraw report and White's inability to make a positive identification. But Wall again denied the soldiers, fifteen months later, in March 2016. This time she ruled that the State did not suppress the Yamacraw report nor have a reason to turn it over to the defense because there was no indication that it had any connection to the murder of Jackson.

Regarding White, she did acknowledge that his identification of the petitioners as the shooters was an important part of the State's case. She also agreed that any information that detracted from the credibility of his trial testimony would be "potentially excul-patory evidence for the defense." But she discredited his recanta-tion, and made no mention of Middleton's testimony that White never made a positive identification of the soldiers throughout the investigation. She omitted that pertinent fact, which was cer-tainly exculpatory and detracted from the credibility of his trial testimony.

Naturally the defense appealed Judge Wall's denial, turning again to the Georgia Supreme Court. This time, on November 9, 2017, the soldiers received what they had sought for the last twenty-six years—justice and exoneration. Overriding Judge Wall's denial, again in a 9–0 decision, the court ruled that, "in light of the totality of circumstances, the outcome of the trial was undermined by the State's failure to provide the Yamacraw report to the defense."

It stated that the Yamacraw report "was evidence that others similar in appearance were threatening a racial attack similar to that suffered by Jackson," and that "if the jury had been presented with information that other persons, not the defendants, were in the area that same night to engage in racially motivated violence, the outcome of the trial might well have been different."

In its opinion the Georgia Supreme Court also pointed out other exculpatory facts: namely, that the defendants were at a rehearsal dinner "over a 50-minute drive away" from the 10:00 shooting until 9:15–9:30; and that the State's case was "heavily dependent" on White's identification of the defendants, "but the investigators conducted no identification lineup, either in person or by photograph. No murder weapon was ever recovered; no firearm was found in the defendant's car, no casings from an automatic weapon were found there, and the forensic scientist who vacuumed the interior of the car looking for gunshot residue found none."

These were indicators that the court, considering the same evidence presented to Judge Wall, had strong reservations concerning the soldiers' guilt. Wall's decisions had egregiously delayed justice for four years.

The day for which the three men and their families had been waiting finally arrived. On Wednesday, December 20, 2017, everyone gathered in the same, now renovated, Savannah courtroom in which the judge had sentenced the men to life in prison almost twenty-six years earlier.

Defendants whose convictions have been vacated by a higher court have a right to be released while they await the prosecution's decision to retry them. Legally speaking, at this point they stand indicted, not convicted. As when originally arrested, however, they must have the financial ability to meet whatever bail the trial judge sets.

Among the attendees nervously sitting side by side in the courtroom were Mark's mother, sixty-five-year-old Deborah McGill; Kenny's seventy-six-year-old mother, Betty; and Dino's seventy-eight-year-old father, Roger, and his uncle Burt. All had driven great distances from Texas and Ohio. All were hoping to take their sons home if the judge set a reasonable bond.

There was a gasp when the three defendants filed into the courtroom, handcuffed one behind the other in white jail jumpsuits, wearing ankle and waist chains. Aged by the years of false imprisonment, they were unrecognizable. They quietly took their seats next to Peter Camiel and Steve Sparger at the defense table. You could hear a pin drop as everyone waited for the judge to take the bench.

Everyone was relieved and somewhat surprised when the prosecutor told the judge, "The State leaves the issue of bail entirely to the discretion of the court." That meant the DA was not going to take an adversarial position. The men were halfway home.

Knowing that the families were unable to post a bond in an amount likely to be set by the judge, Centurion had arranged with a New York City benefactor to post a $100,000 bond—$33,000 per defendant. If needed, he was on standby to immediately wire that amount of money to the Chatham County sheriff's office.

When the judge set bail at $30,000 for each man, the benefactor sprang into action and wired the money, with the assurance that it would be returned to him once the case had concluded.

Excitement grew by the minute because all of us were now confident that the former soldiers would be released without restrictions before the end of the day, free to go home with their loved ones as they awaited the DA's decision on whether to retry them. And that's exactly what happened. Together they walked out of the Chatham County jail at 3:32 that afternoon wearing Centurion-provided T-shirts emblazoned with the words I DIDN'T DO IT.

Surrounded by a sea of supporters cheering loudly in the jail's lobby, the first to greet them was Mark's mother, Deborah, who hugged her son so tightly you couldn't tell them apart. Holding on to him for dear life, she exclaimed for all to hear, "Except for his birth, this is the greatest day of my life." Except for the birth part, that was how we all felt, too, as we took our turns to embrace the three, one by one, and record the moment with photographs.

The sheriff was kind enough to allow the three men to take over the jail lobby for this impromptu party. That night we celebrated at the beautiful Savannah home of John Watts, Jr., Mark Jones's former trial lawyer, who had worked hard alongside Centurion, assisting in our effort to free his former client. Also celebrating that night were Dino's trial lawyer, Bill Cox, and Kenny's former attorney, John Watts, Sr. All three had testified at the 2013 hearing. Bill Cox brought tears to my eyes when he told Judge Wall, "I'll go to my grave thinking these guys didn't do this. I brush my teeth and think about them. I'll never forget 'em."

The next day everyone returned home. It was going to be the first Christmas since 1991 that Mark, Kenny, and Dino could celebrate as free men, and with their families.

Now there was nothing more to be done except wait and see if the DA was going to retry them. Even though their case had been eviscerated, a prosecutor might do anything in an attempt to save face. It took seven months, but finally the DA announced she was not going to retry the former servicemen and would petition the judge to dismiss all charges and thus end the case against them. On July 18, 2018, this was done.

The Sword of Damocles that had been hanging over their heads had finally been removed. For the first time, they could breathe easily, secure in the knowledge that this interminable nightmare had really ended. Now they could begin to start life all over and make their way in the free world.

Their new life, though, would be shaped by their life in prison. All three had spent twenty-six years as model inmates with hardly any disciplinary write-ups. This was extraordinary, practically unheard of, especially for such a long stretch of time. As one of many examples, for several years Dino even worked as an assistant chef in Governor Sonny Perdue's kitchen, and one year shared a Thanksgiving meal with the governor and his family.

What kept these men going all those years with no assurance they would ever get out? When this question was separately posed to each of them, all three had the same answer: their families' rock-solid belief in their innocence and unwavering support and love, from the day of their arrest until the day of their freedom. Mark had his devoted mother, Deborah McGill; his father died in 1995. Kenny had his mother, Betty, and father, Carroll, who died in 2015. Dominic had his father, Roger, and his uncle Burt; his mother, Gayle, died in 1995. Without that support, they simply would not have survived, especially in the early years of imprisonment.

Hope was another friend, never constant but, like a flickering candle, refusing to be extinguished. Kenny was more or less resigned to his fate until Centurion's investigation started to pick up steam. Then his hope came alive, only to fade again with Judge Wall's denials. The second Georgia Supreme Court decision allowed his hope for freedom to finally flourish.

For the first several years after the initial verdict, Dominic believed that the system would see the error of its ways and recognize their innocence. He was convinced the courts would soon see the truth and correct their mistake. The other thing that kept him going was a dream that, once that truth came out, he and his two friends would be the beneficiaries of a multimillion-dollar lawsuit. It took some time before this illusion evaporated and reality set in.

And then the parole board kept denying his requests, giving him eight-year hitches until his next review; and the courts continued to deny his appeals. *Okay,* he decided, *that's it,* although he hadn't completely given up. It was his fighting spirit that impressed Centurion when he wrote us a second letter in 2003, saying, "You told me to come back in a couple of years. It's been a couple of years and this time I'm not taking no for an answer. If McCloskey is retired send somebody else down here to help us out."

But the two denials by Judge Wall were finally too much. Dominic had decided to end his life by suffocation with a plastic bag if the Georgia Supreme Court also ruled against them. If that happened, there would have been no way out, and he didn't want to live for decades more with no hope of freedom.

Mark freely admits that, when his appeals were denied and parole was a dim prospect, he accepted his fate as an innocent man living and dying in prison. Settling in with that mindset, he was determined to make the best of a bad situation by finding "comfort" in the day-to-day prison routine through teaching and playing sports and board games. That was how he chose to cope.

His hope was rekindled at the onset of the 2013 evidentiary hearing. Although he had no confidence that Judge Wall would rule in his favor, after the strong hearing he did believe that the higher court would, especially when it sent the case back to her instructing her to rule on the merits with a unanimous 9–0 vote.

From 2013 until they were sent back to Savannah for the December 2017 bond hearing, Mark, Kenny, and Dominic were housed together, not only in the same prison, but in the same dormitory, one that was exclusively for veterans. This made them feel safe and secure, knowing that they had each other's back. It also gave them a sense of confidence that maybe, just maybe, the wheel of justice was beginning to turn their way. During those last four years they trained together as Braille transcribers to convert English text to Braille for the blind. They were doing this until their transfer to the Chatham County jail.

Despite family and mutual support, twenty-six years of false imprisonment deeply affected the men. Now in their fifties, finding gainful employment was a real challenge. None had a job history or a marketable skill. In completing an application, how were they to explain the twenty-six-year void in employment?

With some luck, and through the good offices of a local Cleveland Veterans Administration counselor, the VA hired Dino as a full-time telephone receptionist with full medical benefits. He lives by himself in the house where he grew up. Mark and Kenny share a four-bedroom house in Corpus Christi recently purchased by Mark. Kenny pays him rent. They are employed as Domino's Pizza delivery drivers.

The men also suffered from a history of inept and poor medical attention while in prison. Since his release, Mark was hospitalized for two months with a near fatal case of bacterial spinal meningitis, Covid, and double pneumonia. He miraculously recovered, but with a loss of hearing in one ear. Kenny suffers from arthritis in the ankles, knees, hips, and shoulders, which is worsening. In addition to a recent diagnosis of diabetes, Dino has recently undergone a hernia and gallbladder operation.

All three suffer from PTSD. Each has continuing nightmares about prison. Kenny dreams he is either back in prison or going back; and once he is there he can't get out. Dino dreams that someone is coming to his cell to wake him up. He has flashbacks that are triggered by a smell or a jingling of keys. In Mark's dreams he is in his jail cell dreaming he has been exonerated, only to discover, while still in the dream, that his exoneration never happened. Knowing that it is completely irrational, Kenny and Dino still have it in the back of their minds that "the state of Georgia will come after them again." They can't shake that fear.

They experience significant depression, anxiety, and stress levels generally, and particularly when meeting new people in unfamiliar settings. Dino, who prior to his arrest was fun-loving and gregarious, now feels inadequate when trying to converse with people. He says that prison "beat the ability to talk to people out of me." He despairs that his time away robbed him of having children and any kind of family life.

Kenny has always been rather shy and a bit of a loner, but those tendencies have noticeably increased. Other than Mark, he has no friends. Talking to someone he doesn't know "ramps up" his stress levels to the point that sometimes his "knees start to shake." He thinks it will be several years before he attempts to date again. When not working, he stays home at night watching animation programs on TV or reading fantasy and science fiction books, habits going back to his days before incarceration.

To this day, Mark's biggest regret is the loss of Dawn Burgett, whom he calls "the love of my life." They both lament that they were unable to have kids and raise a family together. He says losing her was "a heavy price that can't be fixed." She is a hole in his heart, as he is in hers. As friends they still speak periodically on the phone.

Thinking it was best for her and her future, after several years in prison Mark unilaterally broke off their relationship, and did it in what he regretfully described as "a mean way." That broke Dawn's heart. It has taken many years for her to recover and emerge from anxiety attacks and severe depression, brought on by the unresolved and traumatic separation from Mark. She has married twice since then, her second marriage a happy one.

But there is good news, too. In the spring of 2023, the Department of the Army issued Mark and Kenny honorable discharges, enabling them to take full advantage of VA benefits. Dominic had earlier received an honorable discharge, because he had officially left the army prior to his conviction.

Financially, the former soldiers are managing. Effective August 1, 2022, the state of Georgia awarded each of them $1,000,000 as compensation for their false imprisonment. This is distributed in monthly nontaxable payments of $2,612 for the next twenty years, which comes to $31,344 per year per man, after attorney's fees are deducted.

It is impossible to view these men today and not think "If only." If only the doorman at Tops Lounge had granted Mark entrance even though he was two months away from his twenty-first birthday. If only the three soldiers hadn't by chance pulled up to the Savannah police building at the exact moment that James White arrived with police officer Deborah Evans. How much pain and suffering could have been prevented? And who knows how bright the lives of Mark, Kenny, and Dino could have become?

UNKNOWN MALE #1

JOHN GRISHAM

C hester is the oldest town in Pennsylvania. It was founded in 1682 when William Penn landed on the banks of the Delaware River and claimed the territory for the British crown. He named the new colony after himself and founded the city of Brotherly Love.

By the early 1900s, Chester was a busy industrial city producing ships, textiles, automobiles, and other consumer goods, but by the middle of that century it had lost most of its factories and half its population. Like many post-industrial cities in the Rust Belt, it has struggled with unemployment, pollution, poverty, corruption, and crime.

Today, many of the downtown buildings are boarded up. In 2022, Chester declared bankruptcy.

Most of its neighborhoods are to be avoided after dark. One of the rougher areas is the western end of town, and in the heart of it, at the corner of West 10th and Clover Lane, a black woman named Henrietta Nickens once lived alone in a small three-room apartment on the ground floor of an old building. She was seventy, single, with a daughter, a son, and two granddaughters nearby. She existed month-to-month on a small Social Security check but always had a few extra dollars if someone needed a meal or groceries. Ms. Nickens was incredibly generous to those around her and was even known to feed strangers. Her health was declining; she suffered severe coronary atherosclerosis and pulmonary emphysema.

On the night of October 9, 1997, Ms. Nickens cooked dinner for her daughter, Carlotta, and granddaughter, Niena. Carlotta's boyfriend, Rufus McKinney, joined them. They ate around 6:30, then moved to the den where they played cards, watched television, and spent an hour laughing and joking. A typical night for them. Around 8:30, her three guests left and Henrietta locked up for the night. Like clockwork, Carlotta called her mother just before 11:00 to say good night. Carlotta knew that her mother would be sitting in the den waiting for *Action News* at 11:00 on Channel 6, her favorite news program.

That phone call was their last conversation.

———

At some time during the night, an assailant, still known only as Unknown Male #1, broke into Henrietta's apartment and attacked, raped, and beat her in her bedroom. She suffered several blunt-force blows to the head, which, because of her existing medical conditions, was enough to kill her.

When she failed to answer the phone the following morning, Carlotta began to worry. Around 2:00 P.M., she and Rufus, along with Niena, entered the apartment and found Henrietta dead, lying in the small hallway that connected the living room, bathroom, and bedroom. She was not wearing underwear; it was found on the floor beside her bed. There was blood on her arms and face. A telephone cord was stretched across her body, and a broomstick was lying next to her. A lower denture was partially dislodged from her mouth. The bedroom had been ransacked.

Shocked, Carlotta backed away in horror and called the police.

———

The crime scene was a mess. Blood was splattered on Henrietta's bed, sheets, and bedroom walls. A towel lodged between the bed and a wall was covered with blood. Objects were scattered about. A plastic stool with a broken leg was near the bed. It was apparent that Unknown Male #1 had entered through the back door, which was open and shattered. The police photographed a partial footprint on the kitchen floor. Henrietta's purse was found, apparently unopened. The television was turned off and had been moved into the hallway.

Unknown Male #1 was apparently one of the less sophisticated criminals loose on the streets of Chester. At some point during his attack, he removed a green jacket, size XXXL, and draped it over the small television. When he was finished with his crimes, he fled the apartment, forgetting in his haste to retrieve the green jacket. The investigators, of course, confiscated it for testing.

The following day, October 11, an autopsy was performed. There were numerous cuts and wounds to the eyes, cheeks, lips, and chin. There was a slight degree of bruising to the outer part of the vagina, and there was "semen in the rectum" although there was no visible trauma to the anus. The medical examiner was of the opinion that, absent her preexisting conditions and poor health, her injuries would not have been fatal.

The semen from the victim was sent to the state crime lab where it was placed in a long waiting line. Nine months passed before the results were sent back to Chester.

———

There was no possible innocent explanation for the semen in her rectum. She was elderly, single, in poor health, and had no male companions. Her daughter, Carlotta, who talked to her daily and knew every aspect of her life, was adamant in her denial that her mother had any boyfriends.

Niena was eighteen at the time and dating a young man named Sam Grasty, who was nineteen. Sam lived nearby and knew her mother and grandmother, and had been a guest in Henrietta's apartment several times. Niena and Sam were in the middle of a lovers' spat because she was pregnant and thought he was the father. Sam wasn't so sure. Things deteriorated when Sam declared he was not the father and didn't want his name on the birth certificate.

The day Henrietta's body was found, Niena told the police that Sam "might have done it."

From that moment forward, the investigation focused on Samuel Grasty. Other than Niena's bizarre suggestion that he killed her grandmother, there was no credible proof or motive. Why would a nineteen-year-old man who was involved in an intimate relationship with an eighteen-year-old woman suddenly decide to attack, anally rape, and beat to death her seventy-year-old grandmother?

If the police had a clue, it was never known. There is nothing in their reports, records, or testimonies to even suggest a motive, other than revenge against Niena for claiming he was the father of her child.

Nonetheless, Sam Grasty became the prime suspect. Twenty-five years later he's still in prison serving a life sentence for a murder committed by Unknown Male #1.

———

The investigation was led by a detective who had recently transferred from Narcotics to Homicide and was working his first murder. He knew the territory, though, and had the usual assortment of informants and snitches.

In a place like Chester, there was no shortage of small-time criminals, street felons, drug dealers, and addicts. Most had been exposed to the criminal justice system and knew its ins and outs. A big crime, like a murder, rape, or drug bust, touched enough street people to generate some interest and create opportunity. A woman named Lisa Foley was one of the first to seep through the cracks and tell the investigators that she had some inside information. Her story was difficult to believe, but the police were eager to believe it anyway. Lisa explained that she was in an abandoned building performing a sex act, perhaps for money, when she overheard some valuable information. A description of the sex act was never given but evidently it was one that did not require a great deal of concentration, because Lisa, while engaged, heard some guys talking on the sidewalk outside the abandoned building.

The boy doing most of the talking was one Rick McElwee, fifteen years old and one of the few white kids who lived in the neighborhood. He had a drug problem and had been smoking marijuana every day since he was thirteen years old. He also peddled cocaine and was being watched by the police. According to Lisa, McElwee was talking about the murder of Henrietta. He was with Sam Grasty; Derrick Chappell, age fifteen; and Morton Johnson, age eighteen. They were allegedly chiding McElwee because he had not entered the apartment with them when they attacked and robbed Ms. Nickens.

There was no police report detailing the conversation with Lisa.

The detectives leaned on their buddies in Narcotics and learned that McElwee had been selling drugs to undercover officers but had not been charged. The detectives arrested him for those charges and took him to the police station. Once there, they began to interrogate him about the Nickens murder. They later claimed they did not question the boy about the murder until his mother arrived. For two hours, McElwee maintained his innocence as the police threatened him with murder charges. He and his mother finally left the police station, terrified.

For the next month, the police continued to pressure McElwee and eventually coerced him into confessing to a fictional story about being sort of involved in the murder.

Rick McElwee became the star witness. His story, or at least the first version of it, was that on the night of October 9, at 10:00 P.M., he was standing on West 10th Street, outside Ms. Nickens's apartment, serving as the lookout as Sam Grasty, Derrick Chappell, and Morton Johnson broke into the apartment through the rear door. Robbery was their motive. They were in the apartment between five and twenty minutes and stole thirty dollars, which they split three ways, giving nothing to McElwee. Sam Grasty hit the old woman. There was no mention of a sexual assault.

After making his recorded statement, McElwee was charged with murder, burglary, assault, and deviate sexual intercourse. It was never clear why he was hit with a sex charge, since he never entered the apartment, according to his bogus narrative. Once again, there were scant police records to rely on.

In exchange for his cooperation and pointing the finger at Grasty, Chappell, and Johnson, he took a plea bargain deal with a reduced sentence of between six and twelve years. He also pled guilty to some drug charges, with the prison term to run concurrent with the murder and burglary.

Aside from getting stoned every day, Rick McElwee's IQ was 69, which is considered mildly intellectually disabled. During his sentencing hearing in 1998, his attorney referenced a report by a Dr. Rowkos who found that McElwee demonstrated cognitive skills between the borderline and mild range of mental retardation, which significantly impaired his ability to learn and function independently. He was easily influenced by others and had a strong need for attention, acceptance, and nurturance.

The police investigation, and later the prosecutions of Grasty,

Chappell, and Johnson, would be based almost exclusively on the concocted testimony of Richard McElwee.

————

On November 13, Carlotta Nickens informed the police that someone had tried to cash her mother's Social Security check at a neighborhood store. If this incident was investigated by the police, there is no record of it.

————

For weeks the investigators talked to the three suspects, all of whom vehemently denied any involvement in the crime. They had alibis for their whereabouts on the night of October 9. They had no serious criminal records, though Niena told the police that Sam Grasty, her boyfriend, was a small-time drug dealer. The three suspects cooperated fully with the police, met with them at the station whenever they were summoned, and provided hair and blood samples.

On December 2, 1997, the police searched, with proper warrants, the homes of the three suspects. They were looking for shoes that might match the print found on the kitchen floor, and any evidence that the green jacket left behind by Unknown Male #1 was in fact owned by Sam Grasty. They were hoping to find some photos of Sam wearing it. As soon as they tagged Grasty as their prime suspect, they convinced themselves the jacket was his, then showed photos of it to every possible witness and referred to it as "Sam's jacket."

From Grasty's home, the police seized five pairs of sneakers/shoes and some other items. The search of Morton Johnson's home yielded one pair of Reebok sneakers. Nothing of interest was found in Chappell's home.

If the mysterious shoe print matched one of Grasty's or Johnson's shoes, the police said nothing about it. Logic would dictate that if there had been a match, the police would have been thrilled with the additional evidence. But there was no match, nor did the authorities bother to inform the suspects or their lawyers of this fact.

The searches produced no photos or other evidence that would aid the police in their desperate attempt to prove the green jacket belonged to Grasty.

———

On July 9, 1998, nine months after the murder, the Pennsylvania State Police crime lab reported its DNA findings on the semen found in the victim's rectum. The three suspects—Grasty, Johnson, and Chappell—were all conclusively *excluded* as contributors, as was McElwee. The semen had been left behind by Unknown Male #1, a man who has never been identified.

At that point, most professional law enforcement officers would call time-out and reassess their case. It was obvious the Chester police were chasing the wrong suspects. Clear biological proof had just destroyed their theories of guilt and stood in the way of further prosecution and, ultimately, convictions. The bogus confession of Richard McElwee had just been exposed as lies.

But the police in Chester had too much invested in their shabby work. Incredibly, they changed their strategy to one that said, in effect: *The victim was not robbed, raped, beaten, and murdered; she was only robbed, beaten, and murdered. There was no rape.*

No rape? Therefore the sex was consensual? A seventy-year-old widow with pulmonary emphysema and severe coronary athero-sclerosis, and no known boyfriends or close male friends, consented to unprotected anal sex either before she had dinner with her family or sometime thereafter?

The theory was so beyond absurd that it was preposterous, but it allowed the police to continue their investigation of Grasty, John-son, and Chappell. They needed witnesses and found plenty. The favorite method was to concentrate on kids who were already in trouble and therefore vulnerable. They intimidated the kids, lied to them, threatened them with serious criminal charges, and even showed them photographs from the crime scene, all in an effort to frighten them into providing false testimony against Grasty, Chappell, and Johnson.

Will Morgan was twelve years old at the time of the murder. Eighteen months later, when he was fourteen, he was in a juvenile facility on a larceny charge when the police arrived without notice and got him.

They took him to the station where he was interrogated about the murder. The police showed him photographs from the crime scene, including one in which the victim was lying on the floor with a telephone cord near her body. The police accused Will of being in the apartment at the time of the murder with Sam Grasty, Derrick Chappell, and Morton Johnson. As was their habit, the detectives showed Will a photo of the green jacket and referred to it as "Sam's jacket." Will said he wasn't sure if he had ever seen it.

The police then met with Will's mother, outside his presence, and told her that the kid had information about the murder and had better cooperate or "things could get very bad."

Will knew nothing about the murder. He was terrified he was about to be charged if he didn't tell the police what they wanted to hear, so he told them what they wanted to hear. In another false statement, he said he had overheard Grasty talking about someone who was about to get robbed and that since he, Grasty, knew the person, he would not be suspected.

Will Morgan later recanted fully and signed an affidavit admitting his story was false.

Boyd Burke, another juvenile, was in custody because of a shooting. He was interrogated and threatened by the police, and suddenly realized he had information. His incredible story was that he'd bumped into Sam Grasty as they were standing in line in a crowded deli. It seemed like the appropriate time for Grasty to admit to a murder, and so he confessed to Boyd. However, when Boyd was called to testify in Grasty's trial, he denied all of this and said he didn't remember talking to the detectives or giving them a statement. The prosecution, though, was allowed to get the false statement admitted into evidence anyway, through the testimony of a detective.

Boyd was shown a photo of "Sam's jacket," but did not recognize it. So the detectives interrogated another juvenile, Lanier Moore, age fifteen.

They showed Lanier the file and photographs, and said they had talked to people who claimed he knew a lot about the crime. A detective told Lanier that the case was going before a grand jury, that he would be called as a witness, and that if he lied he would be charged with perjury. The detectives accused him of withholding information and threatened to charge him as an accessory after Grasty, Chappell, and Johnson were arrested. They showed him a photo of the victim with a phone cord nearby, and badgered the kid to tell them what Sam Grasty and the other two had told him about the murder. Lanier held his ground and said he had not talked to anyone about the murder. When they showed him a photo of "Sam's jacket," he said he did not recognize it.

———

Months dragged by, then another year. Rick McElwee was away in prison serving his six-to-twelve-year sentence. In September 1999, almost two years after the murder, criminal complaints against Grasty, Chappell, and Johnson were finally issued and they were arrested. Each was charged with first-degree murder, second-degree murder, third-degree murder, burglary, criminal trespass, and conspiracy to commit all of the above.

In Pennsylvania, a murder that is premeditated and planned is first-degree. Killing someone in the commission of another crime is second-degree. Third-degree covers all other types of murder.

———

Armed with no physical or biological proof against Grasty, Chappell, and Johnson, the prosecution faced an uphill battle. It was forced to rely almost entirely on the testimony of Rick McElwee.

The monumental question glaring at the prosecution was obvious: Who contributed the semen? Clearly, it was not the three men who had been charged with murder and were about to face their juries.

To protect its fraudulent investigation, the prosecution had no qualms slandering the memory of Henrietta Nickens, a generous lady who lived alone and modestly, took care of her friends and family, and died a horrible death.

The prosecutors concocted a series of stunning, fantastical scenarios that belong somewhere in the record books. To explain away the biological evidence, and to convince the judges and jurors that Unknown Male #1 had some form of sex with the victim but did not kill her, the prosecutors actually presented, in open court and in written filings, throughout the trials and appeals, the following:

OUTRAGEOUS SCENARIO NUMBER ONE

On October 9, 1997, at some time before the daughter, granddaughter, and Rufus McKinney arrived at her apartment for dinner at 6:30, Henrietta Nickens engaged in consensual, unprotected anal sex with Unknown Male #1. After her guests left, she went to bed and was later attacked, robbed, and beaten to death by Grasty, Chappell, and Johnson.

This scenario was impossible. The semen would drain from the rectum, especially from a woman who was busy cooking dinner and entertaining guests. There was no semen on her underwear found beside her bed.

Years later, during an evidentiary hearing on newly discovered evidence, Mr. Alan Keel, an expert in forensic biology, DNA analysis, and crime scene analysis, testified that the semen in the victim's rectum was deposited at or near the time of her death. There was no drainage onto her underwear or house dress. If the victim had been walking around and moving about after having sex, the semen would have drained onto her underwear or clothing.

Mr. Keel said, "The fact that there is such a large amount of semen still present within her rectum when the swab was collected, and the absence of any semen that would have drained from her rectum . . . in my opinion, demonstrates the semen was deposited in her rectum at or near the time of her death. There was not a lot of activity happening after the semen was deposited."

Additionally, Ms. Nickens had no close male friends and had not dated or "seen" anyone for many years.

OUTRAGEOUS SCENARIO NUMBER TWO

Carlotta testified at least four times that her mother watched the eleven o'clock news every night, then went to bed. Carlotta called her every night a few minutes before 11:00 to say good night, as she did on October 9. However, in McElwee's version of events he watched as the gang of three entered the apartment at 10:00 P.M. Regardless of the time, this scenario maintained that at some point after her guests left at 8:30, and before the gang broke in at 10:00, the victim allowed Unknown Male #1 into her apartment for anal sex. Afterward, he left, and then she was attacked at 10:00 by the gang of three.

This scenario was also virtually impossible, for the reasons stated for the first outrageous scenario.

Shirletta Moore was a close friend of Henrietta's who lived nearby. They visited often and confided in each other. Shirletta helped Henrietta with her paperwork, took her to the doctor, and cooked meals for her. When asked by the police if the victim had any boyfriends, she said, "Definitely not." She was too old and too sick for any activity remotely romantic. Shirletta would know if anyone came around Henrietta's apartment, and the only people who visited other than family were Shirletta, Rufus McKinney, and Sam Grasty.

OUTRAGEOUS SCENARIO NUMBER THREE

After beating the victim to death, the gang of three suddenly became worried about the police tracking them down, so they left the apartment and went somewhere in Chester, late at night, and found a freshly used condom that they took back to the crime scene where they managed to unload its contents into the victim's rectum. Such a shrewd maneuver would certainly throw off the police.

This one defies analysis.

Where does one go in Chester, or anywhere else for that matter, to find a freshly used condom, one with its payload intact?

Here the prosecution's bogus narratives collide and contradict themselves. According to Rick McElwee, the star witness, his job during the crime was to serve as a lookout and whistle a warning if he saw the police. He testified in all four trials and struggled mightily to keep his false details straight. But he did cling to his testimony that he watched the gang of three come and go through the rear door of the victim's apartment. He saw them kick in the door, enter, stay between five and twenty minutes, then exit the same rear door.

At no time during any of the trials or hearings did McElwee say anything about the three leaving, then returning, then leaving again.

OUTRAGEOUS SCENARIO NUMBER FOUR

After beating Ms. Nickens, and finding thirty dollars to steal, the three left the apartment, but only for a moment. On the street they bumped into Unknown Male #1, who was apparently some sort of rapist-for-hire, and convinced him to go with them to an apartment he'd never seen before and anally rape Ms. Nickens while she was either dead or dying, and, of course, while they waited and perhaps watched.

Where do you even begin poking holes in such an absurd story?

Again, McElwee, the ace lookout, never mentioned the three leaving and returning; and he certainly never mentioned a fourth male, the unknown one, returning with them.

How could the three, who had just severely beaten a woman and perhaps killed her, convince Unknown Male #1 to go with them to commit a rape while three witnesses looked on?

And what about the green jacket? In the prosecution's fictional world, Sam Grasty wore it into the apartment, took it off, draped it over the television set, then left it behind. But numerous times? Coming and going under these wacky scenarios, did Sam keep forgetting his green jacket? Did any of his codefendants realize the green jacket was being left behind?

OUTRAGEOUS SCENARIO NUMBER FIVE

After beating the woman to death, the three left the apartment, for good. Of course they left the rear door open, the one they had just kicked in. After they were gone, Unknown Male #1 happened upon the scene, entered the apartment, and assaulted the victim, who was either dead or dying.

These are not the rantings of an unhinged author. During Sam Grasty's trial, the prosecutor argued to the jury:

> It is frustrating, we don't know if Mrs. Nickens had some type of relationship with someone that day before her daughter arrived for dinner. We don't know if she was raped that night. We don't

know if perhaps somebody in that neighborhood, or perhaps one of these guys [Grasty, Chappell, Johnson] that went in there, picked up a used condom somewhere to throw the police off track. We don't know how it got there. We don't know that she was raped. And because we don't know that she was raped, the fact that this Defendant's [Grasty's] DNA does not match that semen does not in any way exclude him from the crime of burglary, theft, and murder. It simply means that he did not rape Mrs. Nickens, if she was raped at all.

———

The three cases were severed and set for trials a few months apart. In January 2000, Derrick Chappell went first. But, before his trial he was offered a plea bargain: In exchange for a plea of guilty to the murder, and for his cooperation in the trials against his two codefendants, he would be sentenced to six to twelve years in prison. Because he was already in jail, he would serve about four more years and walk out. Derrick maintained his innocence, refused to rat on his pals, who were also innocent, and said no to the offer. He was convicted of second-degree murder, burglary, theft, trespass, and conspiracy and sentenced to life without parole. Samuel Grasty went next, and his trial on first-degree murder charges ended with a hung jury. The prosecutor scrambled and three months later tried him again for second-degree murder. He was convicted and sentenced to life without parole.

By the time Morton Johnson's trial began in December 2001, he had been waiting in jail for fifteen months, and he knew all about the convictions of Sam Grasty and Derrick Chappell. He had not participated in their trials because he refused to cooperate with the prosecutors. The three defendants had steadfastly held their ground and would not rat out the others. There was nothing to snitch about. They knew nothing because they had not been involved in the crime.

The prosecutors offered the same deal to Morton, but, like Derrick, he said no. If Morton had taken the deal and pled guilty, he would have served a few more years and, like McElwee, walked out of prison twenty years ago.

However, since he wasn't guilty he refused to say he was, refused to cooperate, and today he's still in prison with no possibility of parole.

The Grasty and Chappell trials were a whitewash. The judges, prosecutors, police, witnesses, and defense lawyers were all white, as were a majority of the jurors. As fact-finders, the jurors chose to believe the prosecution's star witness, Rick McElwee, who was also white.

Morton didn't trust the system, and didn't like his chances. But when he learned that his judge was African American, he thought his luck might change. R. C. Wright was the only black judge out of twelve. Morton's lawyer was Guy Smith, a criminal defense attorney with the reputation of being savvy and tough. He and Morton discussed trial strategies and decided they would have a better chance with a black judge than a white jury.

And there was another reason. Morton had appeared before Judge Wright on two prior occasions for minor crimes, to which he pled guilty. Judge Wright believed him then, so he assumed Judge Wright would believe him when he pled not guilty.

He and Guy Smith opted for a bench trial; forget the jury.

Morton testified in his own defense and had a solid alibi. On the night of October 9, he had worked until 8:30, took the bus home, where he lived with his mother and her boyfriend. He did not leave that night. His mother vouched for his story. But it was in total conflict with the fiction Rick McElwee had already told Judge Wright. At one point the judge, who was obviously struggling to understand two completely different stories, asked Morton, "Do you know any reason why [McElwee] would make these statements about you, or accuse you in this matter?" Morton said he had no idea why.

Why? How about the obvious fact that McElwee did not want to be charged with murder and chose a much more lenient plea bargain?

It's impossible to know if Judge Wright was simply inexperienced, or naive, or both. Odds are that after a few years on the bench and numerous run-ins with lying witnesses, he was far more suspicious of their motives and testimonies. Perhaps Judge Wright fell into the same trap that snares virtually all jurors. They find it impossible to believe that a witness will walk into the courtroom, put his hand on the Bible, swear to tell the truth, and immediately start spinning fictional stories, many of them created by the police and prosecutors.

Whatever the reason, Judge Wright sided with the prosecution, fell for McElwee's lies, found Morton guilty of second-degree murder, and sentenced him to life with no parole.

———

The convictions rested almost entirely on the testimony of Rick McElwee. There were no fingerprints that matched the defendants' taken from inside the victim's apartment. No shoe print. No physical evidence whatsoever, but for the green jacket that was allegedly worn and left behind by Sam Grasty. He denied owning it, and Chappell and Johnson said they'd never seen it before.

McElwee's testimony varied from trial to trial, but the gist of it was that he teamed up with the three suspects in a scheme to break into the victim's apartment and rob her. Why they would rob a sick, old woman with no money was never clear. Why Sam Grasty would rob his girlfriend's grandmother was never clear. Why he would risk being identified by a woman he knew well was never clear.

Most of McElwee's testimony was never clear. He admitted to being a heavy marijuana user and had been smoking pot every day since he was thirteen. On the day of the murder, he said he smoked only one blunt. (A blunt is a cheap cigar with the tobacco hollowed out and packed with marijuana.) That was his testimony during

Derrick Chappell's trial. But during Sam Grasty's second trial a few months later, he said he smoked three blunts on October 9. In his confession to the police and at a preliminary hearing, he testified that on the night of the murder he left home at 9:00 and met up with the three other suspects. Grasty was talking about doing a robbery. Chappell left, went home, and came back an hour later. While he was gone, the other three wasted time by sitting on some steps. Grasty then told McElwee to stay behind, stand at the corner, and whistle if he saw the police. They left and broke into Ms. Nickens's apartment. At trial, though, he had a different story. The gang met at 9:00 at an abandoned building, then dispersed. Grasty and Johnson left and went home. McElwee went home, too. Chappell lived in the projects and went there. An hour later they regathered at the abandoned building and walked down the street to the victim's apartment. At the preliminary hearing he testified he stood watch at the corner of 10th and Booth Street, but at the trials he changed his location and said he was at the corner of 10th and Clover, one block closer to the victim's apartment.

Abraham Lincoln famously said that no man has a good enough memory to be a successful liar. Few liars were ever laden with as many disabilities as Rick McElwee. With his limited cognitive abilities and history of drug use, he could never quite keep the details of his fiction straight during the multiple hearings and trials. At the preliminary hearing, he testified that from his lookout position he could see the back door of Ms. Nickens's apartment, which was off a small porch. He clearly saw the three suspects walk onto the porch, where Grasty then kicked the door "once or twice." He saw all three go through the door and enter the apartment. A few minutes later he saw the three exit the apartment through the same back door.

However, during Chappell's trial, the first of the three, McElwee testified that he could see the back porch but could not see any of the three suspects once they were on it, and he could not see where they went.

In Grasty's first trial, McElwee added a few extra blows and said Grasty kicked the door four or five times. At Johnson's trial, he was back down to "two or three times." Finally, at Grasty's second trial, he became thoroughly confused and said he never saw Grasty kick the door. When confronted with his earlier testimony, he admitted that from where he was standing he could not see Grasty kick the door. In fact, he couldn't even see him on the porch.

Through his many versions of the events, it was never clear why the fictitious gang needed a lookout to begin with.

According to McElwee, the three assailants were in the Nickens apartment between five and twenty minutes. He saw them exit the apartment, but then maybe he didn't. He rejoined the gang as they walked down 10th Street and Grasty supposedly said, "We only got thirty dollars." Later, McElwee testified there was no conversation about money. Initially, in his confession, he said he saw the thirty dollars and watched as the other three split it. In the preliminary hearing, he testified he didn't see it, as in Grasty's second trial. But in Johnson's trial he testified that he didn't see any money and didn't know if the other three had split it. However, when confronted with his initial confession, he changed his mind and remembered seeing the thirty dollars and watching as they split it. When asked to explain his change in testimony, he said, on the record, "Well, it was probably my mind. I smoke weed."

When the police examined the green jacket and emptied its pockets, they found (1) a red straw that had been chewed on one end, (2) a clear plastic bag of white powder that was later determined to be cocaine, and (3) a white glassine packet of white powder that was not a controlled substance.

The prosecution did not DNA test the chewed straw or the jacket, nor did the defense lawyers.

Years passed before the testing took place.

In 2004, lawyers for Grasty learned for the first time that the jacket had been DNA tested *after* he had been convicted and sentenced to life. They demanded more DNA testing. The prosecution opposed it. The judge refused to allow it.

In 2021, more lawyers representing Johnson, Grasty, and Chappell were successful in obtaining more DNA testing on the green jacket and its contents. A sufficient sample was lifted from the chewed red straw, and it had the same DNA profile as the contributor of the semen taken from the victim. In other words, the straw had been chewed on by Unknown Male #1. It was his jacket after all.

The new testing also found a semen stain on the sleeve of the jacket.

Only Unknown Male #1 knew how the semen stain came to exist on his jacket, but the DNA profile was his as well.

The new testing also found a semen stain on the sheet of the victim's bed. It was mixed with her blood, and, according to an expert, proved that the victim was beaten and raped in her bed by Unknown Male #1.

DNA from Samuel Grasty, Derrick Chappell, and Morton Johnson was excluded from the red straw and the semen stains.

To reiterate, at least four samples of body fluids were collected from the crime scene: (1) a large sample of semen taken from the rectum, (2) a semen stain mixed with blood on a bed sheet, (3) a semen stain from the green jacket, and (4) a saliva sample lifted from the chewed red straw in the pocket of the jacket.

All four were contributed by Unknown Male #1, the man who murdered Henrietta Nickens.

Samuel Grasty, Derrick Chappell, and Morton Johnson were excluded by DNA testing, yet they have served twenty-five years in prison and still have no hope of parole.

In the face of overwhelming evidence, the prosecutors fought on to avoid the truth. They have consistently opposed additional DNA testing, with one exception, in 2021, and since that testing was completed, they have continually opposed the granting of relief for the three inmates.

Under Pennsylvania law, there is a four-step test that must be met by a defendant seeking a new trial because of new evidence. In post-conviction litigation, a defendant is not allowed to return to the old courtroom and argue about what the jury should or should not have done. The jury has evaluated the evidence and pronounced the defendant guilty. But if there is new evidence that (1) could not have been obtained prior to the end of the trial with the exercise of reasonable diligence, and (2) the new evidence is not merely corroborative or cumulative, and (3) is not merely impeachment evidence, and (4) is of such a nature that its use will likely result in a different outcome on retrial, then, and only then, will a new trial be granted. Each of the four requirements must be met.

The semen found in the victim was old DNA evidence. It was known at the trials and considered by the jurors, all of whom found the three defendants guilty in spite of it. It cannot be re-litigated.

The new DNA evidence is (1) the semen stain on the bed, (2) the semen stain on the jacket, and (3) the saliva from the red straw.

Today, the prosecution concedes that the new DNA evidence is timely and could not have been discovered at the time of the trials. Step One is met by the defendants.

Step Two: The prosecution argues that the new DNA evidence is merely cumulative to what was known during the trials; to wit, the semen in the rectum did not belong to the three defendants. It was left behind by Unknown Male #1. Thus, the new stains and the saliva, all from the same man, are really nothing new because the jurors basically ignored the testimony during the trials. The prosecution claims the defendants have failed Step Two.

Attorneys for the defendants argue that with today's enhanced DNA testing methods, the evidence is even clearer that Unknown Male #1 acted alone when he broke into the victim's apartment, beat and raped her, left her for dead, and left behind his green jacket with even more DNA proof. Thus, the new evidence is not merely corroborative or cumulative, and Step Two is satisfied.

Step Three: The defendants argue the new evidence is not merely for impeachment, and the prosecution does not contest this.

Step Four: Would there be a different outcome on retrial? With the new evidence, the defendants would like nothing better than another chance in court. The prosecution continues to claim there was and is sufficient evidence to prove their guilt. They are not entitled to a new trial. Justice has been served.

As recently as November 2023, the prosecutors argued strenuously, in a fifty-page brief, that the DNA doesn't matter; that there may not have been a rape; that they, the prosecutors, are not sure how the semen landed where it did—but the three defendants are still guilty.

———

Among innocence advocates and lawyers, it is often said that it is much easier to convict an innocent person than to get one out of prison. To convict, all that's needed is an arrest, with the ever-present presumption of guilt, then a trial in which the authorities rely on lying witnesses who will say anything to avoid more time behind bars. Undoing such a mess takes years of pro bono labor by dedicated innocence lawyers, and hundreds of thousands of dollars for testing, experts, and investigators. It also takes some luck.

For Sam Grasty, Derrick Chappell, and Morton Johnson, luck with the criminal justice system has been elusive. They were wrongfully convicted in the state courts of Delaware County, Pennsylvania. Their wrongful convictions were upheld by the Commonwealth's appellate courts. Their habeas corpus efforts in the federal courts were just as fruitless.

The numbers have been reported so many times that most Americans are weary of them. Hardly a day goes by that a major newspaper or news magazine does not remind us of our pathetic reliance on punishment to cure problems that we cannot otherwise solve. There are approximately 2.3 million Americans behind bars, the highest rate ever known. We lock up more of our own people than any country in the history of the world. This inflicts enormous social and economic harm on our most vulnerable citizens—poor people of color.

The causes of mass incarceration are well known and much studied.

———

Since we started the "war on drugs" in the 1970s, the number of prisoners has skyrocketed, while drug use has hardly declined. Tough politicians have passed tough-on-crime laws with longer sentences for minor crimes and burdensome restrictions after release. These laws and policies have failed miserably. We've lost the war on drugs and our casualties are either dead or in prison.

Poor, uneducated black men have borne the brunt of mass incarceration. They are 13 percent of the U.S. population but 35 percent of the incarcerated population. More than 80 percent of their arrests are for low-level, nonviolent offenses.

Racism is a major cause of mass incarceration. It is a simple yet complicated fact that black suspects are treated harsher than white ones. From suspicion, investigation, arrest, bail, indictment, jury selection, blacks are handled differently.

The Chester case is a perfect example. The police and prosecutors were white. A majority of the judges and jurors were white. They, the authorities, chose to believe the lies of a fifteen-year-old, cognitively challenged, drug-using white boy over the evidence presented by Sam Grasty, Derrick Chappell, and Morton Johnson, all of whom had solid alibis and no motive.

Rick McElwee told the lies the police prepared for him. He served six years in jail and was released almost twenty years ago.

Sam and Morton told the truth and have been locked away for twenty-five years. Barring a miracle, they will die in prison. Derrick was a juvenile when he was sentenced, and will be eligible for parole in four years.

———

But miracles do happen. Luck can appear when least expected.

On March 28, 2024, Judge Mary Ann Brennan of the Court of Common Pleas surprised the three defendants, their lawyers, and the prosecutors with an astonishing ruling. She vacated the guilty verdicts and ordered new trials for Sam, Derrick, and Morton. The district attorney had thirty days to appeal her ruling or accept it.

The district attorney, Jack Stollsteimer, waited until the thirtieth day and appealed Judge Brennan's ruling. In Pennsylvania, such appeals take at least a year to be decided by the appellate court.

TALE OF THE TAPES

JIM McCLOSKEY

James Buckley, a nineteen-year-old gas station attendant, met a violent death on Sunday, January 2, 1983, while working the graveyard shift at a Vickers service station in Dellwood, Missouri, in the suburbs of St. Louis. Buckley was a high school graduate who attended a local community college and lived with his mother, Gloria. Since June 1982, he had worked all night at Vickers three times a week.

Buckley was found around 2:00 A.M., lying on his back in the inside storage room. He was shot seven times with a .22 caliber rifle at close range, once through the heart and several times in the chest, left arm, and abdomen. He had a deep gash in the top of his head that went through the entire thickness of his scalp.

No weapon was recovered, but pieces from the rifle and its spring were found on the floor by his side, as were several shell casings. Buckley's wallet was missing, and, mysteriously, so was the four-foot crossbar used to secure the storage room's back door from the inside. No forced entry was observed.

No fingerprints or any other physical evidence was found that linked anyone to the crime. Neither the office nor the storage room was unduly disturbed. Money was not taken from the cashier's cage or the office, where $361 lay in an unlocked safe, suggesting that the killers were interrupted in their crime by someone entering the service station. Several small bags of marijuana were found under the cash drawer countertop and in Buckley's car.

Dellwood is a one-square-mile town, one of eighty-eight municipalities that make up St. Louis County, each one with its own police force. Buckley's murder was all over the TV, radio, and newspapers. In the previous eighteen months, a wave of gas station robbery/murders had swept St. Louis. Eleven service stations were hit, with six attendants killed and another wounded. Buckley's became the seventh death.

Dellwood's police department requested activation of the Greater St. Louis Major Case Squad (MCS) to take control of the Buckley murder investigation. The MCS was a multi-jurisdictional task force drawing on detectives throughout the region to provide forensic and investigative services to homicide cases when requested by local police. In the Buckley case the commander of the MCS happened to be a fifteen-year veteran of the tiny Dellwood police force itself, Captain Dan Chapman. Twenty detectives were assigned to Chapman's command. They would work full-time on the case in the ensuing weeks.

During the last hour before Buckley's death, several customers and friends visited the service station. The first was Donald Brunner, Buckley's best friend and former high school classmate. Brunner told police that he got to Vickers around 12:30 A.M. and departed an hour later. During his visit, a friend from high school, Kathy Brockhan, arrived, hoping Buckley would give her some free pot. He told her he had none to give. She left after spending about ten minutes with the two men inside the station. Later, Kathy told police that Brunner and Buckley seemed nervous and hesitant to continue their conversation during her visit. She said Buckley appeared "stoned," but Brunner was "straight." She also said she knew that Buckley purchased marijuana by the pound for $360 to $450 from a wholesaler, whose identity she claimed not to know.

Minutes after Kathy left, two male customers in their early twenties, an Asian and a white man, came in together. Although they were strangers to Buckley, he offered to sell them some pot. They bought "half a dime bag" and departed. Brunner and Buckley then smoked a couple joints in Buckley's car, after which Brunner left for home. It was close to 1:30 A.M.

Between 1:30 A.M. and 1:40 A.M., two more customers visited the station, looking to buy cigarettes—first Anthony Longo, then Ken Main, who arrived shortly after Longo left. Both of them saw a black man wearing a green army jacket leaning against the cashier's counter across from Buckley, who was inside the cage. Their descriptions of the man differed slightly. Main thought he was between thirty and forty, Longo in his mid-twenties; but both agreed he was tall—between 6'0" and 6'3"—and that he wore his hair in a medium-length Afro. Longo noticed that he was wearing black boots. Longo declined Buckley's offer of weed, thinking it strange he would ask, and departed with his cigarettes. Main, however, saw something else before he left. Buckley was wearing a look of distress. He seemed to be pleading with his eyes for Main to stay.

A few minutes after Main exited, Jim Abernathy, a videographer, came in to purchase cigarettes. This was about 1:40 to 1:45 A.M., and now no one was anywhere to be seen inside the station. It felt eerie to Abernathy. He could see that the door to the storage room was cracked open a tiny bit, and he felt he was being watched. Rather than call out, he quickly left.

Then Ellen Reasonover arrived, a black single mother who had a two-year-old daughter, Charmelle. They both lived with Ellen's mother, Elizabeth. Ellen was twenty-four years old. Her story of what happened that night remains unchanged to this day.

Earlier that evening, around midnight, she had set out from her family's Dellwood apartment to do the family laundry at a local laundromat. She was accustomed to doing the chore at this late hour, because it was easier for her mother to babysit when Ellen's daughter was sleeping. It took her more than two hours to wash and dry the accumulated laundry, some eight loads. When she ran out of coins for the machines, she went to the nearby Vickers for some change and to buy cigarettes, arriving shortly after Abernathy departed.

When she arrived, she saw a black male sitting at the cashier's window. When he saw her walking toward him, he disappeared into the back of the station. She banged hard and loudly on the window several times trying to get his attention, to no avail. She later described him as between nineteen and twenty-one years old, very light-skinned, and about 5'6" or 5'7" tall. He wore a black-and-red-checkered fishing-like shirt with a matching hat that he took off when he spotted her.

After a couple of minutes she gave up and returned to her car. It was then that she noticed a car parked beside the building. It was at least ten years old, dark in color—either dark blue or black—and had a distinctive set of tires: white walls on the rims and a silver tire on the trunk. She guessed it was a Cadillac or a Buick. She saw two men leave the station by the side door, one wearing an army jacket, and get in the car. A third person was already in the backseat. As she drove out of the station, she noticed their car also leaving, but behind her. She figured they worked there and had finished for the night.

She then went to a nearby 7-Eleven to get change. Coming out of the store, she saw the light-skinned checkered-shirt man and a friend arrive, exit their car, and walk toward the 7-Eleven. As they passed her, she could tell that the light-skinned man's companion was upset with him. The companion wore a green army jacket, army boots, and jeans. He had a light mustache and beard and short Afro hair. He was between 6'0" and 6'2" tall and about thirty years old, with very red eyes. Soon thereafter, when she returned to the nearby laundromat, she heard police sirens in the direction of Vickers.

Buckley's body was discovered shortly after Ellen and the black men departed Vickers. Several customers had gone inside the station looking for an attendant to fix the gas pumps, which were not working. They discovered the body in the storage room and called the police at 2:01 A.M. The police responded within minutes.

When Ellen woke up later that morning, she saw a report about the murder on the TV news. She was alarmed to learn that the victim, a white man, had been killed close to the time she was at the station. She wondered whether she had seen the killers.

Her mother encouraged her to contact the authorities. She did so reluctantly, calling the Dellwood police at 1:42 A.M. on January 3. Initially nervous about revealing her real name, she identified herself as "Sheila Hill." She was afraid that the killers, if she had seen them, might track her down. It did not occur to her that the police might be the real threat.

Once the police officer who took her call realized the possible importance of her eyewitness account, he asked her to call Captain Chapman, who was heading the investigation, for a more detailed interview. After thinking it over, she finally called Chapman at 10:10 P.M. the next night, January 4, still using the name "Sheila Hill." Chapman recorded the conversation without her knowledge. At the conclusion of what was a lengthy and detailed telephone discussion, he persuaded her to come to the police station right away to look at photos. When he dangled a $3,000 reward in front of her, Ellen declined, telling him to give the money to the victim's family. Money was not her motive. She wanted to help. At 11:30 P.M. she arrived, properly identified herself as Ellen Reasonover, and told her story.

Captain Chapman had her view a photo album containing mug shots of 250 black males. She tentatively identified two men as the ones she saw the night of the murder. Her description of the angry man at the 7-Eleven matched Longo's and Main's descriptions of the man they'd each seen speaking to a visibly nervous Buckley shortly before he was killed. All three witnesses said he was wearing a green army jacket and was between 6'0" and 6'3", wearing black boots. Ellen and Main said he was about thirty years old, while Longo estimated his age to be twenty-five or so.

Ellen explained to Chapman why she had used a fictitious name. She thought the two men looked "treacherous," she said, and she didn't want her name in the paper.

The next evening, January 5, Ellen and Ken Main both viewed two lineups, each containing one of the two men whom Ellen had tentatively identified the previous day. One of these men Main also said closely resembled the man with the green army jacket. However, Main was unable to positively identify him or anyone else in either lineup. According to Chapman, Ellen now positively identified one as the light-skinned, checkered-shirt man at the cashier's window but could not identify the other. Ellen, however, insists that she never made a definitive identification of either man in the lineups. As it turned out, both men were in jail when Buckley was killed.

Still trying to help, Ellen told Chapman that the light-skinned suspect could be someone she had met briefly months before at a party, and that her girlfriend who dated him would know his name. Ellen got his name from her friend and gave it to Chapman. The next day, January 6, Ellen picked him out of a photo lineup as the man she saw in the cashier's cage. His name was Willie Love. Love was immediately brought in for questioning.

That same afternoon, the police interviewed an employee of the Dellwood Dairy Queen who had previously reported that two suspicious black males were in and out of the Dairy Queen three times over a two-hour period on December 31, a day and a half before the murder. The employee described one as light-skinned, wearing a beige raincoat, the other as around 6'2" and thirty years old, wearing a green fatigue army jacket. When shown a photo array of ten men, the employee selected Willie Love's photo, saying, "This picture looks like the guy with the beige raincoat." She was asked to sign and date the photo.

The Dairy Queen was located around the corner from Vickers. It stands to reason that these two men were probably the men Ellen saw at Vickers and at the 7-Eleven. The man in the green army jacket at the Dairy Queen fit the description of the man Longo and Main saw speaking to Buckley right before he was shot. And the Dairy Queen employee's identification of Willie Love lent credibility to Ellen's identification of him as the light-skinned companion of the man in the green army jacket.

But that evening, Love was administered a psychological voice stress test, a computer-based examination supposedly able to measure stress in a person's voice as an indicator of deception. Although occasionally used by St. Louis County law enforcement, this test is considered to be highly unreliable by criminal justice experts and is not allowed as evidence in any courtroom. Nonetheless, on the basis of this test, the examiner said that Love had nothing to do with Buckley's death. The same examiner administered the test to Ellen within an hour of Love's and determined that Ellen was a truthful witness.

Love's alibi also checked out. He was cleared and released from custody the morning of January 7.

Earlier, Buckley's friend Brunner had been polygraphed. The polygraph cleared him of the killing, but the polygrapher told MCS that in his opinion Brunner might very well know who did it and why. Brunner's response to two questions—"Do you know who

shot Jim Buckley?" and "Do you know why Buckley was killed?"—
were significantly indicative of deception. In fact, Brunner admitted that he and Buckley sold marijuana together and that they had a
"common problem" related to their drug business.

Four other acquaintances of Buckley and Brunner told police
that the two men dealt marijuana together. Another man, whose
phone number was in Buckley's pocket when he was killed, Louis
Montgomery, told police the morning after the crime that "Brunner
and Buckley were partners at times in the purchase of large quanti-
ties of marijuana." MCS had a powerful lead. But Chapman was
heading in another direction. He dismissed the idea that these two
nineteen-year-olds could be involved in a serious drug business, and
so Buckley's possible drug connections were never fully investigated.

Chapman's new direction was Ellen. He was suspicious of her
incorrect identification of Willie Love (even though the Dairy
Queen employee had identified his photo, too). He decided that
Ellen might have come forward not because she wanted to help, but
because she was trying to distract the police from her own involvement in Buckley's murder.

Several factors had poisoned his imagination. For one, Ellen had
volunteered to him that when she had exited the Vickers station
onto the street, she saw a police car traveling in her direction. She
slowed down to get behind it, since she had a bad taillight on her
1970 AMC Hornet. This gave Chapman the idea that Ellen had
come forward to the police out of fear that the police officer who
had passed her at Vickers would identify her when he learned of the
homicide there. This was a stretch, since it assumed that the officer
in the patrol car would have noticed Ellen's vehicle and taken the
time to remember her before he even knew that a crime had been
committed.

Second, in the first telephone conversation Chapman had with
Ellen, she volunteered that she had worked the all-night shift at

another Vickers station for seven months in 1978. She offered this fact even though it came with baggage. The manager at the station, whose dating advances she had rejected, had accused her of stealing $106. She had denied the accusation and been cleared by the St. Louis County prosecutor's office after an investigation.

Chapman also glommed on to the fact that Ellen's two older brothers, Steven and Mark, had criminal backgrounds. In 1979, Steven was found innocent by reason of insanity in the fatal shooting of his girlfriend and her sister. He had been committed to a state hospital, where he was still residing in 1983. Mark was convicted in 1981 for the attempted robbery of a grocery store and received a sixteen-year sentence as a repeat offender. One can only surmise that Chapman came to believe that Ellen, like her brothers, was a "bad seed," despite the fact that she had no criminal record of her own.

Finally, it came to Chapman's attention that Stanley White, a man Ellen had recently dated, had been arrested a week earlier, on December 29, for smashing her car windows while intoxicated. Since then, Ellen had severed their relationship and refused to see him. The police report of this incident indicated that the vehicle White was in at the time of his arrest—a vehicle that wasn't even his but belonged to a friend—was similar to the car Ellen had seen near the scene of the Vickers murder. It was a dark blue 1974 Buick with a continental kit.

White was brought in for questioning at 10:30 P.M. on January 6. The MCS believed that if Ellen killed Buckley, she must have had male accomplices to subdue him. White fit the description of the man in the army coat in that he was over six feet tall with a slender build. Additionally, according to the police, his alibi did not check out.

As soon as he was brought into the Dellwood station that night, White was placed in a lineup attended by Ken Main, one of the witnesses from the night of the murder. Main wrote in a statement at the conclusion of the lineup that "number 4's [Stanley White's] build reminds me of the man I saw and his profile reminds me of the man, but I only glanced at him at Vickers and I can't be sure it's him." He later said that he only saw the man's full face for "not even a second."

The next day, the police had Main hypnotized by a professional hypnotist. He told the same thing to the hypnotist—that "I just glanced up at the face." At one point during hypnosis, he used the word "nigger" when referring to the black man he'd seen at Vickers, revealing a racial bias.

But Main's uncertainty about the identification disappeared after he asked to have White lean on a counter in the police building so that he could observe him in the same profile he'd observed at Vickers. Now, in a post-hypnotic interview with the hypnotist and an MCS detective, Main claimed that he was "99% positive" that White was the man he'd seen wearing the green army jacket. Interestingly, it appears that the police may have rewarded Main for his help in resolving the Vickers case. Main testified at Ellen's trial that he was recently hired by the St. Louis County Sheriff's Department. Soon after the trial, one of Ellen's trial attorneys was surprised to see him in a deputy sheriff's uniform in a county courtroom. One can only wonder if this new job was a reward for serving as an important witness at Ellen's trial.

At 11:15 P.M., White flunked a psychological voice stress test and was promptly arrested for the capital murder of Buckley. He was placed in a Dellwood jail cell. But on the morning of January 7, Anthony Longo, who had been in Vickers within minutes of Main, was unable to identify White or anyone else in a lineup.

Ellen was now given a second psychological stress test, this one administered by a different detective from the one who had passed her only the night before. According to this detective, Ellen flunked the test. Suddenly, Ellen, a well-meaning witness, became the authorities' chief suspect. To her astonishment, she was arrested on January 7 at 1:00 P.M. for capital murder.

Ellen was placed in a Dellwood jail cell next to her old boy-friend, Stanley White, the man who had smashed her car windows in a drunken rage. They spent the rest of the day into the evening in their respective cells, side by side, wondering what the hell was going on, angry and confused about being suspects in the Buckley murder.

Around 9:00 P.M. that night, Ellen was transferred to a larger jail in Jennings, a nearby town, and placed in a cell with two black women, Rose Carol Jolliff and Marquita Butler. Surprisingly, the next morning, January 8, White and Ellen were both released. While Chapman believed they were guilty, he recognized that Main's identification of White was problematic, and he still had not a shred of evidence against Ellen.

Once free, Ellen thought the police had finally come to their senses; the nightmare was over and she could go about her life. She proceeded to do just that. On January 23, she married Glen Baldwin, an air force serviceman who had loved her ever since they first met two years earlier. He was a decent man, and Ellen, who initially did not share his feelings, thought she could grow to love him. She also wanted her daughter to have a father figure. Charmelle's father, whom Ellen had adored, had been fatally shot seven months earlier.

Unfortunately for Ellen, the same day that she was allowed to go home, one of her two cellmates in Jennings, thirty-one-year-old Rose Carol Jolliff, set her sights on making a deal with the authorities to get a lighter sentence. She told the jailer that she had information related to the Vickers service station homicide.

Jolliff had a long rap sheet dating back to 1975, consisting of charges that included heroin possession, stealing, check forgeries, and numerous counts of passing bad checks. In 1975, she had received a six-month sentence in a federal lockup for altering a U.S. Treasury check. In August 1982, she got ninety days in the St. Louis County jail for a bad check charge. In early January 1983, when she was briefly housed with Ellen, she was awaiting disposition on the charges in a September 1982 indictment, three felony counts of bad checks in St. Louis County. The charges could have sent her away for five years or more as a persistent offender. Up until then, Jolliff had played the system cleverly and managed to avoid a dreaded state prison sentence. She was determined to keep it that way. Indeed, it is possible that Ellen was moved from the Dellwood jail for an overnight stay in the Jennings jail by the police in the hope that Jolliff would offer testimony against Ellen as part of a deal.

Three MCS detectives taped their interview with Jolliff. In bits and pieces, Jolliff claimed that Ellen had told her that she shot the Vickers gas station attendant because she feared he would recognize her, since she lived nearby. Ellen allegedly said she had two accomplices during the robbery, Robert McIntosh and Stanley White, and that McIntosh was her pimp and White was her boyfriend. Jolliff reported that Ellen said one of the men was supposed to distract the attendant at the cashier's window so he wouldn't see her. When he did see her, she had "to get rid of him." She shot him with the rifle seven times. She added that, since Ellen had worked at a Vickers several years ago, she knew the setup. Ellen had said she wasn't going to give up McIntosh or White to the police.

Jolliff was never asked to give a written statement detailing Ellen's alleged confession. However, she told the police to talk to her other cellmate at Jennings, Marquita Butler. In Jolliff's telling, Butler had heard Ellen's confession, too.

Ellen had a very different recollection of her jailhouse conversation with Jolliff. It was Jolliff who had brought up Robert McIntosh, asking Ellen if she knew him. Ellen had said that she and McIntosh had been classmates in middle school, but she hadn't seen him since. The idea that he was her pimp was not only absurd, it was pure projection—McIntosh was Jolliff's pimp. Jolliff had told Ellen she was angry at him for not bailing her out of jail. Perhaps that was why she decided to implicate him in the murder of James Buckley.

Armed with Jolliff's account, Captain Chapman and the St. Louis County trial prosecutor, Steven Goldman, made a run at Jolliff's cellmate, Marquita Butler. Goldman had her brought into his office on January 9. According to a police report, she "failed to corroborate the statement provided by Jolliff" and "refused to cooperate any further." But that didn't deter Chapman. After several attempts to locate her upon her release, he was finally able to speak with her by telephone in a taped conversation on January 13. She told Chapman that she was broke and needed money. Twice, he mentioned that a substantial award was on offer, making it clear that if she cooperated and helped convict Ellen, "you'll get seven thousand dollars."

Marquita finally gave in. She told Chapman that Ellen had confessed to participating in the Vickers robbery, but that it was Ellen's boyfriend who had shot the attendant. Marquita claimed that Ellen said she stayed in the car the whole time. Her accomplices didn't intend to kill him, but the victim knew them; and they had to do it so he couldn't identify them.

But then Marquita's conscience got the better of her and in the same conversation she retracted the lies. In an affidavit she gave to Centurion years later, she said that the police gave her the names of men she had never heard of (Stanley White and Robert McIntosh) and got angry with her when she refused to cooperate any further. They were "mean and rude to me . . . and made me feel little and small." Because she told the truth, Marquita did not receive any part of the $7,000 reward.

Meanwhile, believing she was in the clear, Ellen was busy at home with Charmelle and her husband, Glen, celebrating their marriage before he returned to Eglin Air Force Base in the Florida Panhandle. She and Charmelle planned to join him there later. The St. Louis police, however, were far from finished with her. One month to the day she and Stanley White were released from jail, she was hit with an entirely new set of charges. "They took me away from home and I never came back again," Ellen recalls.

On February 8, 1983, the police descended on her apartment and arrested her for a "till tap," or theft of cash from the cashbox of a Sunoco station in Creve Coeur, a small unincorporated town in St. Louis County. Ellen was stunned. She had never heard of Creve Coeur and was at a loss to understand these new accusations.

The missing link, unsurprisingly, was the investigative zeal of Captain Chapman. After hearing about the Sunoco robbery and learning that the suspects included a black woman along with two black men, he hightailed it over to Creve Coeur, a town outside his jurisdiction, with a pair of photo arrays to show around. In a statement to the county police, the gas station's manager, Chuck Zeiter, had originally described the female suspect as young—twenty-five to thirty years old—fairly tall and heavily built—about 5'10" and 150 to 160 pounds—and having dark skin and short, curly brown hair. When Chapman arrived, with the photos, in spite of the differences between Ellen's physical appearance and his original description of the thief, Zeiter identified twenty-four-year-old Ellen—only 135 pounds, with light skin and black hair—as the female thief. Shortly afterward, at Chapman's invitation, Zeiter viewed a pair of live police lineups and fingered Ellen and Stanley White as the perpetrators.

White was arrested immediately and charged with "stealing over $150." Ultimately, however, Zeiter told the police that he wasn't exactly sure it was White. Two weeks later, the charges against White were dismissed. Once again, he was set free and never bothered again on the matter. The same was not true for Ellen.

On February 9, she was placed in a holding cell at the county courthouse to await arraignment on the Sunoco stealing charge. Here, she had the misfortune of being put in the same cell as Mary Lyner. Like Rose Jolliff, Lyner was a career criminal looking for a deal to lighten her sentence and avoid prison.

Prior to her arrest on November 18, 1982, Lyner was, in the words of her arresting police officer, Sgt. Ronald Klein, the kingpin of one of the largest credit card theft rings in St. Louis history. When Sergeant Klein arrested Lyner in her apartment, besides finding her in a drug-induced stupor moaning for another fix, he found hundreds of stolen credit cards and checkbooks and a closet full of stolen purses. During his investigation, which included lengthy interviews with Lyner, Sergeant Klein tracked down at least $350,000 in fraudulent purchases. Lyner and her boyfriend would purchase things like TV sets, cameras, VCRs, and other high-priced items with the stolen credit cards and checks, then sell them on the black market and use the money to feed their all-consuming heroin habit. At one point Sergeant Klein stopped counting; he estimated that if he tracked down all their purchases, they would have exceeded a million dollars. He characterized Lyner as a "major criminal and a severely addicted junkie with a $1,000-a-day habit." The last Klein heard concerning the disposition of Lyner's crimes was that the city had turned the prosecution over to St. Louis County. He assumed she would get thirty years in the pen.

Once Ellen was removed from the cell, Lyner told a jailer that Ellen had talked to her about her crimes. This prompted the St. Louis County trial prosecutor, Steven Goldman, to visit her at the county jail. It was during this visit that Lyner implicated Ellen in both the Sunoco theft and the Buckley murder. She claimed to Goldman that as soon as Ellen arrived in the courthouse holding cell, she sat down next to Lyner and blurted out, "Those motherfuckers picked me out of a lineup. I told him we should have blown their brains out."

Lyner said Ellen told her, "We robbed a gas station and killed a man. You know, that Vickers station. I stay right down the street from there." Following this, Lyner and Goldman made a deal: He would recommend that she receive a one-year sentence in the county jail for all of her pending charges, including five felony forgery charges, if she cooperated with the State and testified against Ellen at the Sunoco and the Vickers trials, both of which would be tried by Goldman.

Lyner kept her end of the bargain, as would Goldman. She, along with Zeiter, testified at the Sunoco trial in mid-July 1983. Zeiter identified Ellen as the woman who stole $423 from his station's cashbox. Lyner told the jury what Ellen had allegedly said to her on February 9 about getting picked out of a lineup and having told her accomplice that they should have killed the witnesses. Prior to the Sunoco trial, Lyner was released on her own recognizance pending disposition of the charges against her from Sergeant Klein's 1982 arrest and her five felony forgery charges. Ellen was convicted and sentenced to seven years. Prior to sentencing her, the judge asked Ellen if there was any reason why he should not proceed with the sentence. She responded, "Because I am innocent."

The Sunoco "till tap" conviction gave Goldman exactly what he wanted. It would now be very hard for Ellen to testify in her own defense at the Vickers trial, because the Sunoco conviction would have an obvious prejudicial effect on the jury. With the Sunoco conviction, Goldman had laid the foundation for the real prize—a capital murder conviction in the Vickers case, and a possible death sentence.

Four months later, in late November 1983, the State of Missouri put Ellen Reasonover on trial for the slaying of James Buckley. The prosecutor was fully aware that there was no physical evidence tying Ellen to the murder, no eyewitness who had seen her at Vickers that night, and no taped confession. His capital murder case would rely solely on the testimony of two career criminals who had been offered incentives to lie.

One of the State's two star witnesses was Mary Lyner. As she had in the Sunoco case, Lyner told the jury about Ellen's alleged jailhouse confession. By the time of the trial, Lyner had secured a secretarial position at a law firm. She was well educated and well spoken on the witness stand. She also happened to be white, as were all the jurors. On cross, she admitted her twelve prior felony convictions since 1978—the forgery, stealing, and passing of bad checks. She further conceded that, as a persistent offender, she could be sentenced to ninety years in prison for her five pending forgery cases. Her life, it should have been clear to all, was in prosecutor Goldman's hands.

As damning as this was, Ellen's defense attorneys were missing a key piece of impeachment material hiding in plain sight. Two years previously, in 1981, the *St. Louis Post-Dispatch* had published a five-part biographical series on Lyner with her permission and full participation. The paper, however, had disguised her identity, calling her "Anne."

She was raised in an affluent middle-class home and spoiled by her mother and a father who was an executive for the prestigious Chase Park Plaza hotel in St. Louis. She graduated from Webster University magna cum laude in 1971. She became a successful real estate agent living in the western suburbs of St. Louis with a husband and young daughter. In 1975, at the age of twenty-seven, divorced and bored with the real estate business, she joined Archway House, a drug treatment facility, as a counselor to make use of her college social work degree.

There, she fell head over heels in love with one of her clients, a recovering heroin addict who was on probation for robbery. "Bowled over" by him, it didn't take long before she let him move into her apartment. He persuaded her to try heroin with the rationale that she would then better understand the euphoric feeling felt by its users, which would enable her to be a more effective drug counselor. Before she knew it, she was hooked. By the middle of

1977, the two of them were unemployed with a collective $250-a-day heroin habit financed by her savings and the sale of her assets.

Although Lyner made several attempts to escape his spell and return to the "straight" world, he would always reappear and convince her to let him back into her life. The last time was in October 1980. She had lost her most recent job when the company moved to Dallas, and he had just been released from prison after a two-year stretch for robbery. They soon began their daily life of credit card thievery and crimes of deception, which included stealing purses out of offices and forging bad checks. That two-year crime spree ended with her arrest in November 1982 by Sergeant Klein. As she told the *Post-Dispatch,* she was a "smooth talker" and "knew how to tell a good story." She could talk her way into and out of any situation. As an example, she told of the time she went into a high-end store and convinced a salesperson that she was Mrs. August A. Busch III—wife of the then-president of the Anheuser-Busch Companies and a member of St. Louis royalty. She walked out with a $5,000 piece of jewelry without having to show identification.

Now, in exchange for her false and damning testimony against Ellen, Lyner was rewarded with a sentence of one year in the county jail for the entirety of her crimes, per her arrangement with Goldman. Neither the jury nor Ellen's trial attorneys knew about Lyner's theft of hundreds of credit cards and checks, or that she had headed up one of the biggest criminal operations in St. Louis.

Rose Jolliff also testified at Ellen's trial. Earlier, Goldman had promised Jolliff's public defender that he "would not burn her" if she continued to cooperate in the Reasonover case. He didn't. On December 1, Jolliff told the jury about Ellen's supposed "confession" at the jailhouse and said Ellen's accomplices had been Stanley White and Robert McIntosh. As soon as she'd concluded her testimony, Jolliff was escorted to another courtroom, where she pled guilty to the September 1982 indictment of three felony bad check charges and received "bench probation" of six months. Such a light sentence was unheard of for a persistent offender like Rose Jol-liff, who was now free to return to her South Bend, Indiana, home unsupervised. This sneaky arrangement was never revealed to the defense. Once again, Ellen's defense lawyers and the jury were in the dark. Jolliff had told the jury that she was not testifying in exchange for a reduced sentence in the 1982 bad check case.

At trial, Ken Main and Anthony Longo identified two different black males as the man they saw leaning against the counter wearing a green army jacket and speaking with Buckley. Ken Main identi-fied Stanley White as the man; Anthony Longo identified Robert McIntosh. Longo had identified McIntosh earlier in the year at a lineup. No evidence was presented to show that McIntosh and White even knew each other. In fact, they had never met.

Despite the fact that Main and Longo disagreed about the iden-tity of the man they saw, Prosecutor Goldman characterized them to the jury as "really good identification witnesses." He told them that Buckley was "abducted right there by Stanley White, [Ellen's] boyfriend, and Robert McIntosh." He added that Buckley was "dis-tracted at the window by Stanley White and Robert McIntosh and there is no way that Rose Jolliff isn't telling you exactly the truth in this case. The identifications, what they do," he added misleadingly, "is corroborate the names [Jolliff] gave of the two people who have been identified." How the man in the green army jacket could be two different people and yet the witnesses be "really good" boggles the mind.

What the jury did not know is that neither White nor McIntosh was ever charged or prosecuted for any involvement in the murder or robbery of Buckley. They were used as straw men to strengthen the case against Ellen, to tell a better story at trial. Years after the conviction, Chapman conceded to Centurion that he didn't have confidence in either identification.

Ellen's defense attorneys were privately retained and represented Ellen at both trials. They, and the few witnesses they presented, were ill-prepared. They did very little investigation, if any. Ellen's mother, Elizabeth, testified that Ellen went to the laundromat the night of January 1 with dirty bags of laundry, and the next morning the laundry was clean. She also said that she encouraged Ellen to tell the police what she saw at the Vickers station. Elizabeth's friend Dewey Williams, who stayed at the house the night of January 1, told the jury that he and Elizabeth arrived home from a party at midnight, and that he helped Ellen carry the laundry bags out to her car about that time. He estimated that Ellen returned home from doing the laundry at about 2:00 A.M.

Inexplicably, the defense attorneys did not attempt to interview Ellen's other cellmates besides Jolliff and Lyner, nor did they bring in Dellwood police officer Marsha Vogt, who had testified at a pre-trial hearing. At that hearing and in a police report, Vogt related that Goldman and Chapman had wired her up and placed her in Ellen's holdover cell on February 25, 1983, in an undercover capacity, to see if Ellen would make any incriminating statements. While in the cell, Ellen told her that she was in jail for a theft she didn't commit; and this was the first time she'd ever been arrested.

Twenty minutes after Vogt showed up to eavesdrop, Chapman had appeared with news for Ellen: She was being charged with capital murder. Chapman pulled Ellen out of the cell for an interview. When she returned to the cell, she was crying and told Vogt that they were saying she'd killed "some big guy and broke a gun stock over his head." She went on to explain what she had seen at Vickers and the 7-Eleven that night, exactly what she originally told Chapman. As always, she proclaimed her innocence. Vogt recorded every word of the conversation. Later, the police claimed that the recording was unusable on account of a malfunction. Because Ellen's trial attorneys failed to bring Vogt in to testify, the jury did not get to hear her story, so opposite to those told by Jolliff and Lyner.

After a six-day trial, on December 2, 1983, Ellen was convicted of capital murder. All this because she came forward with information she thought might be helpful to the police in their investigation. If she had not reached out to the police, they never would have known of her existence.

The next day, the jury had the onerous task of deciding Ellen's punishment. Two options were available—a life sentence without the possibility of parole for fifty years, or death by lethal gas. In his summation at trial, Goldman had vouched for Lyner's and Jolliff's credibility, claiming that Lyner "couldn't possibly make those statements up" and Jolliff got "absolutely nothing for testifying here. There is no reason for her to lie." Now, at the sentencing stage, in his final argument to the twelve jurors, Goldman argued forcefully and repeatedly for the death penalty.

He told them that "Ellen Reasonover gunned down Jim Buckley in the back room . . . You have to believe that she was the gun person . . . She stood next to him with a fully loaded rifle . . . She is the one that killed him. The evidence shows she is the actual killer." He then capped off his closing remarks with a supposition as ludicrous as it was erroneous: "Somewhere in Ellen Reasonover's life she decided that killing a person is like taking a drink of water." (Six months later, Goldman was less certain that Ellen was the shooter. Even though he had implored the jury to issue her a death sentence, he told *The Washington Post* for a front-page story on questions surrounding Ellen's conviction, "I wouldn't have felt comfortable [asking for the death penalty] unless I thought she was guilty *or at least involved in the murder if not the actual killer.*")

The prosecutor's plea for the death sentence was preceded by Ellen's plea for mercy. She told the jury, "I'm innocent. I have been framed. I was locked up ten months for nothing. Taken me away from my family. All I tried to do was to be a good citizen. And I have a little girl and a mother and I love my family very much and there is no way in this world I would go out in the streets and do anything wrong. So this kind of thing that happened to me, happened to my family."

After deliberating for just over three hours, the jury was unable to achieve unanimity on a death sentence. Consequently, the judge sentenced Ellen to life without the possibility of parole for fifty years. The vote was eleven to one for death. Juror Donna Ellis cast the lone dissenting vote.

She saved Ellen's life.

Centurion took up Ellen's case in 1993. By then, all of her state and federal appeals had been denied. After her conviction, Ellen had reached out in desperation to the NAACP. George Hairston, a leading NAACP attorney in New York City, had served pro bono as her federal appeals attorney. Now he asked Centurion to take on what he knew would be an extensive investigation. Centurion retained the Kansas City law firm of Wyrsch & Atwell, and they assigned staff attorneys Cheryl Pilate and Charles Rogers to the case. We added criminal defense attorney Rick Sindel of St. Louis to the team. Once our collaborative efforts had developed significant new evidence of Ellen's actual innocence, prosecutorial misconduct, and ineffective assistance of counsel, in 1996 the attorneys filed a writ of habeas corpus in the U.S. District Court presenting these claims. The case was assigned to St. Louis Federal District Judge Jean C. Hamilton. She conducted a four-day evidentiary hearing that began on June 28, 1999.

At the hearing, our team presented the two other women, Rose Winston and Carolyn Coats, who had been in the holding cell with Ellen the day she supposedly confessed to Mary Lyner. Both of them testified that Ellen had done no such thing. Marquita Butler also took the stand. She told the court that Ellen had made no incriminating statements about the Buckley murder the day she and Ellen had shared a cell with Rose Jolliff in Jennings.

The Norfolk Four (left to right): Eric Wilson, Derek Tice, Joe Dick, and Dan Williams (Courtesy of the families)

Clarence Brandley being transferred to Montgomery County Jail from the Conroe city jail on September 2, 1980 (Courtesy of *Houston Chronicle*)

Clarence Brandley in the death row visitation cage, circa 1987 (Courtesy of Centurion)

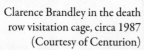

LEFT: Clarence Brandley takes his first step to freedom on January 23, 1990, after a decade on death row. (Courtesy of Centurion) RIGHT: Clarence shortly after his 1990 exoneration (Photographer unknown)

LEFT: Kennedy Brewer post-exoneration at the Martin Luther King, Jr. Memorial in Washington, D.C. (Courtesy of Joe York) RIGHT: Levon Brooks post-exoneration, still wearing the earring (Courtesy of Joe York)

DOMINIC LUCCI   MARK JONES   KEN GARDINER

TOP ROW: Mug shots, January 31, 1992. BOTTOM ROW: Shortly after all charges were dismissed on July 18, 2018. (Courtesy of Centurion)

Mark's mom, Deborah McGill, embracing her son for the first time in twenty-six years at the moment of his freedom at 3:32 p.m. on December 20, 2017 (Courtesy of Centurion)

On December 20, 2017, Kenneth Gardiner, Dominic Lucci, and Mark Jones (left to right) celebrating freedom immediately upon release from jail (Courtesy of Centurion)

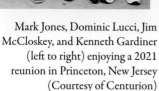

Mark Jones, Dominic Lucci, Jim McCloskey, and Kenneth Gardiner (left to right) enjoying a 2021 reunion in Princeton, New Jersey (Courtesy of Centurion)

Derrick Chappell in prison (Courtesy of the Pennsylvania Innocence Project)

Morton Johnson with his Innocence Project lawyer, Vanessa Potkin (Courtesy of the Innocence Project)

Samuel Grasty (Courtesy of the Innocence Project)

In July 1983, Ellen Reasonover's husband, Glen Baldwin, visiting his wife in prison (Inmate photograph)

Convicted of capital murder, Ellen Reasonover on January 11, 1984, several days before being sentenced to life without the possibility of parole for fifty years (Courtesy of the St. Louis Mercantile Library at the University of Missouri–St. Louis)

In 1986, while incarcerated, Ellen Reasonover earns a Legal Research and Writing Certificate. (Inmate photograph)

Ellen Reasonover celebrates her freedom at the Centurion Princeton office in the fall of 1999. (Courtesy of Centurion)

Joe and Mickey Bryan of Clifton, Texas (Courtesy of Joe Bryan)

On May 1, 2024, Joe Bryan visits Mickey's grave for the first time in thirty-five years. (Courtesy of Joe Bryan)

David Alexander and Harry Granger with their defense team at the Angola state prison in Louisiana, circa 1998 (Inmate photograph)

Harry and David in Princeton honoring Jim's retirement in 2015 (Courtesy of Centurion)

David with his mother, Iris Alexander, in 2018 at his New Iberia home (Courtesy of Centurion)

Twenty-one-year-old Kerry on July 4, 1977, several weeks after Linda Jo Edwards's murder. Linda's apartment mate saw the killer and described him as having "silver hair, cut in a medium, touching-the-ears fashion." (Courtesy of Rhonda Orms)

Forty-one-year-old Kerry with Jim McCloskey and Paul Nugent on November 13, 1997, exiting jail after twenty years on Texas's death row (Courtesy of Centurion)

Kerry and Sandra on their wedding day, March 25, 2000 (Courtesy of Judge Maryellen Hicks)

With death row several years behind him, Kerry and Sandra enjoying family life with their pride and joy, three-year-old son KJ, in 2003 (Courtesy of the family)

Todd Willingham on death row (Copyright © Ken Light/ Contact Press Images)

The aftermath of the Corsicana, Texas, fire in December 1991 (Courtesy of Texas State Fire Marshal's office)

Stacy and Todd Willingham and their three daughters (Courtesy of the Todd Willingham family)

Two other inmates, Barbara Taylor and Ellen Palmer, were in the lineup with Ellen when she was identified by Zeiter as the Sunoco "till tap" thief. Taylor remembered Ellen crying and becoming quite upset upon learning that an eyewitness had identified her as the Sunoco culprit. As in her other jailhouse conversations, she protested her innocence. Palmer told Judge Hamilton that Ellen never made any incriminating statements in front of her at the time of that lineup or in the county jail. All of these jailhouse witnesses had been available and willing to testify at the time of Ellen's trial, but her defense attorneys never spoke to any of them.

What finally broke Ellen's case wide open was the discovery of two police tape recordings in the prosecutor's files that had never been shared with the defense. Both exposed Jolliff's "jailhouse confession" testimony as a lie and completely upended the State's case against Ellen. It is important to note that prior to trial, as part of a discovery motion, Ellen's attorneys had asked for any electronic surveillance records of conversations in which she'd participated. These two tapes were not provided.

The first one was a secret recording of the jailhouse conversation between Ellen and Stanley White on January 7 after each had been separately interrogated as suspects for the Buckley homicide. Ellen's appeals lawyer George Hairston first learned about this recording in the late 1980s, when witness Ken Main told Hairston's investigator that the police had played it for him during an interview. The State refused to turn it over, maintaining in its appellate briefs that it was not discoverable because White and Ellen did not discuss anything of substance concerning the killing, and because it contained nothing exculpatory or of evidentiary value.

In 1996, after repeated requests, the prosecutor's office finally provided Ellen's habeas defense team with the recording. It is quite apparent that Ellen and White had no idea they were being recorded. During the conversation they were both agitated and angry at the police for falsely accusing them of a heinous crime, for trying to get them to incriminate each other, and for threatening them with the gas chamber. More than twenty times they spoke of their innocence. As an example, in one exchange, White said, "I told the police if I do go to the gas chamber I say a innocent man gonna go in there . . . I'm not gonna sit here and tell you something I didn't do." Ellen responded, "That's what I told 'em, too. I say you can't lock me up for murder . . . I ain't did a motherfuckin' thing and I ain't know a motherfuckin' thing about no Vickers shit with Stan."

Both showed ignorance of the crime scene. Stanley didn't know what they were talking about when they asked him what he did with the missing board from the back room. A bewildered Ellen asked White, "What board?" Ellen told White the police told her White was "gonna spill the beans" on her so she might as well "spill them on him first." White responded, "Ain't got no beans to be spillin.'"

Ellen told White how bad she felt when the police showed her photos of the victim. She said, "Then they showed me that little white boy picture . . . He looked all pitiful layin' down there. I said, 'Man, whoever killed him that was cold . . . really cold. These pictures really fucked me up.'" (Since Buckley was 6'8" and almost 200 pounds, Ellen's reference to a "little white boy" was further evidence that she'd never seen him alive.)

Ellen told Stanley she'd said to the police that "the last time I seen you was the last time you came over to knock my motherfuckin' window out. Those motherfuckers is crazy. Think you gonna rob and kill a young white boy, kill him, take his life . . . I know you ain't did no shit like that." Stanley responded, "If I knew something I would tell the motherfuckers. I don't know shit and I'm not lyin.'" Ellen agreed, saying, "If I had somethin' to do with that shit, I'd a snitched on you and everybody else I thought was involved." It went on like that for an hour.

At the hearing in 1999, attorney Rick Sindel subjected Goldman to a methodical but withering cross-examination. By this point, Goldman was no longer working in the prosecutor's office. He had served the last eleven years as a St. Louis County judge.

Initially, he claimed that a police officer—whose name he couldn't remember—had mentioned a tape recording that had captured a conversation between Ellen and White while they were in the lockup. The two had been complaining about being in jail. The officer, however, told Goldman that he couldn't listen to the recording because it had been taped over. On cross, Goldman backtracked. He denied any knowledge of the audiotape, claiming, "I wasn't aware that it was in existence." That's why he never informed Ellen's trial counsel about it, he said. When pressed, however, he admitted that the police officer who told him about the recording might have been Captain Chapman. For his part, Chapman testified before Judge Hamilton that the White/Reasonover tape had no evidentiary value because it didn't show they were guilty. Apparently he believed that evidence supporting innocence doesn't count.

Goldman said he had recently listened to the tape for the first time and admitted that it is indeed "of an exculpatory nature." He also admitted that it was of such import that if Ellen had testified at trial, he could not have credibly cross-examined her about her alleged statements to Lyner and Jolliff. Ellen's trial attorney told Judge Hamilton that if she had had that recording, she most definitely would have put Ellen on the stand to impeach the jailhouse witness testimony. In other words, had the White/Reasonover recording been available at trial, the State's case would have evaporated. Goldman quite likely would have dropped the charges.

There was another recording, too, one that never saw the light of day until the hearing. On June 29, the second day of the 1999 hearing, Judge Hamilton ordered the prosecutor's office to produce its entire file by the end of the day so that Ellen's defense team could examine its contents. We were stunned when we discovered and then listened to the audiotape of a January 12, 1983, telephone conversation between Jolliff and Ellen. Apparently, at the behest of the police, Jolliff had called Ellen at home in a surreptitious attempt to elicit incriminating statements from her. This was five days after Jolliff first told the police of Ellen's "jailhouse confession" in the Jennings jail on January 7–8.

As in the White/Reasonover taped conversation, Ellen repeatedly professed her innocence over ten minutes, five times to be exact. She said things like "Why they trying stick me with something I didn't do?" She complained that "I was really trying to help that motherfucker, man," and that they tried to get her girlfriend to say, "She told me she did it." She repeated to Jolliff what she had told Chapman, that the men she saw at the 7-Eleven may have been the same men she saw at the Vickers station. She said, "When I had got up to the 7-Eleven, the niggers I has seen coming in looked like the nigger I had seen coming out that was goin' in the back when I was pulling up there."

As attorney Cheryl Pilate wrote to Judge Hamilton in a July 6, 1999, post-hearing brief, "It defies reason to believe that Ms. Reasonover would confess to Rose Jolliff on January 7, 1983, while protesting her innocence to Stanley White earlier that evening and telling Rose Jolliff five days later that the State was unfairly trying to pin on her a crime she didn't commit." Thus, the State had in its possession two police-taped statements by Ellen proclaiming her innocence that bracketed in time the alleged "confession" to Rose Jolliff for which the court had only Jolliff's word. Not only did Ellen proclaim her innocence in these secret police-taped conversations, but she once again described her activities and what she observed the night of the crime in a consistent manner, as she had in each and every conversation she had with Captain Chapman, Stanley White, Rose Jolliff, and Marsha Vogt. She never deviated from her honest account of that night. To its shame, the State concealed the tapes from the defense.

When questioned about his knowledge of the Jolliff recording, Goldman claimed to have "no recollection of that." He again stated, "I wasn't ever aware of its existence." Yet we found this tape in his files, labeled ROSE/ELLEN, 1/12/83, COPY. He conceded that it should have been turned over to the defense. While watching Goldman squirm on the stand, Ellen thought: *Finally, this man is paying the piper for what he did to me.*

On August 2, 1999, only a month after Ellen's evidentiary hearing, Judge Hamilton filed a seventy-five-page opinion tossing Ellen's conviction. This was not only an extraordinarily fast turnaround (most judges take four to six months to file such opinions), but it was three times longer than a typical opinion, strongly suggesting the judge's desire to get Ellen out of prison as quickly as possible. In her opinion, Judge Hamilton stated that "the contents of the White/Reasonover tape discredits the trial testimony of Rose Jolliff," and that it "contains a candid, reliable account of Petitioner and Stanley White's actions before, during, and after the murder of James Buckley." She concluded that based on the contents of the White/Reasonover tape alone, no reasonable juror would have believed Rose Jolliff's trial testimony.

Judge Hamilton also listed twenty-one factual questions that Ellen's trial counsel could have asked Jolliff if counsel had had the Jolliff/Reasonover tape. The judge stated, "Each of these facts is favorable to Petitioner, and tends to prove that Petitioner did not confess to Rose Jolliff on January 7, 1983." She also concluded that the Jolliff/Reasonover tape's "suppression resulted in significant prejudice to Petitioner. Had the tape been disclosed, the Court concludes that it would have played a prominent role at trial. The contents of the tape would have had a devastating impact on Jolliff's credibility at trial." It is interesting to note that Rose Jolliff was subpoenaed to the hearing. When questioned under oath in Judge Hamilton's chambers, she took the Fifth, refusing to incriminate herself, twenty-eight times.

On August 3, 1999, the day after Judge Hamilton vacated her conviction, Ellen was freed and exonerated after sixteen and a half years of false imprisonment. Eagerly awaiting her release were her husband, Glen; her mother, Elizabeth; her eighteen-year-old daughter, Charmelle; and her two sisters, Hilda and Valerie. Her legal team, along with hordes of supporters and reporters, were also there for the big moment. The juror Donna Ellis, whose lone vote in 1983 had saved Ellen's life, appeared in the media with Ellen. Recognizing that Ellen needed some peace and tranquility, Donna and her husband invited Ellen to live with them. Ellen stayed at their home for six months until she felt capable of living on her own again with Charmelle. Donna and Ellen remained good friends until Donna's death in 2014.

After her liberation, Ellen brought a lawsuit against the City of Dellwood, alleging civil rights violations and wrongful imprisonment. The City of Dellwood settled the case before trial, paying Ellen $4.5 million after legal fees. She was also graced with the arrival of two grandchildren—Harlem and Jour'nee.

For a stretch of five years in the 2000s, Ellen suffered from fibromyalgia, a painful and debilitating chronic disorder. Thankfully, it disappeared as mysteriously as it came upon her. On August 3, 2024, she will celebrate her silver anniversary of freedom. She is sixty-six and lives comfortably and in reasonably good health near her sisters. She and Glen long ago amicably divorced, but remained the best of friends until he died in 2020. Her mother died in 2011. Ellen loves her grandchildren and looks forward to their frequent visits.

Mary Lyner didn't live to see Ellen's exoneration. Nearly a decade before Judge Hamilton took up Ellen's case, Lyner jumped off the balcony of a high-rise apartment she shared with her mother, while her mother and her daughter were in the next room. She was forty-two when she died. Her best friend, Virginia Druhe, a trusted confidante of the Lyner family, in an affidavit filed with Judge Hamilton, described Mary as a person "capable of great deception who lived her life by telling lies boldly and frequently."

Former Dellwood chief of police Dan Chapman died in 2014.

Steven Goldman retired in 2016 after serving twenty-eight years as a St. Louis County judge.

The two black men Ellen saw at Vickers and then at the 7-Eleven have never been identified. The murder of James Buckley remains unsolved.

THE ABSENCE OF MOTIVE

JOHN GRISHAM

When Joe Bryan was in the second grade he met his future wife, Mickey Blue, who was in the first. Obviously too young to even think about a romance, they nonetheless kept an eye on each other as they grew up in their small, neighboring Texas towns. Mickey was popular in school but very quiet and studious. Joe seldom met a stranger and thrived on interaction with others. He often had the impression that he was watching Mickey a lot more than she was noticing him. As teenagers, Mickey dated Joe's twin brother and he dated her cousin. Other romances came and went, and at some point they realized they were dating the wrong people. When Joe finally asked her out she quickly accepted and within weeks they were inseparable.

Both wanted to be teachers and went away to different colleges with the same goal. They loved children and believed that learning was the key to happy, successful lives. When they married in 1969, Mickey taught in an elementary school and Joe taught Latin and English and coached the swim team. He had a small faculty apartment and they spent some of their happiest years there. Their lives were consumed with each other and the kids they taught. They dreamed of starting their own family, but after three years of marriage received the sad news that Mickey could not bear children. They were devastated, but this made them even closer.

In 1975, they returned to Mickey's hometown of Clifton, Texas. Her parents still lived there and the family was respected and well known.

Mickey had been voted Miss Clifton High her senior year and she quickly renewed old friendships. She got a job as a fourth-grade teacher and Joe became the high school principal. They loved living in Clifton and were active in the community, especially the First Baptist Church and, of course, the schools.

Joe was out almost every night at some school function. He never missed a football game, home or away, and Mickey was usually with him. Their days revolved around their classes, their students, and school activities. They were rarely apart and were often seen taking their long evening walks through Clifton. At home, Joe often helped Mickey grade papers and prepare lessons.

He even helped her decorate her classrooms.

With no children at home, they doted on each other and were determined to keep their marriage fresh. They watched so many of their married friends drift apart with time, pulled in different directions by children and careers. They stayed close to their families and were always ready for another gathering. For Thanksgiving each year, Joe and Mickey hosted her family for a traditional dinner, and for each Christmas they visited his family for the festivities.

———

Mickey was always the first teacher to arrive at Clifton Elementary School, often at her desk at 7:00 A.M. She enjoyed the quiet of the early morning before the real day began and the hallways were filled with the eager voices of young students.

On Tuesday, October 15, 1985, Mickey did not arrive at the school.

Oddly, her classroom was still dark and empty when a colleague, Susan Kleine, a fifth-grade teacher, walked by and noticed the door was closed. It was also locked, and Susan assumed Mickey was in the copy room on the other side of the building. At 8:00 A.M., though, there was still no sign of Mickey, and Susan knew something was wrong. She hurried to the office of the principal, Rex Daniels, and informed him Mickey was absent. Susan assumed she had called in sick and Rex had forgotten to summon a substitute.

But Rex said he had not heard from Mickey. His first inclination was to call Joe, but he remembered that his friend was out of town.

Joe, in fact, was 120 miles away in Austin, attending the annual gathering of the Texas Association of Secondary School Principals. He had spoken to Mickey at 9:00 P.M. the night before when he called from his hotel room in Austin. As always, he had told her he loved her, and that he would be home the following afternoon.

Rex asked his secretary to call the Bryan home, which she did, but there was no answer. He asked her to call Mickey's parents, Otis and Vera Blue, who lived nearby. They answered the phone, said they had no idea where Mickey was but assumed she was at work. They had seen her the previous afternoon when she had stopped by. They left immediately to go check on her.

As did Rex Daniels, who arrived at the Bryans' first and saw that Mickey's car was parked in the garage. The morning papers lay in the driveway. He rang the doorbell but no one answered. The Blues arrived with a key and they all went inside. Vera went first and called her daughter's name. When she stepped into the master bedroom, she screamed at a ghastly sight.

Blood was splattered across the ceiling and four walls. Mickey

lay across the bed, covered in blood, obviously dead. Rex grabbed
Vera and Otis, led them to the living room, and sat them on a sofa.
They were horrified, inconsolable, almost unable to speak. Rex
returned to the doorway of the bedroom but did not step inside.
For a moment he looked at Mickey's body lying across the unmade
bed. She was naked from the waist down and her pink nightgown
was pulled up to her thighs.

Rex managed to gather himself, found the phone in the kitchen,
and called the police.

Around 10:00 A.M., as Joe was attending a session of the conference in Austin, Harold Massey, the organization's executive director and a longtime friend, asked Joe to step outside the room. In a
foyer, Massey told Joe that his wife had been shot to death in their
home. Joe fell into a chair and mumbled, "Mickey Bryan of Clifton, Texas?" Three other principals who knew Joe well helped him
upstairs to his room where he lay in the bed, shivering in his suit
and tie.

Clifton was at least two hours from Austin, a fact that would
become important later. Joe was in no condition to drive. Two
friends from Clifton arrived around noon to take him home, and
when he saw them he broke down and began crying again. One
friend later recalled, "Very little was said. Joe sat in the back with
his head down and cried the whole way."

As they entered Clifton, Joe looked out the window at the streets
and houses and buildings he knew so well, and dreaded the awful
moment when he arrived at the home he and his beloved Mickey
had built ten years earlier. As they approached it, the first thing he
noticed was the police cars parked everywhere. Law enforcement
officers were crawling all over the place and the bright yellow crime
scene tape was strung around trees and light poles. City police-
men, county deputies, state troopers, and crime scene technicians
were busy with the investigation. The fabled Texas Rangers were

already on-site, always ready to help the local boys with a homicide investigation.

The neighbors watched in muted disbelief. Word of the murder had spread quickly, as it always does in a small town. Joe recognized the sad and frightened faces of his people.

Still stunned and sleepwalking, Joe gamely tried to answer the first wave of questions from the investigators. Yes, he kept a gun in the house, a .357 Magnum pistol loaded with birdshot to kill rattlesnakes and copperheads that sometimes got too close. He told them he and Mickey kept $1,000 in cash in a metal box.

After a few more questions, Joe was driven to the home of Vera and Otis Blue, where shocked and grief-stricken friends were gathering. When Joe saw Susan Kleine, he asked her again and again, "What am I going to do without Mickey?"

Later that night, Joe went to his mother's home in the small town of Elm Mott, forty miles away near Waco. Distraught, bewildered, and emotionally spent, he lay awake in bed and kept asking himself, *Who in the world would want to hurt Mickey? And why?*

———

At the crime scene, investigators worked feverishly late into the night.

Some details emerged: Mickey had been shot four times at close range; Joe's .357 Magnum was missing; lead pellets were in Mickey's wounds and all over the bedroom, indicating the pistol was probably the murder weapon; there were no witnesses; the neighbors had heard and seen nothing; there were no suspicious fingerprints; no boot or shoe prints; no semen was found with vaginal swabs; there were no signs of forced entry into the home; a cigarette butt was found on the kitchen floor, though neither Mickey nor Joe smoked.

When the investigators realized that Mickey's gold wedding band, watch, and diamond ring were missing, along with Joe's pistol, they assumed she had been the victim of a burglary-turned-homicide. But there was little evidence to support this theory, or any other for that matter.

They found few clues. Mickey's body was removed, leaving behind a blood-soaked mattress and carpet and a bedroom splattered with blood. The sheer volume of blood convinced the police that they needed an expert.

Robert Thorman was a detective with the police department in nearby Bell County, and four months earlier had received his certificate as an expert in "bloodstain pattern analysis." The Bryan murder was his first fee-paying job moonlighting as an expert. Through the good-ole-boy network of police and sheriffs, word was out that Thorman had passed his tests, got his diploma, and could now study bloodstains and see things invisible to other investigators.

Those who practiced bloodstain analysis, at least in 1985, believed that a bloody crime scene was filled with clues as to what happened and who-done-it. By carefully analyzing the drops, spatters, sprays, drippings, trails, prints, and smudges of the victim's blood, a seasoned expert could find crucial evidence.

Thorman had been certified after taking a one-week, forty-hour crash course for which he paid four hundred dollars to a private company that specialized in training "experts" in all types of forensic disciplines. His classes were held in a hotel ballroom in Beaumont, and, remarkably, every "student" in the class earned high marks, got the certificate, and was ready to testify.

When Thorman arrived at the Bryan home Tuesday night, he immediately went to work doing what he had just learned in the hotel ballroom. He studied the specks of blood scattered around the walls. He took photographs. He tacked strings here and there, took measurements, and spent over two hours in the bedroom.

But his thorough examination yielded nothing of substance. His visit produced little, but he would be back.

What it *did not* yield would become far more significant.

Like most homeowners, Joe and Mickey owned an assortment of flashlights—large and small, old and new, close at hand but rarely to be found when needed.

No flashlight was found at the crime scene. Joe and Mickey's bedroom was searched from top to bottom for hours by different investigators, including the expert Thorman, and not a single person ever mentioned a flashlight.

One of the Bryans' flashlights, though, would become a crucial piece of evidence, its significance exaggerated by the investigators.

———

When Joe was overcome with fatigue, he fell asleep, only to be awakened by another nightmare. *This can't be true,* he kept telling himself. After a fitful night, he finally got out of bed Wednesday morning and braced himself for another awful day.

His first chore was to visit the funeral home to discuss the arrangements for burying his wife. While he was there he was told that Joe Wilie wanted to talk to him. Joe was driven to the police station and entered, without a lawyer. Taking a lawyer had never crossed his mind.

Wilie was a former state trooper who had been promoted to the Texas Rangers, the state's elite and legendary crime-fighting unit. Typical of a Ranger, Wilie carried himself with a self-assurance that some considered cockiness, an aura of believing that he could solve any murder. He began the conversation by asking Joe some routine questions about his life with Mickey. Joe, fatigued and emotionally spent, was initially struck by Wilie's total lack of sympathy. Peering from under the brim of his obligatory white Stetson cowboy hat, he was brusque, cocksure, and to the point. No one observing would've had a clue that the Ranger was talking to a man whose wife had just been brutally murdered.

Joe wanted to know how the investigation was going. Dammit, he wanted to know who killed his wife. But Wilie was tight-lipped and gave almost no details. He did say they had found the metal box but there was no cash in it. No, Joe had no theories about who might have wanted to kill Mickey. He still could not believe anyone would want to.

As unpleasant as it was, the interview was not confrontational. The accusations would come later.

―――

Unknown to Joe, and without his consent, the investigators had removed from the home all of the Bryans' valuable papers and documents: bank statements, insurance policies, checkbooks, bills, wills, virtually everything. The bank statements revealed a frugal lifestyle that came as no surprise. Joe and Mickey saved their money and had about $35,000 in various accounts. The mortgage on their home was approximately $36,000 and covered with a life insurance policy. Upon the death of one, the mortgage would be paid off. The couple had purchased inexpensive term life insurance policies on each other for about $150,000. Their retirement benefits through the Texas Teacher Retirement System were $26,000, payable to the survivor.

Joe would see none of the money.

―――

The murder of a well-known person is shocking news regardless of where it happens, but in a place like Clifton, with 3,000 people, practically all of whom knew one another, Mickey's death was impossible to digest. A local girl from a fine family, a much admired and beloved schoolteacher, and the wife of a popular school principal—if she wasn't safe, then who was? Mickey Bryan's murder was terrifying.

Adding to the fear that gripped Clifton was the haunting death of another woman only four months earlier. Back in June, Joe Wilie was called to Clifton to investigate the murder of Judy Whitley, a seventeen-year-old whose nude body was found in a thicket less than a mile from the Bryan home. The teenager had been bound, gagged, raped, and murdered by suffocation.

Were the two murders linked? For a safe, peaceful community with little serious crime, the news of Mickey's death jolted an already jittery population. And it put even more pressure on Joe Wilie and his team of investigators. The truth was that they had no solid clues. They were working around the clock and chasing every lead, but so far had nothing.

Then Charlie Blue entered the picture. Charlie was Mickey's older brother, who lived in Florida where he was a vice president of an agrochemical company. On Tuesday, upon learning of his sister's death, he flew from Florida to Texas and drove to Clifton.

According to Joe, Mickey and Charlie had never been close. He was an aggressive corporate executive accustomed to being in charge and getting his way, a marked contrast to Mickey's quiet and unassuming personality. As brothers-in-law, Joe and Charlie managed to get along but gave each other plenty of space. There was no animosity in the family. Charlie lived a thousand miles away and they seldom got together.

Charlie stayed with his parents, Vera and Otis, and cared for them as the family mourned. He asked Joe if he could borrow his car, a Mercury, while he was in town and Joe was happy to oblige. Joe was still in no shape to drive and was being ushered around by family members. By Friday, the day after the funeral, Charlie was frustrated by the investigation's lack of progress and decided to do something about it. His company had on retainer a retired FBI agent named Bud Saunders, who worked as a private detective. Charlie called Saunders and asked him to drive to Clifton, said there were some things that were bothering him about Mickey's death. He told neither Joe Bryan nor Joe Wilie that he was bringing in his own private investigator.

Saunders arrived in town Saturday afternoon and met Charlie at the Dairy Queen. They got into Joe Bryan's Mercury and went for a long ride to discuss the case. Somewhere out in the countryside, they stopped to relieve themselves beside the road. In the process, Saunders stepped in some mud and soiled his boots. Looking for a cleaning rag, Charlie opened the trunk. There, in a cardboard box, was a flashlight with the lens pointing up. There were tiny specks of something on the lens. Charlie took it and looked it over. As a corporate executive, he had zero experience with bloodstains or crime scenes, but nonetheless surmised that the tiny specks were droplets of blood. He gave it to Saunders, who readily agreed. They drove back to Clifton and called the Rangers from a pay phone.

Late that night, still Saturday, Joe Wilie executed a search warrant on Joe Bryan's Mercury. The flashlight was taken and sent to the state crime lab for analysis. The car itself was in immaculate condition, with no bloodstains inside or out. Joe loathed a dirty car.

Wilie released the Mercury to Charlie, who drove it to the Bryan home and left it in the driveway around 4:00 A.M. Sunday. He and Saunders then left town. Charlie caught a flight from Austin to Tampa.

Joe Bryan knew nothing about any of this. When he picked up his car Sunday afternoon, it had been out of his possession for four days and had been thoroughly searched by Joe Wilie and his team.

Wilie's big break came when the state crime lab reported that the specks on the flashlight lens were human blood type O, same as Mickey's but not Joe's. DNA testing did not exist in 1985. Wilie was suspicious, even though half the world's population has type O blood. When a crime lab chemist also found some tiny plastic particles on the flashlight lens and suspected that they had the same characteristics as the birdshot shells found at the crime scene, Wilie was convinced the flashlight had been used in the murder.

The Ranger had his man.

On October 23, eight days after the murder, Joe Bryan was at his mother's home in Elm Mott, watching television with her in the den, when Wilie unexpectedly arrived at the door. With him were the Clifton chief of police, Ron Brennand, and the Bosque County sheriff, Denny Proffitt. Joe was relieved and glad to see them, and hopeful they had good news about the investigation.

Instead, Joe Wilie said, "You're under arrest for your wife's murder."

At first Joe was unable to speak, then managed to ask, "On what evidence?"

Wilie had no response. Joe was handcuffed, placed in the rear seat of a patrol car, and driven to nearby Waco, where he was processed. He was then taken to the Bosque County jail in Meridian, where he was stripped naked and photographed. The police were looking for scratches and bruises, possibly to indicate a desperate last-minute fight by Mickey.

No such evidence was found.

———

The news of Joe's arrest was met with widespread disbelief. In fact, no one who knew Joe believed for a moment that he had killed Mickey, a woman he loved, cherished, and was thoroughly devoted to. Their colleagues at the school were incredulous and angry. Current and former students were vehement in their protests. Joe was known for his lack of anger and cool head in every situation. He had neither the temperament nor the motive to harm anyone, certainly not his wife.

It's not clear whether Ranger Wilie and his team felt a backlash after the arrest. They had rushed the investigation, found no witnesses and no credible clues, ignored a clear alibi, and were now preening for the press. Once again the heroic Ranger had ridden into town on a white horse and saved the people by arresting a cold-blooded killer.

Implementing their "indict first, investigate later" strategy, Wilie and his team busied themselves trying to prove the one element of the crime that begged for attention: motive. There was absolutely no evidence or even gossip about Joe and Mickey's marital problems. They had none. They were inseparable, got along with their relatives, had little money to bicker over, loved being together, and would rather spend time by themselves than with friends.

To cast doubt on the couple's closeness, the investigators decided that Joe was a homosexual. Since they believed he had homosexual tendencies, then, obviously, he had homicidal ones as well.

The smear was on. One of their more bizarre theories was that Mickey had somehow found out about Joe's sordid double life and was planning to confront him, then divorce him, and so on. There was not a shred of evidence anywhere to even suggest this, but that didn't matter. The case was completely devoid of any hint of a motive, so it was imperative that the cops create one.

Fueling the smear campaign was something Joe Wilie had found in the trunk of Joe Bryan's Mercury when he was searching for the flashlight. It was a Chippendales pin-up calendar with color photos of partially clad male dancers posing for each month. (Joe and Mickey had bought it, together, as a gag gift for a friend, then forgot about it and left it in the trunk.)

What further proof was needed?

———

After Joe was arrested and released on bond, the investigators fanned out through the community looking for proof that he was gay, and in the process did not hesitate to spread all manner of salacious rumors.

When Joe Wilie interviewed Susan Kleine, Mickey's close friend and teaching colleague, his first question stunned her: "Do you think Joe is effeminate?" Before she could answer, he followed up with "There are rumors that Joe is gay."

Susan was close to both Joe and Mickey and was adamant in her belief that he would never harm her. She knew them well, knew their friends and families well, and had never heard anyone say anything about Joe being gay. Not until it was mentioned by Joe Wilie.

She pushed back hard and said no, Joe was not, in her opinion, effeminate, and he was definitely not gay. And, no, she had never heard such a rumor until now. Kleine became rattled when Wilie kept asking similar questions about Joe's sexuality. She knew the truth, and she also knew how devastating the rumors could be for someone like Joe. She finally warned Wilie that he was on thin ice and should be careful with a person's reputation.

Wilie and his team were anything but careful. In dozens of interviews with friends and acquaintances, they repeatedly returned to the "gay" theme in Joe's life, though not one witness knew the first thing about it. The cops got even more creative and asked questions about "rumors" of Joe being involved with a male student, and Joe stealing away to New Orleans for weekends of debauchery in gay bars. The rumors, all created and fomented by the cops, were repeated, passed around, embellished, and took on a life of their own.

The investigators' notes contain such observations as "Homo tendencies?" and "He gay?" and "Queer?"

As the investigators dug through every aspect of Joe's private life, they obtained his phone records. It was one of those moments when thoughtful detectives would realize they were on the wrong trail. Not so with Wilie and his posse. Joe's phone calls in the month before the murder were to Mickey, his mother, his older brother, a cousin, a vitamin shop, a contact-lens store, and a hospital. There was not a single call that was even remotely suspicious.

Thoughtful detectives, though, were not in charge. The arrest had been made, they had their man, and now they were desperate to prove it.

———

Joe Bryan was a happily married straight male who had never been unfaithful to Mickey. Throughout their marriage they had enjoyed a close, intimate relationship. Like most marriages, the earlier years had seen more activity, especially when they were "working" hard to reproduce. When they learned Mickey could not get pregnant, they were deeply saddened, but they were only in their late twenties and much too young to give up on sex.

When the gay rumors finally made it to Joe at his mother's home in Elm Mott, it felt like just another rotten blow to an innocent man. *What can they do next?* he asked himself.

————

The people of Clifton were law-abiding folks who placed great trust in the authorities: the police, the prosecutors, the judges. A nasty rumor passed along by an average citizen may or may not have traveled far, but one uttered with the authority of a policeman, let alone a Texas Ranger, carried much greater weight. It didn't take long for the rumors, thoroughly unfounded, to get repeated and passed around. As always with rumors, the more sensational they were, the faster they traveled.

As the smear campaign gained steam, Joe stayed away from Clifton.

The school put him on paid leave, and for the first time in many years his days did not center around his students and the school schedule. He missed them greatly, and he missed his friends, many of whom were slowly withdrawing.

Most of all, he missed his beloved Mickey, his wife and best friend.

Once a week he went home to Clifton to mow his yard. He was beginning to feel like a trespasser in his own town. His neighbors were still friendly, but others kept their distance. He often stopped by the cemetery, where he sat next to Mickey's grave and wept. Losing her was a raw, jagged hole in his life. Being accused of killing her made the pain unbearable.

His Christian faith had always sustained and guided him. He prayed more than ever and read his Bible, searching for help. He continued worshipping in his church and was strengthened by the closeness he felt with the other believers. That bond, though, was shattered one day when his pastor telephoned and, after a friendly chat, finally got around to the real purpose of the call. Several members of First Baptist Church had complained that they were uneasy with Joe's presence. Did he mind staying away until the trial was over? It was another painful slap at Joe and he withdrew even deeper into his own dark world.

Not long afterward, the school superintendent paid a visit and asked Joe to resign.

To make bad matters worse, Charlie Blue reappeared and again inserted himself into the proceedings by filing a lawsuit to protect Mickey's estate and keep Joe from spending their savings on legal fees. The judge agreed, and Joe had to borrow money from his siblings to pay his lawyers. Otis and Vera, Mickey's parents, cut off all communication with Joe.

———

Six months after the murder, the trial began in the Bosque County Courthouse in the town of Meridian, the county seat and even smaller than Clifton. Joe's lawyers had made the crucial decision not to request a change of venue. They reasoned that their client was well known and respected in his community, an accused man who deserved to be judged by his peers. The decision proved to be prudent when most of the prospective jurors raised their hands when asked if they either knew or had heard of Joe Bryan.

To his family and friends, he was a startling sight sitting at the defense table between his two lawyers. At times he appeared sad and confused, and at other times he appeared almost belligerent and combative because everyone knew the trial was a sham, he was innocent, and he just wanted to hurry things along and get the trial over with. Since the day of his arrest, it had never for a single moment occurred to Joe that he would be found guilty of murdering Mickey.

At times he feared it might happen, trials being so unpredictable, but he knew the truth and was certain it would absolve him. He didn't belong in the courtroom, dammit, someone else did.

The case was prosecuted by Andy McMullen, the elected district attorney, who had little experience in murder. The evidence handed to him by Joe Wilie and his team was so lame, circumstantial, and riddled with gaping holes that a guilty verdict looked doubtful. McMullen, though, was not about to stand in the way of a Texas Ranger who claimed to have solved a high-profile murder.

McMullen's task was an uphill slog from the opening gavel. He had no direct proof, only circumstantial at best. There were no witnesses; no one saw or heard anything unusual the night Mickey was killed. To convict Joe of the murder, the State would have to convince the jurors to believe an incredible theory: (1) On the night of October 14, Joe and Mickey talked by phone around 9:15 and said good night; (2) Joe then sneaked out of his hotel room in Austin, 120 miles away, and drove two hours to his home in Clifton; (3) Joe made the drive in spite of a heavy thunderstorm, and in spite of a vision problem called corneal erosion, a condition that made it difficult for him to see at night; (4) Joe arrived home around midnight, parked his car in his driveway, then unlocked the door with his key and entered the kitchen; (5) Joe moved through the dark house while Mickey was asleep, found his .357 Magnum pistol, loaded it with buckshot, found the flashlight, then eased into their dark bedroom where he shot his wife four times; (6) while firing away, he was holding the flashlight in such a manner that Mickey's type O blood spattered, or backsplashed, onto Joe, the walls, the ceiling, and the flashlight itself; (7) Joe, covered in blood, bathed, changed into clean clothes and shoes, threw away the bloody ones, and left his home; (8) while making his getaway, he took the pistol, which was never found, and the flashlight, which he placed in the trunk of his car, evidently unaware that the back-spatter had also landed on it; (9) Joe also "stole" the wedding band he'd given to his wife, along with her watch and diamond ring; (10) having killed his wife, Joe drove back to Austin in the early morning of October 15, sneaked into his room without being seen, slept a few hours, then arrived promptly at 8:30 for a breakfast session with friends as if nothing had happened.

With great effort, much of this outlandish scenario could almost be explained. For example: Joe chose October 14 because he would be out of town and his alibi would be well documented; he made the four-hour round-trip drive with his vision greatly impaired but was determined to do so anyway; he knew the town would be fast asleep after midnight on a Tuesday so there was no need to hide his car; he entered his own home quietly because he had a key; perhaps he had pre-loaded his pistol and had it ready; instead of turning on the light in his bedroom and giving Mickey a chance to wake up and resist, he attacked in the dark so she would have no defense and never know who killed her; he knew the scene would be bloody so he had a change of clothes and shoes ready for his getaway. And so on.

Each detail could be debated back and forth. However, in a criminal trial a conviction must be reached beyond a reasonable doubt and cannot be based on what *might have or could have* happened. Solid proof is required, and in *State v. Bryan* the State had almost none of it to offer.

Missing also was a motive. During the trial, the State would be unable to produce even the slightest scintilla of evidence that Joe and Mickey were having marital problems. The opposite was true. After months of questioning their friends and families, the investigators had not dug up a single hint of conflict or a word of discontent.

As for the homosexual angle, it, too, had fizzled. Regardless of the innuendos, rumors, and loaded questions they had floated around the county, the investigators had found zero proof of bad behavior by Joe, either with men or women. They had tried to smear

Joe's reputation, but the courtroom was packed with his friends and supporters, clear proof that he was admired, even beloved. About forty of his closest friends planned to testify on his behalf.

McMullen's opening statement to the jury was so lacking in conviction and ineffectual that it was almost a surrender, an admission that the State didn't have much of a case. Generally speaking, when prosecutors lack strong evidence they tend to grab the high moral ground, yell a lot, even quote Holy Scripture and Shakespeare, and divert the jury's attention from their weak case. McMullen did not do that. He did not present a theory of the case. He rambled on a bit, offered some platitudes, and thanked the jurors for their service.

The fireworks came next, from another prosecutor, an out-of-town lawyer named Garry Lewellen. When Charlie Blue became frustrated with the slow pace of the investigation, he brought in his own investigator. He was equally unimpressed with McMullen, so he hired his own prosecutor—Garry Lewellen. Texas law permitted the victim's family to hire a special prosecutor, but only as long as the district attorney kept control of the case.

Lewellen was rowdier and feistier than McMullen and barked enough to get the jury's attention. The State's case, though, soon lost whatever momentum he had given it. The jury was shown graphic photos of the crime scene, and diagrams of the bedroom and the house, all of which proved little. Two human hairs found in a cardboard box in the trunk of Joe's Mercury did not match his or Mickey's. Some fingerprints from the bedroom were Joe's, but then it was his bedroom. Some more were found on his flashlight. He had never denied owning it. An unidentified palm print taken from the bedroom was not Joe's and it could not be linked to Mickey because the comparison tests got screwed up. A chemist from the state crime lab testified that she'd examined photographs of the flashlight under her microscope and seen a fragment she believed *could have been* from the plastic shell casings found at the crime scene.

Remarkably, the flashlight was not present in the courtroom. It's not clear where it was kept at the time, but the record is clear that the State did not produce it for the jury to see. All the analysis of the lens of the flashlight was performed by examining *photographs* of the flashlight, and not the flashlight itself.

The first days of the trial dragged on with no damning evidence presented against Joe.

The most important piece of evidence also had the most potential to damage the State's case: the cigarette butt found on the kitchen floor. Since neither Joe nor Mickey smoked, it stood to reason that the killer had calmly had a smoke after, or even perhaps before, he committed his crime.

Regardless, the cigarette butt was a major problem for the prosecution. Someone left it there, and that someone was the killer.

But Joe Wilie was not deterred. He had a new story. He patiently explained to the jury that he himself had stepped on the cigarette butt when he was outside the house and had inadvertently tracked it into the kitchen, where it fell off the sole of his cowboy boot. How the Ranger knew he had stepped on it was not made clear. How he knew he had somehow deposited it moments later on the kitchen floor was never explained. So, the problem was solved. And Wilie even had a witness. A Clifton policeman named Kenneth Fields testified that he had actually seen the cigarette butt fall from Wilie's boot onto the kitchen floor. Of course, Fields did not mention this to anyone at the time, nor did he include it in his written report. Wilie's own twenty-five-page report makes no mention of the sticky cigarette butt.

On the fourth day of the trial, the State called Charlie Blue to the stand.

He and Lewellen, the prosecutor he was paying, went through a well-rehearsed back-and-forth to establish that Blue was the concerned older brother who just wanted to find justice for his sister. He told the jury his story about meeting Saunders, his private investigator, and driving around the county in Joe's Mercury, until they stopped beside the road to relieve themselves. When they opened the trunk, Blue saw the flashlight, noticed the red specks on the lens, and immediately said, "That looks like blood." Not surprisingly, Saunders agreed.

Again, the jurors did not have the benefit of looking at the flashlight. Instead, they were handed color photographs that barely showed some specks that were practically indistinguishable.

———

The State's case plodded on with little drama and no clear evidence of Joe's guilt. The most crucial testimony came from Joe Wilie as he was being cross-examined by Joe's lawyers about the absence of motive. He was asked, "You haven't come up with one motive at all, have you, for this man to kill this woman?"

Wilie replied, "She's worth three hundred thousand dollars to him dead, if you want to surmise a motive."

The statement was not only inflammatory and highly prejudicial, it was also untrue. The policy on Mickey's life paid roughly $150,000. When she died, she and Joe had about $35,000 in the bank and a modest home with a mortgage. To testify, under oath, that Joe's motive, indeed the only possible motive, was financial, was objectionable. To mention the life insurance should have been grounds for a mistrial.

Joe's lawyers jumped to their feet and objected loudly. The prosecutors yelled back. When things settled down, the judge allowed the testimony anyway.

After four days the State had produced nothing but weak evidence that was not only circumstantial but, for the most part, equivocal. The course of the trial changed dramatically on the fifth day, when Robert Thorman took the stand. As a newly certified expert in the field of bloodstain analysis, he would bring scientific certainty to an otherwise murky case.

As most expert witnesses do, Thorman began with a blustery

narrative about his credentials and qualifications: his long career in law enforcement, even the military police, and his training in bloodstain analysis. The jury did not know that he had no scientific training in such analysis and that his sole training consisted of one forty-hour course in a Beaumont hotel four months earlier.

He then laid the groundwork for his expertise by describing the crime scene when he arrived on the evening of October 15. The jury had already seen plenty of the gory photographs and needed to see no more. Thorman said there was a "vast amount" of splattering and there would have been a "vast amount" of blood on the killer, whoever he was.

The flashlight was the crucial piece of evidence, and Thorman soon got around to it. Since it was not available, and no one could ever explain where the damned thing was, Thorman relied on some of the same photographs the jury had already seen. They did not reveal any recognizable blood; rather they showed a series of tiny specks, which, to the average eye would mean nothing. But to a highly trained expert like Thorman, there was an enormous amount of evidence in those specks. They were caused by blowback, or backsplash, or "back-spatter," as he preferred to call it, and, at least to him, they were proof that the victim's blood had reversed course from the angle of the wounds and traveled backward at a high rate of speed. Since some of the blood landed on the flashlight, it therefore stood to reason that the flashlight was at the crime scene.

Thorman went on to say that the absence of spatter on the handle of the flashlight indicated that someone was holding it at the time of the shooting.

This fit neatly into the State's scenario that Joe sneaked into his own home, did not turn on the lights for fear of waking the person he was about to murder, then entered his bedroom with the flashlight in one hand while firing his pistol with the other.

Using some of the scientific words he had just learned, and also throwing in the usual jargon, Thorman was certain the flashlight was a crucial part of the murder. After the shooting, Joe had hidden it in the trunk of his car, but only after neglecting to wipe off the blood. Since Mickey's blood was O-positive (like that of billions of others), then it was clear, at least to Thorman and the investigators, that Joe had killed his wife.

On cross-examination, Joe's lawyer asked Thorman how, in spite of the "vast amount" of blood that had back-spattered onto the killer, Joe's car, the Mercury, could have been so spotlessly clean when it was examined by the investigators. There was not a trace of blood anywhere. And, also, how did the killer manage to leave the crime scene without tracking or leaving a trace of Mickey's blood? The crime scene team found no bloody fingerprints, nor boot or shoe prints.

Here, Thorman began to improvise. He speculated that Joe bathed and changed clothes and shoes, and also found the time to thoroughly wipe down his car.

Thorman's alleged expertise was with bloodstain analysis, the parameters of which were set by the crime scene itself. He had a certificate to prove it. From where, then, did he gain the knowledge to predict what a killer might do after he left the crime scene? How could he possibly know, for a fact, that the killer bathed, changed clothes and shoes, and scrubbed his car to get rid of bloodstains?

It was all speculation. Thorman was reaching far beyond the scope of his field. That portion of his testimony was prejudicial and inadmissible, and should have been stricken from the record, with an admonishment to the jury to disregard it. Joe's lawyers objected loudly but the judge admitted the shaky testimony anyway.

Robert Thorman saved the State's case by grounding it in scientific certainty. Until he testified, the prosecution had floundered through a mishmash of hearsay, speculation, half-truths, and innuendo. At the last minute, though, a certified expert had placed the flashlight taken from the trunk of Joe's car and made it a vital part of Mickey's murder.

Thorman had turned the tide dramatically.

For five days Joe had sat at the defense table and looked on help-lessly as the State tried to piece together an unconvincing case that, in the end, did not prove his guilt. How could it? So many times he wanted to stand up and scream, "I'm innocent! I didn't do it! You've got the wrong guy! The killer is still out there!"

He did not kill Mickey and he'd been confident a trial would prove it. But after five days of being accused by the respected author-ities, even a Texas Ranger, he was afraid. His fear was caused by the faces and reactions of the jurors, who appeared skeptical at first, but, after hours of hearing the accusations against him, began glancing at Joe with suspicion. The expert testimony from Thorman seemed to get their attention.

Joe began to understand the presumption of guilt. It went some-thing like this: In a murder like Mickey's, the community is shocked and wants immediate justice. The people want the murderer caught, locked up, and punished. When a suspect is arrested, the public is relieved and rushes to judgment—the suspect must be guilty, or at least involved, otherwise the police wouldn't arrest him. Once pre-sumed to be guilty, the suspect is hauled into the courtroom where he faces the power of the State—the police and prosecutors—the very authorities the public is brainwashed into trusting. The jurors, average folk selected from the community, place much greater cre-dence in the testimony of the authorities than in anything offered by the defendant, who, of course, is fighting for his life and will do or say anything to save his neck.

Joe realized he was presumed to be guilty. The trial was not fair. The field was not level.

He insisted on testifying for himself. He had done nothing wrong and certainly had no criminal record to worry about on cross-examination. He was unimpeachable and his lawyers agreed he could speak for himself. He began by denying everything the jury had just heard. He was in a hotel room 120 miles away when his wife was murdered. He did not kill her, had no reason to, no motive. To suggest otherwise was outrageous. He owned the flashlight but did not put it in the trunk of his car, nor could he remember how it got there.

He was emotional at times, especially when talking about Mickey, but he held himself together and survived the direct examination.

On cross-examination, Robert Lewellen attacked with an endless barrage of accusations that portrayed Joe as a liar. Joe held firm and insisted he had never left his hotel room that night. Time and again he said, "I don't know, I don't know. I've never understood any of this." As Lewellen hammered away, Joe broke into tears and kept saying, "I did not kill Mickey and I don't know who did."

Lewellen had the final word, and the last thing the jury heard was his loud and angry summation, ending with "Mickey didn't go to bed and leave the house unlocked that night. She locked the door, and a man came in with a key, and after all hell broke loose in that bedroom, he cleaned up, changed clothes, wiped up the lavatory, threw his clothes in the bag, walked out the front door. Then he went right back, walking in the front door of the Hyatt Hotel, whistling Dixie."

———

The jury deliberated for only four hours and found Joe guilty of murder. He was sentenced to ninety-nine years in prison. A week later, he was placed in the rear seat of a patrol car and driven 160 miles to the prison in Huntsville, home of the State's busy death chamber. The prison was built with high, redbrick walls and guard towers and looked like a medieval fortress. Joe's first glimpse of it was a frightening shock, but by then he was almost numb to another blow to the truth and his freedom. And, oddly enough, he was not frightened. He knew God would protect him.

In April 1986, Joe Bryan, age forty-six, entered the Texas prison system, where he would remain for the next thirty-four years.

———

Prison is a dreadful place even for those who deserve it. For an innocent person it is a continuation of an unimaginable nightmare. For Joe, it was the endgame, the final stop, the place he would never leave. Robbed of the person he loved, falsely accused by trigger-happy cops, wrongfully convicted by a corrupt system, and banished to a hellhole where he was supposed to die, he immediately fell into a state of dark, endless depression. In his first days and nights at Huntsville he was numb to his surroundings and withdrawn. He felt like a zombie, sleepwalking through the daily routines while trying to convince himself that through some miracle the nightmare would end. The loneliness was achingly painful. Predators attacked him twice but he fought them off and was left alone.

His cell was five feet by nine, a tight space for any man, but Joe had a cellmate, a "cellie," who took the bottom bunk by the rules of seniority. Avoiding physical contact required nimble feet and patience. When one needed to use the toilet, the other one disappeared.

Before long, Joe realized that a week had passed, then another. Then a month. He was slowly becoming institutionalized and moving through each day as he was told. Virtually every aspect of his life was dictated for him: waking up, eating meals, showering twice a week, working, exercising, visiting with family and his lawyers. In his sparse free time he played the piano in chapel services, taught other inmates seeking their GEDs, tutored officers taking college courses, and read at least two books a week.

His lawyers professed optimism for his chances on appeal, though they knew firsthand the harsh reputation of the Texas criminal appellate courts. Joe relived his case, reading and studying everything—the briefs filed by his lawyers, the court transcripts, the motions, and the rulings from the judge.

He met with his lawyers as often as they could make it to Huntsville. In their filings they argued strenuously that the State's case was insufficient, that Thorman's work lacked scientific integrity, and that there was simply no reasonable cause for accusing Joe, the husband, as the suspect.

Joe Wilie's cocky testimony caught the attention of the appellate court.

He was dead wrong when he suggested to the jury that Mickey was worth $300,000 to Joe if she was dead. The actual amount of her life policy was about half that, but such testimony was prejudicial, regardless of the amount.

Two years after the trial, Joe's conviction was overturned. He was ecstatic, and thought—for a moment—that the injustice might be coming to an end. However, the State moved quickly to indict him again and schedule a second trial.

It was a repeat of the first, with the same prosecutors and witnesses.

Robert Thorman was even more certain of his findings and once again ventured far away from his field of "expertise." The only significant difference was the lack of support from Joe's friends. Only a few volunteered to testify on his behalf. The rest had waved goodbye.

In July 1988, Joe was found guilty of murder and again sentenced to ninety-nine years in prison.

———

As bloodstain analysis became more popular in the 1980s and '90s, it also became more controversial. Defense lawyers attacked it relentlessly as bogus science. Other experts, real scientists, studied it and found no shortage of flaws. Several notorious cases cast serious doubt on its reliability.

Perhaps its most egregious abuse was in the case of David Camm, an Indiana state trooper who spent thirteen years behind bars for a horrible crime he had nothing to do with. On a spring night in March 2000, Camm was playing basketball with some friends, and when the game was over he drove home. In his garage, he found a bloody scene that was indescribable—his wife and two children had been shot to death. In spite of a lack of motive, and in spite of the testimony of numerous alibi witnesses at the basketball game, the authorities believed Camm was the killer. They found eight specks of blood on his T-shirt, and they also found a couple of experts who testified that the specks were "high-velocity impact spatter." In other words, the T-shirt was present at the murders. Camm's lawyers produced experts who sharply disagreed and testified that the eight specks were "transfer stains," or bloodstains caused when Camm was frantically trying to render aid. He was put on trial, found guilty, appealed, won a reversal, was retried, found guilty again, appealed again, won another reversal, and was tried for the third time. At the end of his third trial, thirteen years after he was arrested, he was finally acquitted and walked free.

A burglar with a rap sheet was convicted when his DNA matched evidence from the crime scene.

More notorious wrongful convictions followed, and bloodstain analysis grew even more controversial, as did other types of shady forensics such as the analysis of hair, boot prints, arson, and bite marks. Criminal courtrooms in America were flooded with unscientific testimony offered by unqualified experts paid nice fees by prosecutors. With time, many of the wrongful convictions began to sour as defense lawyers and innocence advocates hammered away and DNA testing became more widespread and accurate.

In 2009, the National Academy of Sciences issued an exhaustive report with seismic implications in the field of criminal law. In response to a tidal wave of complaints from defense lawyers, legal scholars, and forensic scientists, and also in response to the growing number of sensational DNA exonerations of innocent men and women, the NAS went to work and put the forensic disciplines under the microscope. What it found was unsettling.

Much of what passed for expert testimony was highly speculative and not grounded in scientific research. Regarding bloodstain analysis, the report issued a number of critical warnings and ended with: "The uncertainties associated with bloodstain-pattern analysis are enormous."

———

Joe's appellate lawyers, Walter Reaves and Jessica Freud, took his case to federal court with a writ of habeas corpus. To be successful, they would have to present new evidence of his innocence. They convinced the court to allow DNA testing of the cigarette butt and flashlight lens. Both proved futile—no DNA profile could be obtained from either. However, one test revealed a startling conclusion: There was no proof that the blood on the lens was actually blood!

In 2017, in a hearing to determine if Joe should be given a new trial, his lawyers stunned the courtroom with an affidavit from Robert Thorman, since retired. Thorman wrote: "My conclusions were wrong. Some of the techniques and methodology were incorrect. Therefore, some of my testimony was not correct." But, he concluded, "in no way did I lie in my report or testimony, as I was doing what I thought was correct as a result of my training at the time."

During the same hearing, a DNA analyst from the Texas crime lab testified that he'd tested six tiny stains on the flashlight lens. Five were negative for the presence of blood. The sixth was positive, but it could not be determined whose blood it was. DNA samples were taken from the handle of the flashlight. Joe and Mickey were both excluded.

Walter Reaves and Jessica Freud destroyed the State's case against Joe.

Nonetheless, his request for a new trial was denied.

As were his requests for parole. In spite of his near-perfect record in prison—no misconduct, no reprimands, nothing but high marks from his guards, bosses, and fellow inmates—Joe was denied parole seven times.

By March 2021, Joe had developed congestive heart disease and was in failing health. Plus, the Covid epidemic had prison authorities on edge. The parole board, for reasons it never explained, reversed itself and set Joe free.

He was welcomed by his family and went to live with his older brother in Houston.

———

Who killed Mickey Bryan? Because the investigation was so thoroughly botched, the truth will never be known. Once the investigators decided Joe was gay and therefore capable of murder and therefore willing to kill his wife to keep her quiet, and also to collect her life insurance, they arrested him a week after the murder. At that point, gripped by a severe case of tunnel vision, they abruptly stopped looking for other suspects. They had their man.

Instead of following several suspicious leads, they poked around for any trace of Joe's sordid secret life. They found nothing. The real killer remained free.

If they had bothered to look closer, they might have found the killer in their midst. Strong evidence pointed to a rogue cop named Dennis Dunlap, a Clifton city policeman.

Judy Whitley was the seventeen-year-old who was raped and murdered four months before Mickey was killed. Her nude and bound body was found less than a mile from the Bryans' home. Joe Wilie was also in charge of that investigation, which remained open. The pressure from the first murder could have motivated Wilie to act quickly to "solve" the second one.

Dennis Dunlap was a drifter who worked for several small-town police departments and had trouble keeping a job. He had a history of violence against women and was known to harass and stalk them while on duty. He was not a homicide detective and did not investi-

gate the Whitley murder, but he surprised his colleagues by knowing so much about the case, even to the point of describing how the
victim suffocated. He was briefly considered a suspect, but when
he abruptly resigned and left town the investigators lost interest in
him. The evidence in the case was stored in a police locker, and it,
too, disappeared. He was known to return to Clifton periodically.

Joe Bryan has always suspected that the Clifton police told Dunlap to leave town to prevent an embarrassment. Once he was gone,
he was no longer investigated.

In 1996, Dunlap was working as a janitor in the town of Rosen-
berg, Texas. His girlfriend called 911, and when the police arrived
they found him in the garage hanging with a cord around his neck.
He did not leave a suicide note, but shortly before he died he admitted to his girlfriend that he had killed Judy Whitley. He had bragged
to his ex-wife, not his girlfriend, that he'd had an affair with Mickey
and was with her the night she was murdered.

When the police went through Dunlap's personal items, they
found letters and newspaper clippings that led them back to the
murders in Clifton. A new police chief there reviewed the Whitley
case and interviewed Dunlap's former associates. They recalled his
intimate knowledge of the most gruesome aspects of the rape and
murder. In June 1999, fourteen years after the murder, the Clifton
police declared the crime solved. The headline in the town's newspaper declared: DUNLAP OFFICIALLY NAMED MURDERER OF
WHITLEY TEEN.

There would be no justice for Mickey Bryan, nor for her husband. The police have not reopened the case because Joe's conviction still stands.

———

May 1, 2024. Joe lives with his older brother in Houston and is still
on parole. To visit Clifton and Bosque County, he must obtain written approval from his parole officer. He is free to travel anywhere in

the state except Bosque County. Approval is granted, and Joe has the paperwork in his car.

He has not visited Mickey's grave in thirty-five years. It is in an old cemetery in a remote part of the county, near the land her family has owned for decades. The cemetery is neglected, poorly maintained, and as he steps through weeds and around old gravestones, he mumbles to himself, "Mickey would not approve of this."

He finds her grave, steps closer, then stops and begins weeping as the memories return. The feelings of loss are overwhelming: the loss of his true love and best friend, the loss of all those years in prison, the loss of a career he thoroughly enjoyed, the loss of friendships.

But he refused to lose his Christian faith. He still prays and reads Scripture every day, same as in prison. Always the teacher, he leads Bible study groups, same as in prison. He will even play the piano for the choir, if asked, same as in prison. He survived hell behind bars because of the strength he found in his faith. God protected him, as he knew He would.

And Joe has long since forgiven those responsible for his persecution. He can never forget people like Joe Wilie, Ron Brennand, and Robert Thorman, but he has forgiven them.

Staring at Mickey's name on the gravestone, he wipes his eyes and shakes his head and softly asks the same questions he has lived with for almost forty years: "Who in the world would want to hurt Mickey? And why?"

THROUGH THE LOOKING-GLASS

JIM McCLOSKEY

⸻

The small town of New Iberia sits on a bayou in southern Louisiana, surrounded by sugarcane fields, not far from the Gulf of Mexico. It was first settled in the 1700s by French immigrants, later known as Cajuns, who were exiled there from Nova Scotia by the British. Today, the town has around 30,000 residents, approximately half black, half white, and is the seat of Iberia Parish, "parish" being Louisiana's word for county. New Iberia is the hometown of famous novelist James Lee Burke and his fictional detective Dave Robicheaux, an investigator for the Iberia Parish sheriff's office. The town takes pride in being near the original home of Tabasco sauce, Avery Island.

On March 30, 1976, on the rural outskirts of New Iberia, shortly before three o'clock in the afternoon, Louis Gladu was robbed and murdered while doing what he did every day, operating the Hasty Mart, a convenience store he owned. He was found lying in a pool of blood by Katherine Eldridge, a customer who had just arrived with her two children, a five-year-old and a baby, to buy some soda. Although near hysteria, she managed to call the sheriff's office using the store's pay phone.

The store was soon swarming with sheriff's officers and forensic criminalists, twelve in all, including the Iberia Parish sheriff himself, Gerald Wattigny, who had first been elected to his job more than twenty years before. The investigation was led by Captain Horace Comeaux, chief detective for the sheriff's office. This was a big case. It was a particularly senseless and unprovoked murder that shook the small community. Gladu, a sixty-two-year-old white man, had sustained a two-inch laceration above the right temple that knocked him to the floor. He was then shot twice at close range while on his back, once in the heart and once in the nose, by a .32 caliber Clerke revolver. He died immediately.

The cash register drawer was left open, and $200 had been stolen. In their haste, the killer or killers had missed the $1,100 in Gladu's wallet and another $695 in nearby paper bags. Cigarette packages that had been displayed on the counter by the cash register now littered the floor. Gladu's glasses lay nine feet from his body. Fresh tire tracks were discovered in a gravel driveway seventy-five yards down the road, on the opposite side from the Hasty Mart. The police made plaster casts of the tracks.

On her way to the Hasty Mart, Eldridge told police, she had passed a light blue car about to turn out of the gravel driveway onto the state highway on which she was traveling, called Sugar Mill Road. No sooner had she pulled off Sugar Mill into the store's parking lot than that same car sped by, going very fast. Nineteen-year-old pregnant Ellen Abney lived in a house trailer along the gravel drive. Her dog's barking awakened her from a nap shortly before 3:00 P.M., when she saw what she thought was a four-door dark blue car occupied by four black men turn around at the dead end of the driveway and pass her trailer on the way out.

Captain Comeaux had his office put out a BOLO (*be on the lookout*) to all units for a light blue, old model, four-door car occupied by four black males.

Six days of fruitless investigation followed with no suspects. With Sheriff Wattigny pressuring Comeaux for an arrest, Deputy Sheriff Eddie Moore, the only black person on the force, came to the chief investigator's rescue. Moore called himself "Shaft," after the suave and successful black detective featured in the film series *Shaft*. To live up to that image, Moore routinely wore three guns: one on his shoulder, one on his hip, and one on his ankle. Looking to impress his boss, on April 5 he brought in Mary Arceneaux, a black woman and career criminal who claimed to have information on the Hasty Mart murder.

———

Mary was thirty-five years old and already had an extensive criminal record. In 1973, she had pled guilty to twelve counts of issuing worthless checks. She received a suspended four-month prison term and was placed on a two-year probation. In May 1974, she was charged with nine new counts of forgery and seven new counts of issuing worthless checks. She pled guilty to one count of forgery and to all seven counts of bad checks. The judge sentenced her to eighteen months on the forgery charge and an additional forty-two months on the check charges. He suspended these latter charges, however, provided she abided by a two-year supervised probation that would begin after she had served her eighteen-month prison term. The judge observed at sentencing that her "widespread propensity . . . to wrongfully obtain money is the result of her association with drug dealers."

Released from prison in 1975, Mary began her two-year supervised probation. She attempted to skip out on her probation in January 1976 but was eventually caught through a connection of Deputy Moore's. Her actions placed her in a legally vulnerable position: She was now facing a return to prison to serve the forty-two-month sentence that the judge had originally suspended. By April 5, 1976, when she met with Captain Comeaux, she figured that if she could help him solve the Hasty Mart crime, he could wipe away her charges and keep her out of prison.

Comeaux questioned Mary about the murder, although she'd spent some time beforehand in a prep session with Deputy Moore and Deputy Chief Jim Desormeaux, who briefed her on the details of the crime. During the interview with Comeaux she claimed that on March 29, the night before the Hasty Mart robbery, a man she had dated for fourteen months named Harold had picked her up at her house in St. Martinville, nine miles north of New Iberia. Two men she didn't know were also in his car. One was introduced as Vinny, but she was never told the name of the other man. Harold drove them all to New Iberia; during the drive the three men talked of "hitting a store to rob it and kill that man and kill five people." She said they were in a blue, "not exactly old" and "not too dark" four-door Chevrolet. After a while, Harold drove her back to her home in St. Martinville.

The next day, Harold picked her up with the same two men. When asked what time, she replied "around dusk." Comeaux made it clear he didn't like this response (it would have been after the murder), letting her know it must have been "around twelve o'clock." Picking up on this, she quickly agreed it was "around lunchtime." After riding around for some time, she said, Harold drove the car onto a gravel road and parked there, seventy-five yards down the highway on the opposite side of the road from the store. Despite being extremely obese and moving with difficulty, she claimed she had wanted to go in with the men, but was told to stay in the car.

Vinny and Harold arrived back at the car "full of blood," the unknown third man having mysteriously disappeared. Vinny scolded Harold for not giving him a chance to shoot the victim, too.

Although she would have had an unobstructed view of the store from the car, Mary said she didn't see the third man run away.

Mary then suggested that the three of them drive to her deceased grandfather's property on Cypress Island, where Harold could bury his gun and bloody shirt.

During the interview, Mary was shown a book of mug shots out of which she picked a photo of David Alexander as the man she knew as Harold. Comeaux discovered a little later that Alexander was never called Harold by anyone who knew him. He was commonly called "Bro" or "Cool Bro." Even though she said that she had dated him for more than a year, Arceneaux had no idea where Alexander lived, nor could she name any of his acquaintances.

At one point during the interview, she identified Photo #3 in a photo lineup as the third man who went into the store with Harold and Vinny. According to the photo, his name was Sammy Derouen. A few minutes later, when Comeaux wanted to know more about Derouen, she changed course and said he'd stayed in St. Martinville and never came with them; it was another man who had participated in the robbery and then disappeared.

She then told Comeaux that she could take him to where Alexander had buried the evidence on Cypress Island. With lights and shovels, Comeaux and four other deputies drove north to the island and dug where Mary directed. They found nothing.

Comeaux returned from Cypress Island close to 11:00 P.M., but his night was just beginning. By mistake, Herbert Derouen had been picked up for questioning instead of his brother Sammy, whom Mary had identified as the third person in Harold's car. Recognizing that they had brought in the wrong brother, the police brought in Sammy, too, and showed him to Mary. She now insisted that Herbert Derouen was actually the third man in the car, not Sammy.

Although Mary's shifting stories had at one point left Herbert Derouen behind in St. Martinville, Comeaux nonetheless interrogated Herbert for hours through the night, the whole thing witnessed by Deputies Moore and Steve Woodring, as well as Mary, through a two-way mirror. For several hours Derouen insisted he was innocent and knew nothing about the Hasty Mart crime. Comeaux kept reciting Mary's account of the crime, attempting to get Derouen to repeat it in a confession. Frustrated by Derouen's persistent denials, Comeaux once slapped him hard across the face. Still, Derouen refused to confess. Finally, Deputy Chief Desormeaux took over the interrogation in his office alone with Derouen. To this day no one knows how he did it, but by 4:30 A.M. he had extracted a verbal confession from Herbert Derouen, which he converted into a typed confession statement by 8:45 A.M. that morning. Derouen was a twenty-year-old with no criminal record. He had lived with his grandmother since he was twelve. With only one year of grade school and an IQ of 61, he was illiterate and could not tell time. He worked part-time for a family friend as a carpenter's assistant.

As hard as the police tried to get Derouen's story to align with Mary's, his differed in several ways. In contrast to Mary, he claimed that there had been a second car involved in the crime. Not only a second car, but a highly identifiable taxicab. Although Mary had Derouen staying behind in St. Martinville, Derouen said that he and a man named Ronnie Miller had gone to the Hasty Mart in Miller's taxicab with a third man whose name he didn't know; he referred to this unknown man as the "bumper-face boy" because he had bumps on his face and neck. Miller had supposedly followed the car David Alexander was driving to the Hasty Mart. He parked in front of the store while Alexander parked across the street. According to Derouen, Alexander had two people with him in the car—the "fat lady" (Mary) and another man whose name he didn't know. He made no mention of the third man Mary had placed in Alexander's car.

Derouen said that Alexander entered the Hasty Mart with three companions—Ronnie Miller, Bumper Face, and a man from Alexander's car he did not know. Derouen stayed outside the store by the front door. Through the window, Derouen saw Alexander pull out a pistol and shoot the store's proprietor. Derouen panicked and ran away, but Bumper Face chased him down, pulled a knife, and forced him back to Miller's cab. The two groups returned to St. Martinville for a short while. Then Miller drove Derouen home.

Despite the absence of a second car in Mary's story, Deputy Woodring arrested Ronald Miller, alleged driver of the purported second car, at his home at 4:40 A.M. that morning, April 6. Dumbfounded at his arrest for murder and armed robbery, Miller insisted on his innocence. No statement was taken from him. He was a thirty-year-old taxicab driver for the Williams Cab Company of New Iberia with no criminal record and a college degree. He owned a white 1969 Plymouth sedan that he had driven full-time as an independent driver for the last three years. As required by city ordinance for all "vehicles for hire," his car had WILLIAMS TAXI CO. and its telephone and city permit numbers prominently lettered on both the driver and passenger doors. It hardly seemed the kind of vehicle a criminal would use in the commission of an armed robbery and murder, leaving it parked in front of the crime scene in broad daylight.

Deputy Moore and Deputy Woodring also arrested twenty-six-year-old David Alexander at his home at 2:23 A.M. that same day. In 1967, Alexander was one of the first two blacks to graduate from New Iberia's Catholic High. He drove a dark blue Buick and since graduation had worked as a full-time taxi driver for his parents' cab company, the Alexander Cab Company, a rival of the Williams Cab Company. In 1972, he had pleaded guilty to possession of marijuana, and in 1974 to aggravated assault, wherein he had brandished a .22 pistol at a drunken man who was threatening him and his younger brother while they sat in their car following a barroom argument with the man. For that, he spent several months in jail in a work release program and was barred by law from owning a gun, which he gladly obeyed. Still, this earlier crime had landed him in a book of mug shots that made him vulnerable to Mary's accusation. Booked at 3:00 A.M. for armed robbery and murder, Alexander insisted he had nothing whatsoever to do with the Hasty Mart crimes.

By the dawn of April 6, twelve hours after Comeaux had interviewed Mary, three people had been arrested and charged with the armed robbery and murder of Louis Gladu. One was David Alexander, allegedly the driver of the blue car, and the other two were supposedly in the taxicab, Herbert Derouen and Ronald Miller. Three suspects were still at large and unidentified—Vinny and the third man from Alexander's car, and Bumper Face from the cab.

Up all night, Comeaux was not yet finished. With the aid of daylight, at 6:45 A.M. he once again took Mary to Cypress Island, still looking for the buried gun and bloody shirt. They dug at several other places she indicated, but to no avail. Finally, she admitted that she had lied about burying anything on Cypress Island. Trying to soften the blow, at least temporarily, she told Comeaux that her boyfriend, Raymond Sam, had the gun used to kill Gladu. But when Sam confronted her in front of the police, she broke down and admitted she had made up her boyfriend's involvement.

Her lies and erratic accounts of the crime were wearing thin with some of the investigators, particularly Deputy Steve Woodring, but Captain Comeaux was in charge and determined to clear the case. Regardless of any misgivings, he didn't give up on Mary, who was finally able to identify the third man in Alexander's car from a chance encounter. Returning from Cypress Island that morning, Woodring, Moore, and Mary had driven by a group of black men conversing. Looking at them, Mary seemed to be setting her sights on one of them. But when a different man left the group, Mary's wandering finger shifted and pointed at him as one of the Hasty

Mart robbers. His name was John Nelson Collins. Mary identified him as the third man who had been with her, Alexander, and Vinny in the getaway car.

Collins was immediately arrested and brought to the parish jail, where Comeaux read him his rights at 10:45 A.M. on April 6. Collins was a twenty-five-year-old married father of three with no prior encounters with law enforcement. He was a truck driver who could only work sporadically due to a congenital heart condition. His father, who died the year before his son's arrest, had been an Iberia Parish deputy sheriff under Sheriff Wattigny for twenty years.

Later in the day, Mary identified Dan Tharpe as a participant, too, most likely as "Vinny" since she had already identified Collins as the third man in Alexander's car. Her identification was bolstered by the fact that Tharpe's mother owned a light blue four-door Chevy. Tharpe was charged with the Hasty Mart crimes and spent a few hours in jail before being released after the police confirmed his alibi. At the behest of the police, Mary then took another shot. She reviewed the mug book again and identified a photo of Harry Granger as the man in the Alexander car whom she had called "Vinny." Woodring and Moore picked up Granger the next morning. He was booked for murder and armed robbery at 3:17 P.M.

———

In her April 5 interview, when asked how tall Vinny was, Arceneaux replied "not that tall, but he's pretty tall." Granger was 5'5"—not remotely tall—and 113 pounds. His nickname was "Joe Willie." He was never called "Vinny" by anyone who knew him. Granger was twenty-two with an eighth-grade education and worked occasional odd jobs while still supported by his family. In 1973, he had pleaded guilty to a misdemeanor theft and received a suspended sentence. He had stolen a valise from the backseat of a car. When he discovered it was a doctor's bag, he returned it. He had had no other charges since.

The next day, Thursday, April 8, Woodring and Moore brought

in yet another person, Rene Jackson, for questioning. How he became a suspect is unknown. Derouen positively identified him as the third man in Miller's cab, whom he had referred to as Bumper Face. Jackson was booked and charged with murder and armed robbery at 12:25 P.M. that day. Like Derouen, he had no criminal record and could not read or write. He could only make a mark for his signature. Up until his arrest, at age twenty-three, he had lived with his widowed and caretaker father. With little schooling and unemployable because of his mental disability, he rarely left his neighborhood, and then only to go fishing. His sole means of travel was his bicycle. His face was scarred with extensive acne (perhaps why Derouen identified him as "Bumper Face").

According to a report prepared by DA investigator O'Neil "Sonny" Tyler, the illiterate Jackson was turned over to Comeaux and eventually "confessed." Tyler's report describes Jackson's suspiciously detailed and coherent confession to the chief detective, which provided specifics on the Hasty Mart crimes, naming all of those involved and their roles in the murder of Gladu, including his own. His purported confession coincided perfectly with Derouen's account of what transpired that day at the Hasty Mart.

Also included in Tyler's report, however, was an extremely emotional confrontation between Jackson's father (who had rushed down to the jail when his son was arrested) and Comeaux, who told him of Jackson's confession. His father demanded to see his son immediately. With Comeaux standing there, Jackson, weeping uncontrollably, told his father, "I didn't do it. I didn't do it. They're trying to frame me." While the deputies were booking Jackson, his father and brother were "raising hell" and had to be restrained. Jackson's father told Comeaux, "I'll go to my grave knowing Rene did not do this."

The case was now managed by prosecutor Dracos Burke, first cousin of mystery writer James Lee Burke and the top trial prosecutor in the district attorney's office that covered Iberia Parish and two other parishes. On May 10, 1976, a grand jury indicted the six men, all black, for the first-degree murder and armed robbery of Louis Gladu—David Alexander, Harry Granger, and John Collins allegedly in Alexander's dark blue car; and Ronald Miller, Herbert Derouen, and Rene Jackson allegedly in Miller's white taxicab. Mary was also indicted, but she and Derouen were given immunity in exchange for their testimony against the others. While Mary was freed, Derouen remained jailed because the authorities, mindful of his acute cognitive deficiencies, needed easy access to him for grand jury and trial preparation.

It had been one thing for the sheriff's investigators to hitch their wagon to Mary's and Derouen's nonsensical stories, but it was no sure thing that a man of Burke's intelligence and experience would do the same. Imagine seven people traveling in two cars, one parked seventy-five yards away, the other, a white taxicab with its company name, telephone, and city permit number emblazoned on both sides, parked in front of a store. The three occupants of this white cab—the thirty-year-old owner of the cab and his two young, mentally impaired passengers—had to wait for the three male occupants of the other car to journey three-quarters of a football field's length to join them. Then the six, with no assigned roles, entered the store to rob it. Imagine these six people, most of whom had no criminal record and none of whom had ever associated with the others, walking unmasked into a small convenience store in broad daylight to commit an armed robbery. Why would the supposed two leaders, Alexander and Granger, bring along five other people, two of whom were mentally challenged, to assist in the robbery as accomplices?

Dracos Burke knew his star witnesses had told two different stories. Mary had mentioned only one car and said the three men in it robbed the store. She had a full and clear view of the Hasty Mart from Alexander's parked car; yet she never saw the white taxi, its occupants, or Jackson supposedly chasing Derouen. They were absent from her story. In contrast, Derouen had two cars and six men committing the crime. Burke also knew that neither the sheriff's nor the DA's investigators had developed any evidence or witnesses to refute the defendants' insistence that they had never known or associated with one another. And Burke knew that the police could not disprove Alexander's insistence that he had never seen Mary in his life, let alone dated her for fourteen months; nor had they found one person who called Alexander "Harold" or Granger "Vinny." Yet, unaccountably, Burke went along with this charade and prosecuted the whole lot.

———

What happened next, however, was stupefying. On July 1, one of the actual Hasty Mart murderers, seventeen-year-old Jerry Paul Francis, voluntarily confessed that he and twenty-four-year-old Preston Demouchet had committed the crime. It was just one in a long spree of nearly identical crimes they had committed together.

On May 10 (the same day the six men were indicted), Demouchet and Francis committed a midafternoon armed robbery of a hardware store in Rayne, thirty-eight miles northwest of New Iberia. During the course of the robbery, seventy-four-year-old Curtis Johnson, who'd been working alone in the store, was fatally shot. On May 24, close to three in the afternoon, the duo robbed another convenience store in nearby Jeanerette, eleven miles southeast of New Iberia. Demouchet pressed his .32 against the head of one of the store's two female employees lying on the floor. A car pulled up, causing the men to flee with money from the cash register, and most likely saving the lives of both women.

The bank robbery that ended their crime spree took place around noon on May 26 in the town of Parks, sixteen miles north of New Iberia. Demouchet shot the lone female bank teller, forty-eight-year-old Beverly Chauffe, in the head. She lingered for sixteen months before succumbing to her wound. Both men were caught on the bank's camera exiting the building. Before Demouchet shot her, the teller pleaded with him, "Oh Lord, please don't hurt me. It's only money."

After taking $10,000 in cash from the Parks bank, the two desperadoes ditched their guns in a sewage canal in New Iberia and fled to Demouchet's sister's house in Houston. The FBI apprehended them two days later based on information provided by Francis's mother, who saw him on the bank's camera footage, which was televised. The feds released them to the Louisiana parish authorities on June 23 for prosecution. Francis, realizing the law had him cold, voluntarily gave a detailed confession and led the sheriffs to the canal so they could find the guns.

After a two-day search that included draining the canal, both guns were found by Comeaux and sent to the crime lab for tests. One was a .32 Clerke revolver, which ballistics conclusively established as the gun used to kill Gladu.

Demouchet was a hardened criminal. In 1969, at the age of eighteen, after serving a one-year prison term for aggravated battery, he was sentenced to six years in Angola for several counts of burglary and another of aggravated battery. A few months after his release on parole in 1972, he was arrested for attempted murder, but apparently never prosecuted for the charge. Nevertheless, he was returned to Angola to serve the balance of his six-year sentence due to a number of parole violations. A month after he was paroled again, in August 1974, he fatally shot a woman in a crowded bar. On December 13, 1974, in a sweetheart plea deal with prosecutor Dracos Burke, the charge was reduced to negligent homicide with a three-year term in the Iberia Parish jail, not Angola. His sentencing judge told him, "I think the State is being very lenient with you, permitting you to serve your time here instead of Angola." As it turned out, he served only half that time. By early 1976, he was back on the streets of New Iberia, shortly before the murder of Gladu.

On June 30, a week after confessing to the Parks robbery,

Demouchet's accomplice, Francis, unburdened himself further. Since he was illiterate, he dictated a letter to another inmate to send to Sheriff Wattigny. In it, Francis listed five crimes that he wanted to discuss with the sheriff because he knew his life was "washed up." Although he didn't specifically identify the Hasty Mart, one of the crimes he described was an armed robbery and murder on March 30 at 2:55 P.M. in New Iberia. This got the sheriff's attention. The next day, July 1, Sheriff Wattigny, Captain Comeaux, and DA investigator Sonny Tyler followed up with an interview. In the course of it, Francis revealed many details about the Hasty Mart job that were stunning in their accuracy and could only have been known by the police and the killer. Unlike Mary, he needed no coaching, because he was speaking the truth. Francis said the robbery happened between 2:30 and 3:00. He and Demouchet went in the front door. Demouchet shot the man while Francis was behind the register getting the money. Demouchet hit the man in the back of the head with a gun, then shot him twice where he fell, which was outside the counter area, in "the hall." Francis jumped over the counter and knocked some cigarettes onto the floor. The old man was wearing glasses. They took $200 in cash and a bag of change and left the register drawer open. Also, there may have been a witness who saw their getaway car—a woman in one of the trailers across the street.

Additionally, he told the lawmen that he was with Demouchet when Demouchet shot the lady in the Parks bank and the man in the Rayne hardware store. He added that Demouchet used the same gun to shoot both those two and "the old man" in New Iberia.

He prefaced his confession by telling the police, "You got them six boys in jail for nothing. Them boys didn't do that . . . it don't make no sense. Me and Preston Demouchet and 'Shine' [Malcolm Roy, driver of their car] done that . . . Shine was driving his brother's car." For emphasis, later in the interview he reiterated: "It don't make no sense to let young boys that's up there suffer for something they didn't do." Sensing that these lawmen didn't believe or didn't want to believe his account of who really did the Hasty Mart job, he twice asked his questioners if they were "willing to put your life upon it that I wasn't at that store?" He then added, "I was there!" Francis was speaking from his heart. He was conscience-stricken and hell-bent on setting the record straight.

Knowing that Demouchet would never confess, Francis challenged the police to go see Malcolm Roy. He thought that if Roy knew he had fingered him, then Roy would admit he was there, too. The sheriff's department waited five days before they brought the eighteen-year-old in for questioning. July 6 was a gut-wrenching day for Roy. He gave several statements. As Francis predicted, in the first interview with Comeaux, he readily confessed to his involvement in the Hasty Mart stickup. He said he had borrowed his brother's car and, at Demouchet's instructions, had driven Francis and Demouchet to the Hasty Mart. It was 2:45 P.M. Demouchet told him to wait in the car with the motor running while they went inside "to get something to drink." Next thing he knew, Francis and Demouchet came running out of the store, Demouchet with blood on his hands and a gun, saying he "killed the bitch" (criminal speak for a victim, male or female); Francis was carrying a sack of change. Roy returned to New Iberia, dropped them off at the projects, and went to his mother's house, returning the car to his brother.

His account corroborated important elements of Francis's confession a week earlier. Demouchet was the shooter; Francis emerged with a bag of coins; and the time of the crime was 2:45 P.M. Neither Francis nor Roy knew that an eyewitness had described the getaway car as light blue, which was the color of Roy's brother's two-door 1973 Pontiac LeMans.

And then the unthinkable happened. The police refused to accept the killers' confession. They told Roy that they didn't believe him. In fact, Sheriff Wattigny threatened him with jail for lying.

Under pressure to recant, Roy came up with another story, one that explained his confession to the sheriff. He said he wanted to go to jail to get out of his marriage. Wattigny and his deputies didn't choose to believe this either. They dragged his wife down to the station and watched—no doubt amused—as she chewed out her young husband. At last, dejected and defeated, Roy gave a third statement, this time with the help of the deputies. He said Iran Alexander (David's father) had offered him $45,000 to take the fall for his son; that Iran gave him a one-and-a-half-page typewritten story to memorize and instructed him to burn it, which he did. Once Roy signed this retraction (and false accusation of bribery) at 3:45 P.M., he was free to go home with no charges.

Fearful of where it would lead, the sheriff's investigators did not investigate Roy's bribery claims, nor did they interview the car's owner, Roy's brother Joseph, to see if he had indeed loaned his car to Roy on the day of the Gladu murder. The sheriffs never showed Roy's car or took a photo of it to show to eyewitnesses Abney and Eldridge. They also failed to compare the car's tire treads to those found at the end of the gravel road.

Two days later, on July 8, Francis, too, retracted his confession, telling Comeaux and Wattigny in a statement suspiciously similar to Roy's that he had been offered $4,500 by Theresa Collins, John Collins's mother, to say her son was innocent and that Francis and the others were the guilty ones. He said that she had visited him in jail, giving him her offer in a typewritten note, which he'd had his cellmate read to him. Francis said he flushed the note down the toilet and was never contacted again by Mrs. Collins or anyone else about the offer. Nevertheless, he said this proposal inspired him to recant his confession. No charges were ever brought against Theresa Collins or Iran Alexander for their alleged attempts at bribery.

The prosecution now had what they needed to account for the Hasty Mart confessions of Francis and Roy. On July 14, DA Burke wrote a letter to the defendants' attorneys informing them of the false confessions and the bribery attempts by Iran Alexander and Theresa Collins. In this letter Burke stated, falsely, that Jerry Paul Francis's July 1 confession was "replete with inconsistencies and errors of fact . . . and the falsity of his account was quickly established."

The biggest challenge now for Dracos Burke and the sheriff's investigators was how to get the .32 Clerke out of the hands of Demouchet and into the hands of Alexander so they could make the case that Alexander used it to shoot Gladu. They came up with a "gun swap" story. It began in an interview with Demouchet in Burke's office on June 29 with Comeaux and Moore in attendance. According to Burke's notes, the interview's purpose was to determine how the .32 got used in the Hasty Mart crime by Alexander when the gun belonged to Demouchet. A one-hour conversation resolved the problem. Demouchet said that he loaned the gun to Alexander on March 25 so that Alexander could "pull a job"; and that Alexander returned it to him on April 2. This gun swap became official history when Comeaux took a statement from Demouchet on July 10. Demouchet told of "hocking" the pistol to Alexander on March 23 for twenty dollars with Alexander promising to return the gun to him the following week. Demouchet said he loaded the gun with five .32 bullets at Alexander's insistence. This time he said that Alexander returned the gun to him on April 1.

To make everything appear aboveboard, at an in-chambers meeting with trial judge Robert Johnson and the defendants' attorneys on August 4, Burke briefed them on Demouchet's July 10 statement, adding that the same .32 Clerke was used by Demouchet and Francis in a few other crimes, including "a bank robbery in Parks and a store in Rayne." He then sent them a transcription of Francis's recorded July 8 statement and Malcolm Roy's July 6 statement that recanted their confessions to the Hasty Mart crime and told of the alleged bribery attempts. The cover-up was complete.

David Alexander and Harry Granger were tried together on

September 13–17, 1976. (John Collins and Ronnie Miller were given a later trial date because Collins's attorney needed a medical procedure.) Their original indictment for first-degree murder had carried with it a possible death penalty, but the U.S. Supreme Court declared Louisiana's death penalty unconstitutional in July while they were awaiting trial. Without a death penalty to aim for, the DA decided to try them solely for armed robbery, because that only required ten out of the twelve jurors to vote guilty. In the weeks leading up to the trial, Burke offered Granger total immunity if he would testify against Alexander. Granger refused, telling his lawyer to tell Burke that he had no idea who committed the murder and that he would not lie to point a finger at Alexander or anyone else.

The Alexander family could only gather $8,000 for an attorney. That was enough to retain the prominent Alexandria law firm of Camille Gravel, which assigned a young and promising attorney, Mike Small, to represent Alexander. Harry Granger was indigent and therefore had to depend on a court-appointed lawyer, the inexperienced Jerry Theriot, who proved to be inept and in way over his head, explaining to the jury that he would depend on Small since "Mr. Alexander's defense will be Mr. Granger's." He was hardly heard from again, rarely asking a question during cross-examination. At trial, the defense was hamstrung by Burke's refusal to turn over his witnesses' pretrial statements, maintaining that Louisiana law at the time only required him to provide them if they were "exculpatory." His response to Small's request for this information contained this preposterous line: "The State has no evidence exculpating the defendants."

At trial, Katherine Eldridge testified that she didn't see any cars on the road when she drove from her house to the Hasty Mart. Her testimony conflicted with what she had told others before and after the trial; namely that she *had* seen a light blue car about to turn out of the gravel driveway, which then sped by when she pulled into the

Hasty Mart. This is what she had testified to in her original witness statement and to the grand jury. But now, she avoided mention of the car at the behest of Captain Comeaux, who had a vested interest in the car being dark, rather than light, blue. In addition, although the Acadiana Crime Lab had found that Alexander's tire treads did not match those in the gravel road, the authorities did not reveal this crucial fact to the defense. Such information, in combination with Eldridge's original witness statement, could have refuted Ellen Abney's and Mary Arceneaux's identification of Alexander's car at trial as the one used by the killers.

Mary Arceneaux and Herbert Derouen carried the load for the State. Both enhanced their pretrial statements. Key among Mary's many changes was her story about Cypress Island. Now, at trial, she testified that after the robbery, she and her fellow criminals drove to Cypress Island to kill time, making no mention of her earlier story about burying the gun and bloody shirt there. In fact, she now said she had no idea what Alexander had done with the gun. The last she knew, it was under his car seat wrapped in his bloody T-shirt. According to her, after Cypress Island they had returned to St. Martinville around dusk and gone to the Candle Light Lounge to talk for a while.

Mary also testified that she had never been convicted of any offenses other than the 1974 forgery charge, when, in fact, she had at least twenty convictions when she was in her thirties alone. That's not counting however many she had in her twenties. Burke stood silently by and let that falsehood go uncorrected. In post-conviction appeals, Burke inaccurately asserted that Mary's "trial testimony was consistent with her initial statements to law enforcement officers."

Derouen's trial testimony added significantly to what he had originally told his sheriff's office interviewers. Key among his additions was an account of a so-called dry run by all seven participants, who drove in two cars to the Hasty Mart the night before. Also for the first time, Derouen described Alexander running out of the store after shooting the victim and telling Miller to meet him in St. Martinville at the Candle Light Lounge. According to Derouen, Alexander was still wearing his bloody shirt when they met in St. Martinville and had put the gun under the driver's seat.

Small's cross-examination ridiculed Derouen's nonsensical version of events. Derouen had testified on direct that he got off work that day at 2:10. Small asked him to look at the courtroom wall clock and tell the time. He couldn't. Under Small's cross, Derouen admitted that none of the six who entered the store had any assigned roles to play there; that he just went along for the ride; that he didn't know any of them well; that he never gave any thought as to why six men and two cars were needed to hold up a store in broad daylight; that it didn't bother him that he was going to do something "bad" with people he didn't know; and there had not been any talk the night before about meeting at the club after the robbery. It just happened on the fly when David Alexander fled the store after shooting the man.

Burke intended to wrap up his case with witnesses Preston Demouchet and Jerry Paul Francis, but Demouchet came prepared to double-cross him. Demouchet denied he ever loaned the .32 Clerke to Alexander. He said it wasn't even his gun. He also disavowed the statement he had given the police on July 10 about the so-called "gun swap." Comeaux was the one who came up with that story, he said, and Demouchet had agreed to it just to get Comeaux, who was constantly harassing him, off his back. He concluded his testimony stating, "I've never given David Alexander no kind of pistol. None whatsoever."

When questioned in front of the jury by prosecutor Burke and cross-examined by defense attorney Small concerning his involvement in the Hasty Mart crimes, Jerry Paul Francis pleaded the Fifth a total of twenty-three times, repeatedly asserting his constitutional right not to incriminate himself. Both sides tried to use him to their advantage, asking questions that introduced their version of events. Burke asked him if he'd told Comeaux he was promised money to take the blame for the Hasty Mart killing. Small asked him if he recalled giving a detailed statement to Comeaux admitting that he committed the crime with Demouchet and Malcolm Roy. In both cases he pleaded the Fifth. With that, the State rested.

The defense attempted to establish Alexander's alibi for the afternoon of March 30 through the testimony of one Gail Guidry, who told the jury that Alexander picked her up in his cab at 2:30 to take her to work that day. Under cross, she conceded that she'd had help from the defense recalling that the day was March 30. Alexander's mother, the cab's dispatcher, was ready to present the taxicab logs for Alexander's fares that day, but Small did not call her because he noticed that the log for the 30th was printed neatly, unlike the log's other days. Granger was unable to present an alibi because his witnesses could only account for his presence on the 31st, not the 30th.

The key witness for the defense was Malcolm Roy. One week before the trial, Roy testified at a preliminary hearing, once again confessing to the Hasty Mart crime. Angered by his effrontery, the authorities arrested and charged him with filing a false police report—that is, his Hasty Mart confession. At trial, Small read his confession statement of July 6 and the recantation statement he made that same day. Roy bravely insisted that his confession was true and his retraction was false. He agreed that Small had warned him that by testifying he could be prosecuted for armed robbery and murder, and now for perjury, and that no one at any time had promised or provided him with any kind of benefit for his testimony. He then, once again, told the story of how he had committed the Hasty Mart crime with Demouchet and Francis. Under cross, Burke warned him that he was waiving his right not to incriminate himself. Undeterred, Roy told the jury that he was confessing because he hadn't been able to sleep and it had been on his conscience ever since March 30. He said that he had no idea Demouchet was going to rob the store, let alone kill anyone.

Morris Lee, Derouen's carpenter boss, informed the jury that he was positive Derouen worked for him from 1:00 until 3:30 the afternoon of March 30 and that he always drove him to and from work because Derouen had no means of transportation. He had shown Derouen's work records to Deputy Chief Jim Desormeaux. Under cross by Small, Desormeaux testified that he had known Lee for some time, and had no reason to doubt him, stating, "I thought he was telling the truth." Alexander testified, declaring his innocence. Granger reluctantly agreed not to testify, given his highly agitated emotional state throughout the trial.

Unfortunately, when it came time for his summation, Small was not up to the task. To the defendants' detriment, he gratuitously praised local law enforcement, including the sheriff's investigators and Burke, as men who would not lie or encourage their witnesses to lie. Other than currying favor with Iberia Parish law enforcement, his unwarranted defense of their integrity was inexplicable. He also expressed a hint of uncertainty concerning the defendants' innocence: "If they did this, they deserve to go to the penitentiary." At the same time, Small properly ridiculed the State's reliance on the conflicting and obviously false stories offered by Mary and Derouen, and mocked the State for dismissing clear and convincing evidence pointing to the guilt of Demouchet and Francis. Theriot's summation was incredibly brief—a mere two pages of transcript. He did little more than ask the jury to consider the concept of reasonable doubt that the judge would explain to them in his charge. Absent an advocate, Harry Granger never had a chance.

When the second day of testimony had concluded, the case went to the jury at 8:00 P.M. It is unclear from the record how long the jury was out, but it was the same day, September 17, that in a 10–2 vote, it returned verdicts of guilty for both defendants.

When the verdicts were announced, Granger was so angry that he punched Steve Woodring, who was standing next to him, and then promptly fainted. On October 16, Alexander and Granger, standing together, faced the judge for sentencing. When asked if he had anything to say before sentencing, Alexander replied, "I didn't rob nobody. I didn't kill nobody. All of you here know it. They got a God in heaven, man." When he, too, was asked, Granger simply said, "I agree with him." The judge then sentenced each man to ninety-nine years of hard labor for the crime of armed robbery. Their next stop would be the infamous Angola state prison.

Not knowing what to do with Rene Jackson, the third man in Miller's cab according to Derouen, Burke decided to dismiss all charges against him. On November 30, Burke had Jackson committed to the Central Louisiana State Hospital for clinical evaluation. The treatment team diagnosed him with a severe intellectual impairment and noted that he didn't know his age and could not recite his ABCs or count. The report stated he had spent the last nine months in jail for crimes he insisted he didn't do. He was not considered dangerous by his team of doctors, and they returned him home a completely free man on December 7, one week after admission. This was the same man who Derouen claimed to the police in his first statement had chased him outside the store after the shooting and forced him back to Miller's car at knifepoint. On December 6, the day before Jackson was released from custody, his devoted father, who had vowed that he would go to his grave knowing his son was innocent, died of an asthma attack.

John Collins and Ronald Miller were terrified at the prospect of serving a ninety-nine-year sentence at Angola. Their trial was set for Monday, January 24, 1977. The chances of acquittal were slim, since the same witnesses used to convict Alexander and Granger would incriminate them. Surprisingly, Dracos Burke offered a lifeline. If they would plead guilty to accessory after the fact, he would dismiss the armed robbery and murder charges and allow them to spend their sentence in the parish jail rather than Angola. If the judge gave them the maximum, five years, they would be out in two to three years. He threw in home visits as a sweetener. Because the prospect of Angola prison was more than either could bear, and with the encouragement of their families and friends, they reluctantly swallowed the bitter pill of admitting involvement in a horrible crime in which they had not actually been involved. Collins had a wife and three children to consider and Miller, unmarried, had his mother to think of. Several days before the trial, the judge gave them the five-year maximum. They served two of those years and then came home on parole.

Ironically, both men lied, incriminating themselves, to avoid a possible life sentence in Angola, but earlier had refused to lie in order to incriminate Alexander and Granger as part of an immunity deal offered by Burke.

———

Because of a technicality in Louisiana criminal law, Preston Demouchet and Jerry Paul Francis were tried and convicted of armed robbery, not murder, for both the bank and hardware store crimes. This in spite of the fact that the victims in both instances were fatally shot. Nevertheless, for each crime both men were sentenced to ninety-nine years in prison, where they remain today.

———

By July 1, 1980, there was a new sheriff in town. Errol Romero, a former schoolteacher and political newcomer, ended Sheriff Wattigny's twenty-four-year reign in a bitterly fought contest. The first thing he did was fire Deputies Comeaux, Moore, and Desormeaux, whom he believed to be inept and corrupt. Suspecting that Alexander and Granger may have been wrongfully convicted, he also reopened their case, launching an investigation that would last several years.

Former Iberia sheriff's deputy Steve Woodring was one of the people Romero interviewed. By the mid-1980s, Woodring had become an experienced investigator in the Baton Rouge Armed Robbery Division. In an affidavit offered to Sheriff Romero, Woodring stated reasons why he was convinced all six men were innocent. Among them was something that he had personally witnessed. Prosecutor Burke "desperately wanted Miller and Collins to accept his immunity offer [to testify against Alexander and Granger] and pressed strongly for it." Burke knew that both men would have been far more believable on the stand than the mentally impaired Herbert Derouen or the career criminal Mary Arceneaux. Detective Woodring witnessed Comeaux and Desormeaux, acting on behalf of Burke, make that offer to both men "numerous times." Woodring was deeply impressed by Miller's and Collins's refusal to accept the offer even though they were facing ninety-nine years if convicted. Years later, Collins said he'd refused immunity because "I knew if I lied against those men, I'd never be free . . . not in here," as he tapped his heart.

Woodring had had concerns about Mary's veracity from the very beginning. Later he said that even Horace Comeaux started doubting her truthfulness, especially after she admitted she had lied about Alexander burying the gun on Cypress Island. DA investigator Sonny Tyler had, in his own handwriting, in a document undisclosed at trial, described Mary as "a pathological liar."

Woodring had encountered Mary again, in 1985. His unit was investigating a string of armed robberies at Texaco gas stations in Baton Rouge. Mary, again arrested on forgery charges, told Woodring and his colleagues that in exchange for money and dropping her charges, she would tell them the name of the Texaco robber. She gave them a name and said the man had counted the stolen money in front of her. The actual robber was caught several weeks later. Not surprisingly, he was not the man Mary had falsely named. Steve was amazed and thought, *She's doing it again.*

When he confronted her, mentioning her testimony in the Hasty Mart case, he told her he suspected Deputy Eddie Moore had encouraged her to lie against those boys. She ignored the question, complaining bitterly instead that Moore had taken money off the top of the cash payments the sheriff's office had given him to give her for her Hasty Mart cooperation. According to Woodring, she was paid several hundred dollars a month plus rent reimbursement from April through the September trial.

Sheriff Romero also spoke with one of the eyewitnesses in the Hasty Mart case, Katherine Eldridge. She told Romero that the light blue car she'd seen near the crime scene had been smaller than David Alexander's dark blue Buick, which she had inspected at the impound lot. Deputy Comeaux had insisted that the car she had seen was Alexander's, but she disagreed. She knew cars. She had worked at a mechanic's shop. Comeaux and Burke had rebuked her after she testified to the grand jury that the car had been light blue, warning her "not to pull a trick like that again."

After countless interviews and an extensive file search and review that lasted several years, Romero presented affidavits to prosecutor Burke alleging that Comeaux, Moore, and Desormeaux had "intimidated witnesses, paid witnesses, and brutalized a witness [Herbert Derouen] for the sole purpose of having those witnesses testify to a fabricated story" against Alexander and Granger.

Burke refused to bring charges against the former lawmen, claiming "lack of evidence." This back-and-forth created a firestorm. In 1985, the three ex-deputies filed a civil suit against Romero for defamation. It took four years of discovery and many depositions before the suit was settled in 1989 without a trial. Although the civil suit halted Romero's reinvestigation, the discovery demands forced Burke to produce several exculpatory documents from the Alexander and Granger files that he had kept secreted in his office since the trial, marked DO NOT REMOVE FROM THIS OFFICE. Burke had not given Romero access to the files during Romero's original effort to reinvestigate the murder.

As part of the civil suit against Romero, Herbert Derouen underwent a psychological evaluation in 1987. During his interviews with the psychologist, Derouen continually asserted his innocence and lamented that he had lied, condemning innocent men out of his own fear of going to prison. He claimed he wasn't at the crime scene and had no idea who committed the crimes; that he was working that day for Morris Lee; and that he had spent nine months in jail for no reason at all. The psychologist determined that Derouen's intellectual functioning was consistent with that of a child in grade school, and that he could easily be persuaded to say what others wanted him to say, regardless of the facts. At his deposition in the suit, Derouen testified that he had never been to the Hasty Mart until Comeaux took him there; he lied at trial because the police threatened him with prison unless he "told the truth."

Centurion committed to the case in 1996. By then Alexander's and Granger's direct appeals had been denied, as had two petitions for post-conviction relief. In addition to launching an exhaustive multi-year reinvestigation that included scores of interviews as well as numerous courthouse and attorney archival-file searches, we alerted *60 Minutes* to this gross and obvious miscarriage of justice. In December 1998, the show aired its story, titled "Who Killed Louis Gladu?" Ed Bradley was the correspondent. Steve Woodring, still with the Baton Rouge police, told Bradley, "They are absolutely innocent. I am absolutely certain of what I'm saying . . . Anyone who examines this case reaches the same conclusion, except the sheriff's office and the staff of the DA's office in Iberia Parish." Bernie Boudreaux, the multiple-term sitting district attorney, maintained to *60 Minutes* his steadfast belief that the right men were in jail and were guilty. In the broadcast, Bradley told the viewers that one of the reasons Boudreaux believes the defendants are guilty is because the testimony of Arceneaux and Derouen was "corroborated, consistent, and credible."

When Bradley asked Arceneaux if she got paid for her testimony, she responded, "I sure did. All I can say it was bribery." Bernie Boudreaux, however, said that "she was not paid anything." Woodring said she "received money from the sheriff's department. She was paid." Malcolm Roy told Bradley that "they framed those guys. They knew what they was doing. Not one of them was there. I was stunned when they picked them up because these guys didn't do this." John Collins and Ronald Miller, who had pleaded guilty to lesser charges to avoid life in prison, were interviewed sitting side by side. Collins summed up the case neatly by saying, "Everybody that told the truth done time. Everybody that lied went home."

During our investigation, Centurion located the owner of the Candle Light Lounge, Geraline Mitchell, who blew a hole in Mary's and Derouen's testimony that they and the killers had all gathered there the night of the murder. In an affidavit, Mitchell stated that she knew Mary very well. She remembered telling the sheriff's investigators that Mary was definitely not in her club on March 30, because by then Mary had been banned from the club for running up an unpaid bar tab. Besides, Geraline had closed the club shortly after she opened it around six that evening, after her husband told her about the Hasty Mart shooting and instructed her to close the bar.

In 1997 Jerry Paul Francis explained to Centurion why he had recanted his confession with the fabricated bribery story: because Sheriff Wattigny had told him during the interview that "you're just digging yourself a hole by confessing to something you didn't do. We're just trying to keep you from putting yourself in real trouble by getting a lot more time." He said Comeaux "suggested that I was bribed into confessing. So, I gave them what they wanted."

Tortured by his false testimony against Granger and Alexander,

Herbert Derouen told Centurion that "I think about it all the time. I can't sleep all these years with them boys in prison. It's always on my mind."

Malcolm Roy's brother Joseph swore in an affidavit that he did loan his brother his 1973 blue Pontiac LeMans the afternoon of March 30, 1976. He recalled noticing a large quantity of quarters, eight or nine dollars' worth, in the ashtray the first time he drove it after Malcolm returned the car to him that afternoon. Malcolm had admitted to him that he was involved in the Hasty Mart crime.

Centurion was fortunate to obtain the services of New Orleans attorney Peggy Woodward. Working alongside Centurion investigator Paul Henderson, she was indefatigable, producing a 179-page brief with 133 exhibits in support of a petition for post-conviction relief. In the petition, she told the entire story of the shameful miscarriage of justice that led to the false conviction of David Alexander and Harry Granger. It was filed in September 1999 in New Iberia's 16th Judicial District Court, the original court of conviction. The State responded with a sixty-seven-page brief that largely skirted the petition's factual contentions and relied primarily on procedural arguments. The petition then sat in Judge William Hunter's chambers for two years.

On September 18, 2001, one week after the 9/11 attacks, Judge Hunter issued his denial of the petition. His opinion was an exact copy, page by page and word for word, of the State's brief, only it had his signature, not the DA's. The petitioners were denied two years later by the Louisiana Supreme Court without comment. Following suit with the state courts, the entire federal judiciary rejected their application for relief, without explanation. Without so much as a hearing, Alexander and Granger had exhausted all judicial remedies.

Their only chance for freedom now rested with the Louisiana parole board. Overcrowding at Angola had resulted in a law that allowed parole eligibility to any inmate who was forty-five and had served twenty years. This law qualified Alexander and Granger for parole—by now they had served close to thirty. They knew the board would not look kindly on claims of innocence by its inmate applicants. Parole boards want to hear remorse for crimes committed, not cries of "I didn't do it." Nevertheless, they had what they felt was an overwhelmingly strong case for innocence and decided to go with that.

At the hearings in 2005 and 2006, Detective Woodring and former sheriff Romero appeared before the parole board and spoke with compelling conviction about their belief in the inmates' innocence. Gladu's daughter, Ann Gladu Begnaud, wrote a letter to the board in which she gave a ringing endorsement of their release, stating, "I am convinced that tainted evidence convicted two innocent men of my father's killing." She added that, from the very beginning when she attended the trial, she had had doubts about their guilt and expressed them to both the sheriff and the district attorney.

The men's families also expressed their love and support of Alexander and Granger throughout the past thirty years and promised their support would continue should the board allow them to come home. Last but not least, Centurion included a tape of the powerful *60 Minutes* broadcast for the board's review.

Once the hearings ended, right then and there, after a short caucus, the board announced its decision to grant parole. Centurion later learned that the board had granted parole in large part because the three members of the panel had been convinced by the *60 Minutes* piece that Alexander and Granger were innocent and should never have been in prison in the first place.

Embraced by his mom, Iris, outside the prison gates, Alexander went home on December 23, 2006. His eighty-two-year-old dad, Iran, died of lung cancer two weeks later. Granger's day of freedom arrived on January 19, 2007, when his sister, Eva, picked him up and took him home to his mother, where she was waiting in the house in which he'd been raised. Although his mother died in 2010, Granger still lives in that house and is a kitchen worker on the oil rigs in the Gulf of Mexico. Alexander returned to his old job as a taxi driver for the family cab company. He still drives a cab but is also now in charge of operations. The two men are on lifelong parole with minimal supervision, but each must pay the State sixty-four dollars per month in parole administration fees and secure permission to travel out of state.

Granger is seventy and Alexander seventy-four. Both are in reasonably good health and remain philosophical about their unjust thirty-year incarceration. Granger says that even though the best years of his life were taken from him, he can't play catch-up and has moved on; he's basically enjoying a quiet, peaceful life. Alexander feels blessed. He's in charge of his own life, is self-sufficient and independent. He wonders if what happened to him was "destiny"; and anyway, "everything is in God's hands." He notes with some satisfaction that he has outlived all those men who had a hand in putting him in prison, even Dracos Burke, who died at 102 in 2022. Besides that, he says with a twinkle in his eye, his life now is far better than picking cotton and working in the Angola fields for twenty years at four cents an hour.

Over the years, observers of the case have often asked why the New Iberia authorities insisted on prosecuting David Alexander and Harry Granger when the real killers surfaced before the trial and offered confessions that comported with the facts of the crime. There could be several reasons. One is that it would have been embarrassing, even humiliating, to admit to the wrongful indictment of six people, an indictment that was the result of work done by the entire law enforcement community, including the elected sheriff and the most respected prosecutor in the district attorney's office. Another reason may have been the authorities' fear that if they had gone after Demouchet, the real killer, their past leniency with him, despite his violent history, would come to light. Demouchet was an informant for the Iberia Parish sheriff's office and as a reward was softly treated by the local authorities for his many crimes. But as violent as he showed himself to be, he should not have been on the streets the day Louis Gladu was gunned down. The repercussions of such a revelation could have been devastating to the careers of New Iberia's elected officials.

There is an Alice-in-Wonderland quality to the arrest and prosecution of the six Iberia men. To David Alexander and Harry Granger, for whom it cost thirty years of life each, the experience was like peering through the Looking-Glass. What was happening could not be real, but it was. In his interview with *60 Minutes,* John Collins had perfectly captured the way justice was turned upside down and backward: "Everybody that told the truth done time. Everybody that lied went home."

"OH, WHAT A TANGLED WEB WE WEAVE / WHEN FIRST WE PRACTICE TO DECEIVE"

JIM McCLOSKEY

———

Tyler, Texas, known as the Rose Capital of America for its impressive production of roses, is the seat of Smith County, located a hundred miles east of Dallas in the middle of the Bible Belt. In 1977 this East Texas town had close to fifty Baptist churches amid a population of more than 65,000. Kansas City Chiefs' quarterback Patrick Mahomes, winner of three Super Bowls, hails from Tyler, which is also home to University of Texas at Tyler, known in the 1970s as Texas Eastern University (TEU). This tidy town and university were not prepared for the gruesome news that broke Friday morning, June 10, 1977.

Paula Rudolph had returned home to her Tyler apartment in the sprawling Embarcadero complex at 12:30 A.M. after spending a couple of hours with a friend who was in town on business. As she came through the front door and stepped into her darkened foyer, she came face-to-face with a man standing nine feet away in her brightly lit spare bedroom. He quickly took a step toward her and closed the bedroom door without saying a word. The man wasn't a stranger; at least, that's what Paula thought at the time. He was Jim Mayfield, her boss at the TEU library. She knew why he was there, too—to visit her friend, Linda Jo Edwards, with whom he had been carrying on an affair. Embarrassed, Paula exclaimed, "It's okay, it's only me. I'm going to bed." She then briskly walked across the living room into her own bedroom, and closed the door. Several minutes later she heard the patio door open and close.

In her bedroom the thirty-six-year-old librarian lit a cigarette and fumed. Mayfield had promised Paula that his long-standing affair with Linda was over. Now it appeared that he'd been secretly visiting her. Paula's first thought was *That S.O.B. can't leave her alone.* She felt sorry for Linda, who was only twenty-two and clearly in over her head, too young to handle the stress of a relationship with a married man twice her age. Paula and Linda had talked often about the unsettled, topsy-turvy affair, one that Paula described as "nasty." It seemed that part of Mayfield wanted to break it off, but part of him did not.

Three weeks earlier, on May 19, Linda had attempted suicide after Mayfield left her to return to his wife of twenty-three years, Elfreide. Linda had swallowed eight to ten Dalmane 30mg sleeping pills. Mayfield had found her unconscious the next morning when he came by to get his clothes. He carried her to his car and rushed her to the hospital, where she stayed for six days. Upon her release, Mayfield had convinced Paula to take Linda in until she could get back on her feet, swearing that he and Linda were finished as lovers and that he wouldn't visit her in Paula's apartment.

After the university learned the cause of her suicide attempt, its president, James Stewart, had fired Mayfield from his position as library director and dismissed Linda from her secretarial post in the Humanities Department. Mayfield's firing took place on Monday, June 6, just three days before Linda's murder.

Now Paula read in bed for a few minutes, set her alarm, and

went to sleep. She woke up the next morning at 7:10. Not getting a response after calling for Linda, Paula opened Linda's bedroom door. The sight would haunt her for the rest of her life. Linda lay spread-eagled on her back, practically naked and covered with blood. Paula stuffed her hand in her mouth, backed out of the room, and somehow managed to make two phone calls, first to the police and then to Olene Harned, her trusted friend and a senior colleague at the library, who arrived shortly after the police.

The scene was sickening. Linda was mutilated, every part of her sexual anatomy destroyed. The killer had used three weapons, all from Paula's apartment. With a five-pound statue from the living room credenza, he had repeatedly, at least ten times, smashed her face, mouth, and head, knocking her unconscious. The killer then used sewing scissors from a nearby table to stab her neck at least nine times, severing her carotid artery and jugular vein. He used a vegetable knife ten inches long and three inches wide in a variety of gruesome ways. He sliced both corners of her mouth several inches across each cheek, cut her right breast three times, plunged it deep into her body right below the breast and thrust it three times into her back, almost all the way through to her chest. In a frenzy, he then stabbed her genitalia with the scissors multiple times, obliterating her vaginal cavity and its deeper recesses. He cut and took several inches of hair from her head, apparently as a souvenir.

Linda's jeans were on the floor by the bed, next to her left ankle, clean with no blood, indicating that she or her killer had removed them before the assault. Her blouse and bra were cut with the knife and pulled above her breasts. Her panties were also cut with the knife, pulled off and lying by her right foot. Her right mid-calf-high nylon stocking was missing but her left one was still on. The statue and scissors were on the floor. The vegetable knife—part of an expensive cutlery set that Paula kept in a drawer in the kitchen—was missing at first, despite a concerted search by the police. It was finally discovered by Paula's father five days later when he was cleaning out her apartment. The knife had been sitting all along under a pile of clothes in Linda's bedroom closet.

Small traces of blood were found on the bedspread and pillow, barely noticeable with the naked eye. Minimal blood spattering was found in the room. The bathroom adjacent to the spacious bedroom closet was clean, dry, and spotless. The killer had to have been covered in blood, yet left no trace of it, except a drop on the glass terrarium near the patio door, as he made his exit from the bedroom through the apartment's living room to the patio door. There was no forced entry into the apartment, nor any sign of a struggle in the tiny eleven-by-twelve-foot bedroom. Nothing was out of place or knocked over. The iron was on, sitting upright on the ironing board. The TV was on. The bed, which was only a half-bed on blocks, was made and unruffled. The crime scene was chillingly clean and neat. How the killer achieved this ninja-like feat of a cleanup was a mystery to the forensic experts who analyzed the crime, including the FBI.

One thing was apparent, however: Linda Jo Edwards, six feet tall, 150 pounds, athletic and strong, with no defensive wounds and intact fingernails, was most likely the victim of a surprise attack by someone she knew and trusted.

Paula was taken downtown for a statement that morning and described in some detail the man she had seen the night before. He had "silver hair, cut in a medium, touching-the-ears fashion . . . The body was that of a Caucasian with a tan wearing white shorts . . . The figure was sleek and slender . . . my first impression was that it was my boss Jim Mayfield . . ." In later testimony she consistently described the man's height as one to two inches taller than her almost 5'6" height. Whoever it was, she said, had a very trim figure and moved quickly. He was reasonably proportioned with good-sized shoulders and a visible tan.

Her detailed description fit Mayfield to a T. He had silver hair, cut so that it just touched his ears. At a February 1978 deposition Mayfield agreed that his silver hair was "moderately short, comes down a little over the top of the ears—not quite to the middle of the ear." Paula testified twice in later hearings that Mayfield was 5'7" to 5'8" tall. Mayfield's university colleagues all recalled that he often wore white tennis shorts, was well tanned and lean. Obsessed with physical fitness, he played tennis or racquetball almost every day.

Sergeant Eddie Clark was a detective with the Tyler Police Department. Despite his youth (he was only twenty-six) and his lack of experience with homicides (this was his first), he was assigned to lead the investigation into the murder. Clark had known Linda her entire life. Both were raised in Bullard, a town with one railroad crossing and 500 residents, located eighteen miles south of Tyler. Both went to Bullard High School. Linda graduated four years behind Eddie, along with his younger sister, Susan. Eddie was president of his 1970 graduating class and voted most likely to succeed among his fifty classmates. Bringing Linda's savage killer to justice was personal for him. He felt that he owed it not only to the citizens of Tyler, but also to Linda's family and friends and the folks back in Bullard who expected nothing less.

Linda had been the star basketball player for Bullard High, weighing in at 200 pounds before meeting Mayfield. She was a pretty young woman, gregarious, vivacious, and well liked. Soon after high school she married a local boy, Bobby Lester. For a small-town farm girl, Linda was a spendthrift, running up thousands of dollars in credit card bills for clothing and jewelry. She wanted the finer things in life, which Bobby could not afford. Bobby, who loved her dearly, worked double shifts at the Tyler tire factory to keep them afloat. In November 1975, Linda began working at Mayfield's library as a periodical clerk. It didn't take long for the forty-two-year-old Mayfield, an inveterate womanizer, to notice the beauty and potential sexuality in twenty-year-old Linda. Their affair began at the library's 1975 Christmas party at Mayfield's home with a kiss under the mistletoe. It lasted until the night she died. During its duration, Mayfield remade and molded Linda physically into the woman he wanted. Through a regimen that included pills, diet, and exercise, he got her to lose fifty to sixty pounds, and encouraged her to get contact lenses and change her hairstyle. Under his Svengali-like guidance, she was transformed into a statuesque figure he delighted in, and she was proud of.

Realizing he'd be a suspect, Mayfield contacted Eddie Clark and was interviewed by him at the police station that very afternoon, June 10. He provided a rather understated description of his affair with Linda, which he claimed began when she came to him with her marital problems. Linda had split with her husband in June 1976, and she had gladly accepted Mayfield's invitation to live in his family's Tyler home, along with his wife and their three adopted children, eighteen-year-old Bonnie, seventeen-year-old Charley, and sixteen-year-old Louella.

Mayfield told Sergeant Clark that Linda stopped living with them in January 1977, when the family moved to a new home on Lake Palestine, seventeen miles south of Tyler. Elfreide no longer wanted Linda in the house. So Linda moved in with her grandmother in Bullard, a short distance from the lake. By then, Bonnie had married and Charley had joined the army, leaving Louella the only child at home. Mayfield told Sergeant Clark that the affair continued for the next five months until it culminated in the brief and torrid week in mid-May when he left his wife and daughter and moved into an apartment he rented at the Embarcadero complex for him and Linda, not far from Paula Rudolph, and then, six days later, changed his mind and returned to his family, leaving Linda so despondent that she tried to take her own life.

Sergeant Clark already knew quite a bit about Linda because he was the officer who had investigated her suicide attempt. From her Bullard friends he'd learned she had had other affairs while married to Bobby. He learned that a month before her death, Linda had dated an old friend from high school, and asked her best friend to cover for her if Mayfield called. This same friend told Eddie how possessive Mayfield was. Years later she told others that "he would die if he knew she was seeing someone else." Eddie learned from other sources that when Linda lived with the Mayfield family in Tyler, she and Mayfield carried on their affair right under the nose of Elfreide and their teenage children. Eddie knew that Linda had spent a great deal of time at the Mayfields' lake house as well, often observed by neighbors sunning herself on the pier in a bikini. Eddie also learned that Linda habitually called Mayfield at night and beckoned him to her apartment, much to Elfreide's resentment. They couldn't stay away from each other. He, sexually addicted to her; she, madly in love with him.

Mayfield concluded his story by telling Eddie he was with Linda several different times during the day leading up to her murder. She came to TEU to speak with him late in the morning. That visit spilled over into lunch at the Dairy Queen until 1:30, when she departed for a job interview at a local bank. She returned to his office at 4:00 to tell him she got the job. Then, driving their own cars, at 5:30 they went apartment hunting for her until 6:00 when they went their separate ways. He failed to mention that they had also played tennis that afternoon at the Embarcadero courts. According to him, the last time he saw Linda that day was at 8:30 P.M. when she unexpectedly arrived at his Lake Palestine house. They talked a few minutes in his driveway. She told him about meeting another man—someone called Steve—at the local tennis court and asked Mayfield to fix her car on Saturday. Mayfield told Eddie that he remained home that night with his wife and Louella.

Mayfield agreed to return to the police station the following

Monday, June 13, to take a polygraph. But on Monday he retained the top criminal defense attorney in Tyler, Buck Files, who immediately canceled the polygraph. Files notified Sergeant Clark that he was not to speak with Mayfield or his wife without his permission, effectively excluding the Mayfields from the police investigation.

That same afternoon, Friday, June 10, Sergeant Clark had other visitors who wanted to volunteer information: history professor Dr. Andrew Szarka and speech professor Dr. Judy Freeman, along with their spouses. They were all neighbors of Mayfield's at Lake Palestine, as well as his former colleagues at TEU. Both couples knew Linda well and suspected Mayfield may have been involved in her death. The Szarkas reported that Linda had stopped by their house immediately after she had spoken with Mayfield the night before and stayed a half hour, until 9:00 P.M. Linda spoke of how upset Mayfield had been when she told him she had decided to date other men while still continuing their own relationship. Judy Freeman, ten years older than Linda, had been a confidante to the younger woman. She told Sergeant Clark how possessive and jealous Mayfield was, unwilling for Linda to see other men.

It did not take long for the police to account for Linda's movements the night of her murder. She had made the seventeen-mile, twenty-two-minute drive from the Embarcadero to Mayfield's home, arriving around 7:30 P.M. Since he was not yet home, she went over to a nearby tennis court, and happened upon twenty-five-year-old Steve Nations. Never shy, she introduced herself, gave him her telephone number, and suggested he call her if he wanted to play tennis. She then went by the Freeman home, but they weren't there. After her visit to Mayfield and the Szarkas, she arrived home at 9:30. Paula informed Linda that she was going to shower and get ready to visit a friend at the Rodeway Inn. She would be leaving in about an hour. Linda left the apartment at 10:00 P.M. and went to the nearby Embarcadero tennis courts to see who was there. She bumped into Orlando and Alma Padron, who lived in one of the Embarcadero apartments, and they invited her back to their place for a drink. Linda reluctantly accepted but kept telling them that she had to get back to her apartment before her roommate left for the evening.

Alma Padron years later said that Linda was nervous and jittery that night. Her legs were shaking as she constantly looked at her watch. She seemed troubled as she sat on the edge of the couch. Earlier at the tennis court, before they returned to the Padrons' apartment, Linda had poured out her heart to Alma, whom she barely knew. Linda talked of her divorce, her attempted suicide over her problems with a married man, and his jealousy. She also spoke of a new job she'd gotten at a bank that day, and how she wanted to begin life anew. Alma sensed that Linda was determined to let go of the past, but at the same time was "emotionally torn up." Linda left the Padrons' at 10:25 and was back in her apartment in time to see Paula off at 10:30.

Only two hours later, at 12:30 A.M., Paula arrived home and saw the killer in Linda's bedroom.

In a bizarre twist in the case, it turned out that two weeks before Linda's murder, during the week of May 23–27, sixteen-year-old Louella Mayfield had impersonated a police officer in her Explorer Scout uniform and visited several Tyler apartment complexes, including the Embarcadero. She told apartment managers that she was investigating a murder involving Jim Mayfield and Linda Jo Edwards. The next day, Louella was warned by the police that such behavior was a serious offense. Then, about a week before Linda was killed, Louella stormed into Linda's TEU work area and in front of others loudly confronted Linda, threatening to kill her if she continued seeing her father. She then marched into her father's office, screaming at him that he must stop seeing Linda.

All of Louella's actions had been written up in a police report by a Sergeant Hayden, who ended his report by stating, "I personally know Louella to be mentally and emotionally unstable, very hyperactive and a pathological liar."

Years later Louella told *The Dallas Morning News* that she did these things because "my mom was going through a lot of emotional stress . . . and it hurt." This was certainly true. Elfreide was indeed worn out by her husband's nonstop philandering and devastated by his decision to desert her and Louella and move in with Linda. When she learned of Linda's suicide attempt, she wondered aloud to her best friend, Wanda Joyce, "When will it ever end?"

Jim Mayfield was Elfreide's Coffeyville, Kansas, high school sweetheart and the love of her life. She was determined not to lose him to a woman half her age. On May 19, her forty-second birthday, days after he had moved out, she called Mayfield and implored him to come home. This request threw Mayfield into a frenzy. Torn between his young paramour and the wife of his youth, he started behaving erratically. On that same day, he filed papers to divorce Elfreide, then immediately returned home to her. Mayfield's whiplash broke Linda's heart. That was the night that she, depressed and feeling abandoned, took the pills that nearly ended her life.

Sergeant Clark interviewed Louella on Tuesday, June 14, about her threats to Linda. Louella admitted making them and to pretending to be a police officer. She wanted her father back; his absence was tearing her mother apart. She also told Clark that she, her father, and her mother were all home together the night of Linda's murder. Based on this interview, Sergeant Clark eliminated Louella as a suspect. In any case, the next day attorney Files called Sergeant Clark and told him no more interviews with Louella.

Initially, Sergeant Clark did consider Mayfield and his wife as possible suspects. If Linda had told Mayfield she was cutting off the relationship, Clark reasoned, then out of anger Mayfield might have killed her by destroying her sexual parts; that way no one else could have her. Clark also thought that Elfreide might have had motive to destroy Linda's sexual parts, so Linda could never use them again to destroy her marriage. In the end, however, neither Sergeant Clark nor the Tyler police could bring themselves to believe that the director of the university library or anyone in his family was capable of such savagery. The Mayfields simply did not fit the profile of such a killer. Especially not the one compiled by local psychologist Jerry Landrum, whom Sergeant Clark had used before and who coincidentally lived at the Embarcadero. After viewing the crime scene photos and receiving a debriefing by Clark the week of June 13, it was Landrum's view that the murderer was possibly eighteen to thirty years old, homosexual, impotent, introverted, a drug user, and epileptic. So Sergeant Clark believed it would be a waste of time to interview any of Mayfield's or Linda's university colleagues, or anyone associated with Mayfield's professional and personal life, past or present. Instead, he focused his attention on the Embarcadero apartment complex, convinced that he would find Linda's sadistic killer in those 265 units. Thus he enabled Mayfield to walk free.

At 9:00 A.M. on June 10, Sgt. Doug Collard, the fingerprint identification police supervisor, dusted Paula's apartment for fingerprints. He was intrigued by the clarity of prints he lifted from the patio door, how they "jumped up at him" immediately upon dusting the door. Later that morning, he told Clark: "When you find the man whose prints are on the sliding patio door, you will have your killer." For the next two months, from morning to night, Clark knocked on every apartment door, contacting almost all the residents. He fingerprinted all the men in the Embarcadero, polygraphed several of them, and investigated those who had any kind of criminal record. He was a man possessed.

On August 2 he hit pay dirt. He bumped into James Taylor, whom he had fingerprinted and interviewed earlier. Taylor was an independent truck driver who made frequent out-of-town deliveries of oil equipment for a family company. For the first time, Taylor told him that while he had been away when Edwards was murdered, a guest had been living temporarily in his apartment. His name was Kerry Max Cook. When Taylor returned from his trip that weekend, he learned that Kerry had left Tyler the day after the murder for Jacksonville, a town thirty miles south of Tyler, to visit his parents. Taylor told Clark that Cook had had problems with the law in Jacksonville. He went on to say that Cook returned to Taylor's apartment on Monday, June 13; later that day, Taylor dropped him off in Houston during another delivery run.

Before crashing at Taylor's apartment, Cook had been a bartender in Dallas at a gay bar called Old Plantation. Taylor had met Cook there, and introduced him to his friend, Robert Hoehn, a Tyler hairdresser. Both Taylor and Hoehn were homosexual and attracted to Cook. The fact that Cook worked in a gay bar and was temporarily staying with Taylor is what later led police to believe he was homosexual.

The next day, Sergeant Collard obtained Cook's fingerprints from the Jacksonville police and compared them to the prints on Paula's patio door. Excited, he told Clark they were a match. Eddie and his colleagues thought they finally had their man. This view was reinforced when they learned that Cook was a twenty-one-year-old with a criminal record. No violent crimes, but he had spent time in prison. As a juvenile delinquent in the early 1970s, he had made a habit of running away from home and taking friends on junkets in stolen cars. These escapades earned him a short stint in a Texas prison for first-time offenders. He was released on his eighteenth birthday, April 5, 1974, and returned home to his parents in Jacksonville. There, he got into new trouble when he kicked out a store window after being wrongly accused of robbing the store. For that he was put on probation for "malicious mischief." His probation ended in the spring of 1977. For the first time in four years, he was free and clear of any entanglements with the law.

In the midst of these earlier arrests, Kerry had been sent to Rusk State Hospital for pre-trial evaluation. The man who examined him was none other than Dr. Jerry Landrum, the psychologist who, four years later, would offer Sgt. Eddie Clark a profile of Linda's killer. In his report on Kerry, Dr. Landrum called him a "typical rebellious juvenile" and "an immature, dependent youth who cries for his mother at night." After determining that Kerry was not psychotic and had no other mental disorder, Dr. Landrum saw no reason to confine him and ordered his release.

On August 3, Sergeant Clark took statements from two people who had interactions with Cook in the days leading up to the murder—Randy Dykes, Taylor's seventeen-year-old nephew, and Cook's friend Robert Hoehn. Both recounted a story that caught Sergeant Clark's attention. At one point during his stay, Kerry had seen a girl undressing in the bedroom of a different unit. The girl was Linda Jo Edwards. Hoehn said he'd heard the story from Kerry at 11:00 P.M. the night of the murder, while they were walking from Taylor's apartment to the Embarcadero swimming pool. Dykes told the sergeant that he had heard the story days earlier, also on a walk to the pool with Kerry. Both Dykes and Hoehn now showed Clark the window. Dykes recounted another detail: On June 7, three days before the murder, Cook's neck "was covered with passion marks." Dykes had asked Kerry about the marks, and Kerry said he had met the girl he saw in the window—Linda Jo Edwards—at the pool, and that the two of them had gone back to her apartment and made out.

The stories told by Hoehn and Dykes convinced Eddie Clark that Kerry was a peeping Tom. This, in combination with Dr. Landrum's profile, made him conclude that Kerry was Linda's killer. In fact, there was some evidence that Linda had an exhibitionist streak—two other men in the building testified later that they'd noticed her standing nude in the window as if she wanted to be admired. But, convinced they had their man, law enforcement moved with lightning speed against Kerry. On August 3, Smith County district attorney A. D. Clark (not related to Eddie Clark) issued an arrest warrant for Kerry Max Cook for the capital murder of Linda Jo Edwards. It wasn't until 5:30 P.M. on Friday, August 5, however, that Cherokee County sheriff Danny Stallings of Jacksonville, who knew Kerry and his family, learned of Kerry's whereabouts from his parents. Kerry was working as a bartender at the Holiday Club in Port Arthur, Texas. Sergeant Clark and Sheriff Stallings flew on a private plane from Tyler to Port Arthur at 8:00 P.M. that evening.

With the assistance of local police, at 10:50 P.M. Sergeant Clark placed Kerry under arrest at the club. The police then proceeded to search—Kerry would later say "ransack"—his apartment. As this was close to midnight, Kerry's girlfriend, Amber Norris, with whom he had been living for several weeks, sat on the bed in her nightgown, terrified. Nothing of evidentiary value was found.

Back at the Port Arthur jail Sergeant Clark, Stallings, and the Port Arthur vice squad interrogated Kerry for hours on end, trying to extract a confession. They yelled expletive-laden accusations in Kerry's face and told him, falsely, that his hair and semen were found on Linda's body. One of the locals even plunged Kerry's head into a toilet bowl, continually flushing it, screaming at him to confess. All to no avail. At last, before dawn, they put him on the plane back to Tyler. But his ordeal wasn't over. The Tyler police stripped Kerry of his clothing and locked him in a windowless jail cell with an air-conditioning unit pumping freezing air onto his naked body.

A day or two later Kerry's mom and dad, Earnest and Evelyn Cook, arrived. Although a rebellious youth, Kerry loved them both and greatly respected his dad, who had been a career army sergeant running the motor pools at different army bases in Europe. Kerry and his older brother, Doyle Wayne, whom Kerry idolized, were army brats who moved from base to base throughout Germany in their formative years. In 1972 his dad had retired after twenty-one years of service and moved the family back to Jacksonville, Texas, where he and Evelyn had been raised, met, and married.

During this visit Kerry's dad asked him if he knew the girl who was killed. When Kerry began to tell him the story about meeting her at the pool and going to her apartment, Earnest interrupted him and warned, "Never tell anyone you were inside that apartment or that you even knew her. If you do they will pin that murder on you. Promise me you will keep your mouth shut." For the next fourteen years Kerry followed his dad's dictum, and denied he ever met Linda Jo Edwards. This lie, along with the web of lies spun against him by prosecutors, would ensnare him for years to come.

On September 1, Sergeant Clark went to Port Arthur to interview those who knew Kerry. He spent some time with Kerry's live-in girlfriend, Amber Norris. She told him she first met Kerry on July 1 at a gay bar in Houston when she was visiting friends. She returned to Port Arthur after the July Fourth weekend and Kerry came with her. He got a bartender's job at the Holiday Club on July 7, and they rented an apartment together. She accompanied him to Jacksonville in mid-July where she met his mom, dad, and brother. She told the prying Sergeant Clark that their sex life was very normal and included oral, but not anal, sex. Although she and Kerry had several homosexual friends, she had no idea if Kerry was bisexual or not. He was never impotent with her. On occasion they smoked marijuana; under its influence he became "silly," never angry or violent.

The grand jury met about Kerry's case from August through October 1977. Cyrus Kugler, the manager of the Holiday Club where Kerry worked, testified on September 19. He had nothing but good things to say about Kerry.

The Holiday Club's clientele, he said, was straight, middle-class Americana, not gay. He characterized Kerry as a "very easygoing fellow who made friends with many people around the club." Everyone liked him, men and women. "Girls galore" wanted to go out with him. He was always "nice, polite, with good manners." He was an experienced and excellent bartender who needed no training. To better fit in with the club's customers, Kerry got his hair cut and dressed conservatively.

That same day, September 19, Jerry Landrum also appeared before the grand jury. He expanded on his earlier profile of the killer. He said the perpetrator was most likely bisexual with problems of impotency, a problem that caused him to harbor an inordinate amount of anger and hostility toward females. He believed the offender was a "sexually inadequate" male with a "pathological hostility toward a mother figure." In a contradictory and somewhat incomprehensible analysis, he first stated that the killer, a homosexual, was motivated to mutilate the victim's sexual body parts because he did not have those parts. Then, in the next breath, confusing the grand jurors, he said it was a sexual attack by a bisexual.

Three witnesses—Taylor's nephews Randy and Rodney Dykes, and Robert Hoehn—testified to the grand jury that Kerry had told them he had met Linda at the Embarcadero pool and that she had invited him into her apartment where they made out, giving him the passion marks on his neck. Hoehn testified that Cook told him about his encounter with Linda during dinner at Hoehn's home on Monday night, June 6. Randy testified that on Tuesday morning, June 7, Kerry had told him the same thing when he questioned the marks on Cook's neck. Hoehn also testified that he and Kerry had spent June 9, the evening of the murder, together. The X-rated movie *The Sailor Who Fell from Grace with the Sea* was on cable TV, but Hoehn said that Kerry "wasn't paying any attention to it." He also testified that Kerry was not angry, frustrated, or upset that night. All three men were questioned by A. D. Clark, Sgt. Eddie Clark by his side.

Fearing that this grand jury testimony, which gave an innocent reason for Kerry's prints on Linda's patio door, could undercut his case against Kerry, A. D. Clark unlawfully withheld it from Kerry's trial attorneys. It would not see the light of day for another fourteen years.

———

In June 1978, ten months after his arrest, Kerry's trial took place. His attorneys were Larue Dixon and John Ament. Dixon was the former district attorney of Cherokee County who had prosecuted Kerry and sent him to jail five years earlier; Ament had represented Kerry on some of those charges. As Jacksonville partners they accepted the case for a retainer of $500—all the Cook family could afford. They received no other payments for their representation, making it impossible to pay expert witnesses and investigators to help defend Kerry. The thirty-five-year-old trial prosecutor was Michael Thompson, an overbearing bulldog who would stop at nothing to get a conviction.

The murder of Linda Jo Edwards was the most heinous crime in East Texas history. Thompson and his boss, District Attorney A. D. Clark, were determined not only to convict but to put Kerry Max Cook to death for it. Besides that, Clark, appointed district attorney by the governor after his predecessor resigned, was up for election later that year. Heading into the trial, Clark knew he needed more evidence, and a lot of it, to get a conviction. His political career depended on it.

The first challenge was the patio door prints that were indisputably Kerry's. How and when did his prints get on that door? Was he an invited guest earlier, or did he slip in and kill her? Clark's solution was to convince Doug Collard to testify that those prints were six to twelve hours old when discovered, thus placing Kerry in Linda's apartment at the time of her death. By hiding the three men's grand jury testimony, which offered an alternative account for Kerry's presence at Linda's apartment, and insisting that Collard place Kerry's prints on the patio door at the time of the crime, Clark was well on his way to being able to present the assault on Linda as a "stranger-on-stranger" crime committed by the deranged defendant. He knew full well, of course, that Kerry was no stranger to Linda.

———

Now A. D. Clark needed Paula Rudolph to identify Kerry as the man she saw in the bedroom. Kerry's appearance was vastly different from the man she had described to the police and grand jury. There was even proof of that. On the morning after Linda was murdered, Randy Dykes had taken Kerry to get his driver's license renewed. The Tyler Department of Public Safety took a new photo to process the renewal. It showed Kerry with a full head of bushy dark brown hair that covered both of his ears and ran down the sides of his face. This was a far cry from "silver hair, cut in a medium, touching-the-ears fashion." The photo also listed Kerry's height as 5'11", significantly taller than the 5'7"–5'8" described by Paula. Unfortunately for Kerry, the photo got lost in the mail and was not secured until years later.

Regardless, Paula was never asked to attend a lineup, nor was she shown a photo array for identification purposes. She was never asked at two pre-trial hearings to specifically identify Kerry as the man she saw, despite the fact that Kerry was sitting at the defense table across the room. Nor was she asked if Kerry was the man she saw when testifying to the grand jury on September 19. At Kerry's bond hearing, she was asked if she could identify the man she saw. She answered evasively, "I will not swear under oath who it was." Prosecutors Clark and Thompson knew they needed time to convince Paula that the man they were prosecuting for Linda's murder was, in fact, the killer, and for Paula to agree that the man she had seen couldn't have been Jim Mayfield, because Jim Mayfield couldn't have committed such a barbaric act.

It took almost a year for her to come around, sort of. At trial she was no longer certain that she had seen the man's hair. Her nonsensical rationalization for this significant change was that she'd been looking at a brightly lit room against which she observed only a "reflected silhouette." (Forensic experts agree that standing in the dark and looking into a well-lighted room a short distance away is the ideal visual environment to make accurate observations.) Paula said that she didn't see facial features, only "shadows and planes on a shape, a figure." When asked if the defendant was the man she saw, she replied, "Yes, he fits." Thus, in the end, her identification of Kerry was based on "a silhouetted body shape," which, according to her, Kerry fit.

———

Now allied with the prosecution, Paula backed off what she originally told the police. She was now certain that the man she saw was not Jim Mayfield. But she was still convinced that the man was wearing white shorts. This proved helpful to Kerry when Robert Hoehn testified for the State. But the testimony that came next was absolutely damning in the eyes of the jury.

As they did in their grand jury statements, Hoehn and the Dykes brothers portrayed Kerry to the jury as a peeping Tom. Randy testified that Kerry told him he was passing the girl's bedroom window one night, and from the sidewalk he stopped and watched her undress. He added that Kerry told him she had big breasts and played with herself. On the morning after Linda's death, Randy took Kerry to fill out a job application in Tyler, and then drove him to Jacksonville and dropped him off at his brother's workplace. Although he did not say it at this first trial, Randy testified at a 1994 retrial that on the morning after Linda was murdered, he took Kerry to the local Department of Public Safety to renew his driver's license—not a likely destination for a man who had allegedly mutilated a woman twelve hours earlier.

Hoehn testified at trial that he and Kerry had watched the

X-rated movie *The Sailor Who Fell from Grace with the Sea* on cable TV the night Linda was killed. But this time, in direct contradiction of his grand jury testimony—in which he said several times that Kerry "wasn't paying any attention to it"—Hoehn now disgusted the conservative jury by salaciously describing the oral and anal sex that he and Kerry supposedly had together while the movie was playing, including Kerry masturbating and ejaculating on the floor as Hoehn watched. Hoehn told of one scene in the movie where a little boy peered into his mother's bedroom and watched as she pleased herself. He said Kerry was "rubbing himself" when children in the movie were getting ready to mutilate a cat, and that he held up a butcher knife saying, "Let's cut it out." None of this was true, but the prosecution ran with it, portraying Kerry as a perverted and intoxicated homosexual killer so sexually stimulated by the film, and by the memory of seeing Linda nude in her bedroom window, that he'd gone to her apartment, slid in through the patio door, caught her by surprise, and did to her what the young boys did to the cat in the film. If Ament and Dixon had had Hoehn's suppressed grand jury testimony, they could have knocked down the State's ludicrous presentation.

Parts of Hoehn's trial testimony, however, did help Kerry's case, except by now the jury was so turned off they probably gave it no credence. Hairdresser Hoehn told the jury that Kerry had a full head of dark brown hair down to his shoulders and was wearing the same blue and red boxing shorts that he always wore (not white tennis shorts).

Hoehn also testified that he and Kerry left the apartment sometime after midnight to get a pack of cigarettes. When they returned, he dropped Kerry off at the Embarcadero's front entrance. He was positive it was between 12:30 and 12:35, not earlier and not later. After they purchased the cigarettes, Kerry had suggested that they ride around for a while. Hoehn said no. When he dropped Kerry

off, Kerry invited Hoehn to come in and visit with him a little longer. Hoehn declined because he had to get up early the next morning for work.

So, if Kerry were the killer, he would have had to turn into a
monster in the blink of an eye as soon as Hoehn drove away. On
an impulse, he would have had to dash back to Taylor's apartment,
change into white shorts, run over to Paula's apartment, slip in the
patio door, confront and mutilate Linda, meticulously clean up,
and hardly leave behind a trace of blood.

There was a reason Hoehn testified falsely against Kerry. Inexplicably, Smith County prosecutors were convinced that Hoehn had
joined Kerry in killing Linda. The police interrogated Hoehn so
intensely, and harassed him so ceaselessly, that he retained an attorney to put a stop to it. But prosecutor Thompson still tried. When
the last juror was selected, he asked for a recess and ushered Kerry
and his attorneys into a conference room. He offered Kerry a plea
whereby if Kerry named Hoehn as his partner in the murder, he
would recommend a sentence of twenty-five years instead of death.
Insisting on his innocence, Kerry refused and went to trial.

The fixation of the authorities on Robert Hoehn had no basis in
fact. Hoehn looked nothing like the man Paula described. He had
blond hair thinning on top. He was overweight and soft-looking
with a noticeable belly. He stood close to 5'11" at 175 pounds. His
skin was pasty white with not a hint of a tan. When Kerry refused
to plea out, Hoehn was given immunity to testify as he did. Besides
a murder charge, he avoided prosecution under the anti-same-sex
sodomy law in effect in Texas until 2003, when the U.S. Supreme
Court found the law unconstitutional.

After Hoehn's testimony, the prosecutors had a jailhouse snitch
to share with the jury. Thompson brought in Edward Scott Jackson
(aka "Shyster"). He had been in jail for first-degree murder since
November 1976, awaiting trial. Shyster told the jury that Kerry had

confessed to killing Linda while they were in the Smith County jail together. Shyster repeated gory aspects of the murder Kerry had supposedly told him. For instance, Kerry allegedly told him he cut out Linda's vagina and took it with him along with hair from her head. Jackson recalled that Kerry had a particular hatred for women with dark hair (Linda had long, dark brown hair), but he liked blondes and redheads. He'd say vulgar things about dark-haired women while they perused girlie magazines together, like "this bitch needs her ass kicked for posing like this."

Shyster assured the jury there were no secret deals with the prosecutor for his testimony. Thompson backed this up during summation, claiming, "I will be yelling for [Shyster] Jackson's head right before this rail of justice just like I am this killer and it will fall. I don't make deals with killers." That's not what happened, though. On August 15, 1978, a month almost to the day after Kerry arrived on death row, Shyster was back in court. He pled guilty to involuntary manslaughter, was sentenced to time served, and walked free. He had spent 625 days in the Smith County jail on a murder charge, rather than a life sentence in a Texas state prison if convicted at trial.

The State's last witness was Dr. V. V. Gonzalez, a pathologist who had examined the body at the crime scene and performed the autopsy at a funeral home later that morning. Dr. Gonzalez was not trained as a medical examiner, nor did he formally serve in that capacity. In 1977, Smith County did not have a medical examiner's office. Years later, the renowned Texas forensic pathologist, Dr. Lloyd White, reviewed Gonzalez's work in Linda's case. He described his autopsy report and testimony as "almost unintelligible." Dr. White also characterized Dr. Gonzalez as "incapable of describing any sort of wound or injury in a manner consistent with all generally accepted standards of forensic pathology practice."

Dr. Gonzalez offered one very damning, and highly suspect, finding. Even though he had not made note of it in his autopsy report, he testified that he believed a piece of the vaginal canal had been "cut off" and "was missing." He was able to discover this even though the killer had repeatedly stabbed the vagina and the area around it so many times that her genitalia and rectum all the way into the pelvic cavity had been eviscerated. As soon as Dr. Gonzalez departed the stand, the State rested its case.

The defense consisted of only three witnesses, all Smith County jail inmates. They told the jury that Shyster Jackson had told them he had a deal with the district attorney that would enable him to plead to involuntary manslaughter, get time served, and go home. Which is exactly what happened.

Fearful that Thompson would ride roughshod over Kerry, his attorneys persuaded him not to testify.

In his summation, Thompson used Gonzalez's "missing vagina" finding to tell the jury that this "pervert" took Linda's missing calf stocking, "dropped those body parts in it," and with the stocking in hand exited the apartment. In an outrageous assertion, he then added, "I wouldn't be surprised if he didn't eat those body parts." Thompson branded Kerry a "young sexual psychopath" and implored the jury to "take his warped, twisted and perverted mind out of existence" and "do something about that pervert before he does it again to a young woman in our county."

Thompson told the jury that after Randy Dykes took Kerry down to Jacksonville the day after the murder on June 10, "he [Kerry] kept on running and never came back to Tyler . . . he went like a rabbit from the City of Tyler and hadn't come back." Thompson knew this was false. While James Taylor didn't testify at trial, he had testified before the grand jury on October 3, 1977, that Kerry had returned to Tyler on Monday afternoon, June 13, three days after the murder, having spent the weekend with his family in Jacksonville. Kerry only left Tyler again when Taylor kicked him out of his apartment after hearing that Kerry had had sex with one of his friends. It was a groundless rumor, but Taylor's jealousy got the best of him, and he asked Kerry to leave. Taylor drove Kerry to Houston later that day during a truck delivery run. Kerry called twice from Houston later that week, asking Taylor to let him come back. Taylor refused and never heard from Cook again.

Like Hoehn's and the Dykes brothers' grand jury testimony, Taylor's was kept from the defense for the next fourteen years.

In their summation, defense attorneys Ament and Dixon tried to drive home how much Kerry's physical appearance differed from Paula's initial description of the killer. They argued that Kerry could not have committed the crime, since Paula saw the killer in the bedroom at 12:30 and Hoehn dropped Kerry off at the same time. They ridiculed the Shyster Jackson "jailhouse confession," characterizing him as a "smooth talker" who should not be believed. Dixon predicted, accurately as it turned out, that in two months they would read in the paper that Shyster had pled to involuntary manslaughter and walked free. But Cook's attorneys couldn't get around Collard's testimony that the prints were six to twelve hours old when found. Absent Kerry's admission that he'd touched the patio door when he and Linda had gone to her apartment a few days earlier to make out, Collard's testimony placed Kerry in the apartment at the time of the murder.

The jury reached its verdict at 10:00 P.M. on June 28, 1978, after deliberating through the afternoon and evening. They found Kerry guilty of capital murder. The punishment phase began the next day.

For this, Dr. Jerry Landrum took the stand. He was now a self-employed psychologist, no longer at Rusk Hospital. But he recalled his evaluation of Kerry at Rusk several years earlier. He told the jury he didn't have his notes but remembered that he had diagnosed him as "an anti-social personality." Even though he had not interviewed him since, he added that he would put Kerry in the "severe psychopathic category" and had "no doubt" he was a continuing threat to society who could not be rehabilitated if institutionalized. Since the defense never saw his September 1973 evaluation, they didn't know that Landrum was contradicting his own conclusion that Kerry was "not psychotic," that Kerry was "free of any mental disorder," and that there was "no reason" to keep Kerry confined.

Later, it was discovered that Dr. Landrum consistently misrepresented his résumé and used highly questionable practices. He often testified under oath that he had a PhD in psychology, when in fact his doctorate was in education and personnel administration. In 1982, the Texas Court of Criminal Appeals ridiculed Dr. Landrum's diagnosis of another Texas death row inmate's future dangerousness as "ludicrous," one that "cannot be seriously considered." In that case Landrum rendered his opinion after silently observing the inmate for thirty minutes while sitting alone with him, the inmate refusing to speak the entire time.

The other primary witness against Kerry at the punishment hearing was Dr. James Grigson, a forensic psychiatrist. He examined Cook and also found him to have an antisocial personality, which he defined as a person without conscience who has no regard for another person's life. He went deeper and put him "at the very end, the very most severe [end] where you will find the sociopath," further adding: "You can't come any more severe than that . . . I feel absolutely 100% certain that he is and will continue to be a threat no matter where he is." As it turned out, Dr. Grigson was a career witness for the prosecution. He had testified on behalf of the State in 167 capital trials, nearly all resulting in death sentences. The press dubbed him "Dr. Death." He was eventually exposed as a prosecutorial shill and expelled by the American Psychiatric Association in 1995 for unethical conduct. Professionally disgraced, he died in 2004 at age seventy-two.

But, of course, the jury knew none of this, and Kerry's family had no money to pay an expert to rebut the testimonies of Landrum and Grigson. On June 29, 1978, after only a few hours of testimony, the punishment phase of Kerry's trial concluded: The jury voted unanimously for death. The judge sentenced him immediately, stating, "Your punishment is assessed at death to be carried out by lethal injection." With that, Cook was quickly ushered out of the courtroom by deputy sheriffs and met by a horde of reporters and TV cameras. When someone shouted, "Tell us why you did it" he responded, "I am innocent. I have been framed. But one day I'll prove I didn't do it. If it takes me ten years, or twenty years, I'll prove I didn't do it."

———

On July 18, 1978, Kerry was permitted one last tearful embrace with his parents and brother Doyle Wayne at the Smith County jail. After a deputy sheriff told Kerry, "It's time to go home," the authorities put him in chains and drove him three hours south to the infamous death row unit outside Huntsville, Texas. He was assigned the number 600, meaning he was the 600th person sentenced to death in Texas. His new home was in a wing containing fifty cells. His cell was three-sided with concrete walls, each 5'9" in length, with a sink, toilet, and a front door of steel bars operated electronically. Daily routine was breakfast at 3:30 A.M.; then lunch at 9:45 A.M., capped off by dinner at 3:30 P.M. Each meal was served on a metal tray pushed underneath the door by a trusty inmate (an inmate who had gained privileges for good behavior). Lights out at 10:00 P.M.

Since Kerry's case was widely reported, his reputation as a "homo punk" preceded him. He was constantly ridiculed as a "pussy-eating faggot" by his cellblock neighbors, who yelled and threatened to make him their "bitch." It was terrifying. He was warned by a sympathetic inmate that when—not if—he was sexually assaulted, he must vigorously fight back as if his life depended on it, which it very well might. If he didn't, he would lose respect and become game for all.

Then it happened. Kerry had mustered up the courage to go through the dayroom into the small recreation cage with other inmates. Before he knew it, James Demouchette, a huge black man, instructed Kerry at knifepoint to strip naked while others looked on.

Kerry obeyed and braced for the inevitable. When he was finished, Demouchette carved into Kerry's buttocks *Good Pussy* and his new name for him, *Cindy*. From that point on, he was a lamb among wolves.

Overwhelmed by shame, Kerry cut his wrists with a razor blade. This was the first time, but not the last, that he would attempt suicide. When he recovered, he was moved to the front of the cellblock, closer to the guards' station. But the sexual abuse continued. Perhaps he could have stopped the attacks if he had fought back, but he feared that, if he did, he might kill his tormentor, confirming the prosecutors' belief that he was a killer. He would then never escape the executioner. Instead, he studied legal books from the law library, determined to find a way out by educating himself on Texas criminal law.

Meanwhile, the media had taken notice of Kerry's conviction. The first story to examine the State's case with a critical eye appeared in a local paper in Longview, Texas, in April 1979. Written by Bob Howie and headlined IS THE REAL GUILTY PARTY NOW AWAITING EXECUTION ON DEATH ROW, the article caught the eye of Longview attorney Harry Heard, who offered, pro bono, to appeal Kerry's conviction.

Then, a few months later, in June 1979, *Dallas Morning News* reporters Donnis Baggett and Howard Swindle published a bombshell. Shyster Jackson, the jailhouse snitch who had lied about Kerry on the witness stand, had recanted his story to Baggett and Swindle—and a Texas Ranger named Stuart Dowell—in an interview the previous September. Not only was his story about Kerry's supposed "confession" a complete fabrication, Shyster said that he cooked it up with the aid of District Attorney A. D. Clark in exchange for a sweetheart deal. Instead of the maximum sentence of life that he could receive at his upcoming murder trial, he would be given a get-out-of-jail-free card—a sentence of twenty-one months in the county jail, which time he had already served. Shyster jumped at the chance to walk free, and told his lie to Kerry's jury.

Although Shyster now regretted the false testimony that had sent an innocent man to death row, he refused to sign an affidavit for Ranger Dowell, fearing a perjury charge. He took off for his home state of Missouri, where in 1982 he committed another murder. For that, he was tried, convicted, and received a life sentence after all.

Attorney Heard filed Kerry's appeal and later argued it before Texas's highest court, the Court of Criminal Appeals (CCA), on February 13, 1980. He pointed out to the court that Jackson's admission was indicative of the State's trumped-up case against Cook. His brief encompassed nineteen different errors at trial that he argued rendered the conviction unreliable and unconstitutional. Kerry was cautiously optimistic that the CCA would rule in his favor. But then the years ticked by with no decision. On December 7, 1982, Texas executed its first man since 1964. More years passed, and still the CCA sat on Kerry's appeal. Kerry's only friend on death row, Kenneth Brock, was executed on June 19, 1986, even though the prosecutor who convicted him and the father of the victim appealed to Governor Mark White for a stay on his behalf. Kerry was heartbroken. He felt alone and forsaken.

Then came the real blow. On December 9, 1987, the CCA denied his appeal. The court had sat on his petition almost eight years, the longest time without a ruling for a direct appeal in American history. The CCA's vote to uphold the conviction was 8–1. The court cited Jackson's jailhouse confession, Paula Rudolph's identification, and Cook's patio prints as more than sufficient evidence to convict the defendant. It did agree with one of attorney Heard's arguments, that is, that Dr. Grigson's punishment phase testimony was inadmissible because Dr. Grigson had interviewed Kerry to assess his future dangerousness without notifying Kerry's attorneys or obtaining their permission to do so. However, the court ruled that the admission of Dr. Grigson's testimony had been a harmless error, because Dr. Landrum had offered a similar opinion, finding Kerry beyond rehabilitation.

Justice Sam Houston Clinton offered the lone dissent. At the outset of his twenty-two-page opinion he stated there were "troublesome aspects" to this case, and "a rational reviewer of all the facts is left with serious questions whether a rational trier of fact could find guilt beyond a reasonable doubt." Justice Clinton was particularly troubled by Paula Rudolph's identification. He devoted thirteen pages to analyzing her testimony and questioning its reliability. He was also concerned that the unidentified fingerprint found on the scissors had a whorl pattern when Kerry's print didn't have that characteristic. Also, with the exception of the fingerprint on the patio door, Kerry's prints were nowhere else in the apartment. In contrast, there were five other unidentified fingerprints found— none of them Kerry's. Clinton was not impressed with Jackson's confession testimony, which he believed was the "most incriminating" flaw in the case. Nor did he grant much weight to Robert Hoehn's graphic testimony about the sex acts they had supposedly performed the night of the murder.

Mere days after receiving the CCA's decision, Kerry received more crushing news: His dear brother, thirty-three-year-old Doyle Wayne, was dead—murdered in a tragic misunderstanding. Doyle Wayne had been enjoying an evening at a Longview club with a friend. Around closing time, the friend had yanked a pair of sunglasses from the face of another patron. Thinking Doyle Wayne was the culprit, the man had pressed a .44 Magnum revolver against his neck and shot him dead. (The shooter was caught and would plead guilty to voluntary manslaughter. For taking Doyle Wayne's life, he'd receive sixteen years in prison.) The loss of both sons was almost too much for the Cooks to bear.

Three days after learning of his brother's death, Cook was once again raped. Hopelessness consumed him and triggered a second suicide attempt. Once again he cut himself with a razor blade, this time slashing his wrist, legs, and penis. Miraculously he survived and spent the next two years receiving in-patient treatment from the prison's psychiatric team. Such attention was unheard of on death row. At last, someone showed kindness and compassionate care to Kerry Max Cook.

In 1988, events started to turn in Kerry's favor. In February he attracted a talented lawyer to his cause, Scott Howe of the newly established Capital Punishment Project, which represented death row inmates. Howe's immediate concern was keeping Cook alive. Smith County judge Joe Tunnell, newly assigned to preside over the Cook case, had set a July 8, 1988, execution date. Howe appealed that decision to the U.S. Supreme Court and asked for a stay of execution. On June 28, 1988, eleven days before Kerry was to die, the court granted the stay and remanded the case back to the CCA for reconsideration. The CCA reconsidered. On January 17, 1990, it once again reaffirmed the Cook conviction and sentence. But then, six months later, on June 13, something shocking occurred. This same court had a change of heart. In an almost unprecedented moment of self-reflection that stunned the legal world, it granted Scott Howe's request for a rehearing, and renewed Kerry's hope for a retrial.

Shortly after the CCA reopened Kerry's case, Scott Howe obtained two critical affidavits. One was offered by retired George Bonebrake, former director of the FBI's Fingerprint Section and a nationally renowned expert with more than forty years' experience. After examining Lieutenant Collard's testimony, Bonebrake was disturbed by many of Collard's determinations. He was most concerned that Collard had aged the patio door prints to the hour. He deemed this conclusion "entirely unreliable," stating that it "was impossible to determine whether the print was left on the door two hours or two weeks before it was discovered by the police." He added that "it is an accepted principle in the fingerprint examination field that an examiner cannot determine with reasonable accuracy the age of a fingerprint."

Howe also obtained a sworn statement from Dr. Gary Mears, a tenured professor of psychology at the University of Texas at Tyler, who had chaired the Department of Psychology there from 1973 through 1985. Dr. Mears recounted that Jim Mayfield, a day or two after Linda Jo's homicide, came to his office and asked him how to "beat" a polygraph. Mayfield knew that Mears had a polygraph machine in his laboratory and was a student of polygraph science. In that conversation, Mears confronted Mayfield about a book he had recently stumbled across in the university library called *The Sexual Criminal*. Published in 1949, the book contained police photographs of murdered women whose sexual organs had been mutilated. Chillingly, the photos mirrored Linda's wounds. After finding the book by happenstance, Dr. Mears had discovered that Mayfield himself had ordered the book for the library. Embarrassed, Mayfield had lamely said, "I have more books like that one, too." That same afternoon, Mears reported this conversation to a senior Tyler police officer, who seemed disinterested and never followed up. Not only that, but when Mears bumped into Mayfield the next day, Mayfield told him the police had passed along to his lawyer the tips Mears had given them about the book and polygraph. Mears was stunned. It was as if the police were working with Mayfield instead of treating him as a suspect.

Around the same time, David Hanners, a Pulitzer Prize–winning investigative reporter with *The Dallas Morning News,* was digging into Kerry's case. Hanners left no stone unturned. His inaugural front-page story, published on February 28, 1988, was headlined, INMATE WAS RAILROADED. This and articles that followed touched on all aspects of the case and included interviews with most of those associated with it, including Smith County law enforcement, defense attorneys, and state witnesses. Randy Dykes told the reporter that the prosecutor told him what to say and what not to say. He also swore in a 1991 affidavit that prosecutor Thompson kept yelling at him, insisting he get his story straight. He continued, "I was just a high school kid and he really had me intimidated. I decided that I would just tell him whatever he wanted to hear so that I could get out of there as fast as I could. When I got home, I told my family what had happened." His younger brother, Rodney Dykes, while serving a ten-year sentence for drugs and burglary charges, told Hanners the law "put words in his mouth."

Robert Hoehn had died of AIDS in Dallas on September 12, 1987, but a close friend revealed to Hanners conversations he had with Hoehn on his deathbed. Hoehn told him that the Cook case haunted him, that he "felt guilty for his role in the Cook conviction," that "the wrong man is on death row." He swore to his friend that "Cook was never, ever guilty."

On October 9, 1988, *The Dallas Morning News* ran another feature story that focused on Collard's aging of the patio door fingerprint as further proof of prosecutorial shenanigans. The headline read, KEY TESTIMONY IN COOK CASE SAID TO BE FALSE. This article had a far-reaching effect, sparking an inquiry by the International Association for Identification in 1989. In a thirteen-page response dated May 22, 1989, Collard admitted that when he gave his testimony, he knew that "there was no positive or scientific way that [his aging of the print] could be supported" and that "no other latent examiner would support such an analysis." Nevertheless, when he told A. D. Clark that he had no scientific basis for aging the print, Clark told Collard to offer it as his "opinion." Collard objected repeatedly to this but was met with "full and continued resistance" from Clark. When Collard finally caved, A. D. Clark was able to use his unrebutted testimony like a magic bullet—first to establish probable cause, then to get an indictment from the grand jury, then to set the terms of Kerry's bond, and, ultimately, to obtain Kerry's conviction at trial. With Collard's false testimony that the door print was only six to twelve hours old, Kerry hadn't stood a chance.

In February 1990, Kerry was inspired to write Centurion a sixty-one-page letter in pencil asking for help after learning of our role in Clarence Lee Brandley's exoneration and release from Texas's death row after ten years of false imprisonment ("Guilty Until Proven Innocent"). Hanners assisted Kerry by sending Centurion all the newspaper articles and interview write-ups. After discussing the case at length with Hanners on the telephone and studying the entire record, I had two lengthy visits with Kerry in November. I became convinced of his innocence and committed Centurion to his cause.

Believing Mayfield to be a viable suspect, Centurion spent the better part of 1991 doing what the Tyler police had not done—interviewing countless people who knew him—neighbors, relatives, university colleagues, faculty, library staff, and past associates throughout his career stretching back to Coffeyville, Kansas, where he was raised and began his professional life. We learned that early in his career he had a mental breakdown and would not go out of the house for a year or two. Elfreide supported the family during those dark days.

The people who knew Mayfield recalled one distinctive characteristic: his explosive temper. One of his past colleagues likened him to an "electrical capacitor," meaning he would build up a charge and then let it go like lightning. Another likened him to a "volcano." Another remembered that Mayfield would "shake with red hot rage" when his temper got the best of him. All remarked that he would explode and then an eerie calm would ensue. Most of those with whom we spoke would not have been surprised if Linda had been the victim of Mayfield's wrath. Every woman who worked for him at TEU or at Midwestern University, where he had worked as library director from 1969 to 1973, believed he was fully capable of Linda's murder. Shortly before he left Midwestern, nine women who worked for him signed a letter to the university president asking for Mayfield's immediate dismissal because of his "frequent temper tantrums" and abusive behavior. When Linda was killed, the female library staff at TEU had suspected that Mayfield might have been involved.

Even his adopted son Charley thought Mayfield should be a suspect in Linda's death. He told police that, in his view, his adoptive father's "violent temper" would have made him capable of such a hideous crime. He also predicted that Elfreide would "stand by her husband" despite his mistreatment of her, Charley, and his siblings.

Those who knew the dynamics of the Mayfield marriage understood that Elfreide's sole purpose in life was to cater to his every whim and domestic need. She was a devoted and multitalented homemaker who tailor-made Mayfield's suits from bolts of fabric. Wanda Joyce, Elfreide's best friend, recalled that Elfreide "loved him so much that she'd be happy to live under a rock with him." Elfreide's sister told others the same thing. For his part, Mayfield was utterly domineering toward Elfreide. He ruled his home with an iron hand. Whatever he wanted, he got. According to the female TEU library staff, "he ordered her around like a martinet," and she was his "doormat." Elfreide suffered in silence at his verbal abuse as well as his constant philandering.

Wanda Joyce thought that Mayfield had "cracked, that he went crazy and killed [Linda]." Elfreide never told her that, but she did visit her the week after Linda's death. She looked "drawn and upset," and told Wanda, "They think Jim did it, but we've all taken polygraphs and passed." She added that "the stress is unbearable. It is all a nightmare." But Elfreide stood by him through thick and thin. Ultimately she saved his life as his alibi witness, a debt he owed her until the day he died on July 12, 2019.

Mayfield's executive assistant and successor at the library, Olene Harned, offered insight into Mayfield's mindset in the days before Linda's killing. Mayfield loved his job and his life at the university and on Lake Palestine, she explained. After moving around every three to four years in his twenty-year career, he felt he had finally found his niche and landed a position of respect and standing. At age forty-four, he hoped to remain dean and director of the TEU library for the rest of his career.

According to Olene, when Mayfield was fired, he was devastated. He blamed Linda for "ruining" his career. He told Olene that he and Elfreide had decided to move to Houston and pick up the pieces of their shattered lives. Elfreide had family there. He was afraid Linda was going to follow him to Houston: "If she does, I'll never be rid of her."

Yet Olene knew the truth was more complicated. Mayfield was equally obsessed with Linda and couldn't stay away from her. He was exhausted by the consequences of the affair and wanted to break it off with her. But he couldn't muster the will to do it.

It was apparent to Olene and the other female library staff that Mayfield's sexual appetite for Linda had torn him and his family apart and destroyed his professional life. His secretary, Sophia Lenderman, recalled that "it was common knowledge Jim wanted to get rid of her, that he was tired of the relationship. He talked of giving her up, but somehow couldn't because he was sexually addicted to her."

On the morning Linda was killed, Mayfield arrived at work an hour early, a little after 7:00 A.M. Waiting for him was library staff member Ann White. She had just received a phone call informing her that Linda had been "badly beaten." He insisted that Ann drive him to the Embarcadero. While they sat in the car looking at the police activity outside the apartment, rather than express concern for Linda, Mayfield angrily exclaimed how she had "ruined him, cost him his job, and caused a lot of problems for him." Late Friday afternoon, after he had completed his police interview, Mayfield went to see Chad Edwards, a friend and university music professor, at his home in Lake Palestine. During the several-hour visit, he "came unglued, just crying and crying," and waited until dark for the police to come and arrest him. Close to another nervous breakdown, he returned home to the all-forgiving Elfreide.

On Monday after the murder, he came into the office and told Olene he had failed a privately administered polygraph commissioned by his lawyer, and would try again. He was shaking and crying, with "tears dripping down his chin." Olene realized he was "scared to death for his own hide. It was not grief for Linda." He told Olene, "I'm scared to death that I'm going to be implicated in her murder."

In addition to interviewing Mayfield's family, colleagues, and associates, Centurion spoke to people who were close to Linda. Coworkers said that, in the days after her suicide attempt and just before her death, she told them that she was "having problems with Mayfield" and vowed that she was "going to get him back no matter what." Wednesday, June 8, Linda's second-to-last day on earth, was also Jim Mayfield's birthday. He turned forty-four. That morning, Linda dropped by his office and gave him a set of bells that, ironically, she said brought good luck and would ward off evil spirits. Sophia Lenderman remembered how adoringly, almost worshipfully, Linda looked at Mayfield that morning. That lunch hour they spent alone in Paula's apartment. Linda showered him with gifts, including a new tennis outfit, cologne, socks, and a painting done by Linda. According to Mayfield in an early deposition, they only "necked."

That evening, Linda went to her art class from 7:00 to 9:00 P.M., and then spent an hour or so chatting alone with her art teacher, Gloria Coughenour, a woman twice her age. In the two and a half years that Gloria had been Linda's art teacher, she had become Linda's friend and confidante. Gloria was aware of Linda's history with Mayfield and the trouble it had caused for everyone involved. That night, Linda seemed excited that her brother-in-law had gotten her a job in Baytown, some twenty-five miles east of Houston, where he and Linda's sister, Carolyn, lived. It was Gloria's impression that Mayfield did not fit into Linda's plans, that Linda was starting anew and had let Mayfield know about this and her move to Houston. Coughenour was not aware that on the next day, June 9, Linda had a job interview lined up at a local Tyler bank. No one, except maybe Mayfield, knew exactly what Linda's real intentions were.

—

In April 1990, Kerry lost his father, Earnest, to cancer. His grief put him in a deep funk. But then came good news a year and a half later. On September 18, 1991, the CCA reversed Kerry's conviction and ordered a new trial. The court had decided that Dr. Grigson's testimony was in fact both inadmissible and harmful to Kerry in convincing the jury of his future dangerousness in the punishment phase. A technicality, yes, but an opportunity for freedom after fourteen years of dangerous and brutal confinement.

Scott Howe had accomplished his mission. He also knew he now needed to step aside. His strength was as an appellate attorney, and Kerry needed a trial litigator for this second trial. Scott and Kerry asked me to help them with the selection. I suggested Paul Nugent in Houston. I had worked with Nugent and his partner, Mike DeGeurin, in freeing Clarence Brandley from death row.

Nugent was delighted to take on the case and agreed to represent Kerry pro bono.

———

By the early 1990s, A. D. Clark was long gone from the Smith County district attorney's office. Jack Skeen—Clark's first cousin, their mothers were sisters—was the new DA. He and his top trial prosecutor, David Dobbs, would be prosecuting Kerry. In the fall of 1991, before Nugent came on board, Dobbs and I had traded discovery material. Among the more important exchanges, he gave me the hitherto suppressed grand jury testimony of Hoehn, Taylor, and the Dykes brothers; and access to the eighty-four-page police investigative report. I gave him a twenty-two-page memo on why Centurion believed Mayfield was guilty. I tried in vain to convince him of Kerry's innocence and Mayfield's guilt. Dobbs said he believed Mayfield loved Linda and was impressed that Mayfield would cry whenever he spoke about her. Much to my horror, he revealed to Mayfield my sources of information and what they had said about him.

One evening, Dobbs and I visited the crime scene—Paula's now vacant apartment—and reenacted the moment when Paula came in the door and saw Linda's killer. We re-created the lighting conditions and took turns being Paula and the killer. It was clear to both of us that this was a perfect visual environment to make accurate observations. Dobbs therefore stunned me during this exercise when he said he didn't believe it was Kerry whom Paula had seen, but rather Hoehn, and that Kerry was in the closet where the knife was found. I retorted in shocked disbelief that Paula had described Mayfield to a T, and Hoehn looked nothing like the man Paula described.

Preparing for trial, Paul Nugent gained access to Dobbs's files and discovered the 1989 memo from Collard to the International Association for Identification explaining why he had aged the patio prints to the hour, despite knowing it was wrong to do so. There appeared to be four missing pages from Hoehn's grand jury testimony, and Dobbs assured Paul that he would search for these.

On March 4, 1992, Kerry was removed from death row and transported to the Smith County jail to await trial. Without authorization and behind Paul Nugent's back, Dobbs confronted Kerry when he arrived at the jail. He attempted to interrogate Kerry about his fingerprints at the scene, a blatant and unethical violation of the prohibition against interviewing a defendant without his attorney present. Judge Tunnell later upbraided Dobbs for this misconduct.

Paul attempted to prevent the retrial by arguing that, under the rule of double jeopardy, the State should not be permitted to retry Kerry for the same crime when, in its first prosecution, the State had hidden critical exculpatory evidence from the defense and the court, and suborned perjury from numerous witnesses. If the judge were to agree with Nugent's arguments, a retrial would be precluded and Kerry would be set free.

In order to make his determination, Judge Tunnell conducted a series of hearings in the fall of 1992, focusing on these allegations of police and prosecutorial misconduct, to decide if the rule of double jeopardy applied.

Many witnesses testified at the hearings, including A. D. Clark, Collard, Dobbs, and Eddie Clark. Shyster Jackson was even brought in from Missouri state prison. He recanted his entire trial testimony, admitting, "I lied to save myself," and testified that he was coached, fed information, and shown victim photos by A. D. Clark. His trial testimony had all been a sham. In his jailhouse conversations with Kerry, Cook had always maintained his innocence.

At the conclusion of the hearings, Judge Tunnell flabbergasted the defense by announcing that the trial would proceed, and that he would reserve ruling on the double jeopardy issue until after the conclusion of the trial. That made no sense. It defeated the purpose of the hearings, which was to determine if there should be a trial at all.

Citing the substantial media presence in Tyler, Tunnell granted a change of venue to Georgetown, Texas, at that time a conservative town and the seat of Williamson County in Central Texas, twenty-five miles north of Austin and more than two hundred miles from Tyler.

Judge Tunnell also made a series of pretrial rulings in favor of the State that hamstrung Kerry's defense. The most damaging was the exclusion of the grand jury testimony of Robert Hoehn, James Taylor, and the Dykes brothers that A. D. Clark had hidden from Kerry's first defense team. Thus the jury was unable to hear an alternative reason for Kerry's prints on the patio door: that Kerry had been in Linda's apartment on Monday afternoon, June 6, to make out, the passion marks on his neck being the evidence of their romantic tryst. Without the "passion marks" testimony, Nugent knew he wouldn't be able to make the argument that Kerry left his fingerprints on the patio door days before the murder. He argued vigorously against the judge's prohibition, saying that under Texas evidentiary rules he should be allowed to question these witnesses using their prior statements in order to fully complete their conversations with Kerry, and not limit these to Kerry telling them about observing Linda nude in her apartment. In response, the judge challenged Nugent to put Kerry on the stand if he wanted the jury to hear about the passion marks and Kerry's make-out session with Linda. Of course, such testimony coming from Kerry alone, without his friends' corroboration, would sound highly dubious. Thus Judge Tunnell's ruling allowed Dobbs and Skeen to make the same deceptive pitch A. D. Clark had used in the first trial—that this was a "stranger-on-stranger" crime by a perverted sexual deviant.

The judge also precluded Nugent from telling the jury about the prosecutorial misconduct that had tainted the previous trial.

Nugent was forbidden from mentioning Shyster Jackson's false confession or Collard's unscientific aging of the patio door fingerprints. The past misdeeds of the district attorney's office were wiped clean for this new jury. Judge Tunnell also set tight limits on what the defense witnesses could say about the evidence implicating Jim Mayfield in the killing. For instance, the judge precluded Dr. Mears from telling the jury that Mayfield had asked him days after the murder how to beat a polygraph, and had admitted to ordering the book *The Sexual Criminal,* which depicted wounds from sexual organ mutilation that eerily resembled Linda's. These judicial rulings significantly tilted the trial in favor of the prosecution, just as State-sponsored perjury had prejudiced the first trial.

The second trial began at the end of November 1992, fourteen years after the first. The State's case was a more refined and somewhat expanded version of what it had presented at the earlier trial. Paula was now certain that the man she'd seen was the defendant and not Mayfield. Watching Dobbs examining Paula, I thought back to our conversation in Paula's apartment a year earlier when Dobbs told me he believed it was *Hoehn* whom Paula had seen, *not* Kerry. Yet here he was eliciting from her the exact opposite, that it was Kerry she had seen, not Hoehn.

Since Robert Hoehn was dead, Nugent didn't have the chance, on cross-examination, to hammer away at his testimony about the night of the murder and perhaps to elicit an admission that his testimony at the 1978 trial was false and coerced by the belligerent Michael Thompson. Judge Tunnell allowed attorneys to read most of Hoehn's 1978 trial testimony to the jury, including the more salacious parts. The movie was also played for the jury.

Since Collard had earlier admitted that there was no scientific way to age a fingerprint, he got around this by cleverly describing it as a "fresh print." Dobbs brought in Danny Carter, supervisor of the Latent Fingerprint Department of the Texas Department of Public

Safety, who confirmed that it was Kerry's fingerprints on the patio door. Tunnell decided to ask him outside of the jury's presence if it was appropriate to describe a print as "fresh." Carter emphatically said "no." Calling a print "fresh" was just another way of estimating its age, and a fingerprint examiner could not estimate a print's age. Such honesty from a prosecution witness was unexpected, even if the jury did not hear it. Fingerprint expert George Bonebrake confirmed this point for the jury when he testified as a defense witness.

Now that the prosecution no longer had the false confession of Shyster Jackson, it came up with a brand-new "confession" witness, Robert Wickham, a former reserve deputy sheriff. On September 26, 1991, one week after the CCA had ordered a new trial, he informed the prosecutor for the first time that Kerry had confessed to him in an elevator during the 1978 trial. He repeated his story to the jury in 1992. He said that, while he had been escorting Kerry to the courtroom, Kerry had blurted, "I killed her and I don't give a shit what they do to me." Wickham's excuse for his thirteen years of silence was that he didn't think it was admissible—there was no one else who heard it.

Wickham's account had a glaring flaw. He said that Kerry had been handcuffed and was wearing a jail jumpsuit in the elevator. Yet Smith County had a strict policy that inmates should be escorted into the courtroom in civilian clothes and not in handcuffs, so as not to prejudice the jurors. Also, Wickham's account was transparently self-serving. He managed a restaurant that was a law enforcement hangout. His employees considered him a "wannabe cop." As a reserve deputy sheriff, he wasn't a real deputy sheriff. He was a volunteer who was required to serve twenty unpaid hours a month to keep his reserve status. His testimony at Kerry's second trial elevated his status among the Tyler cops who frequented his restaurant.

As part of maintaining the fiction that Kerry never knew Linda, Dobbs convinced the judge to order the journalist David Hanners to testify. David, who knew very well how Kerry had been framed, reluctantly told the jury that Kerry always insisted he never met Linda, nor was he ever in her apartment. He said his prints got on the door when he was watching her from the outside. This testimony hurt Kerry's defense and was a key example of how this lie came back to bite him. It wasn't until Paul Nugent and I were preparing Kerry for trial in the summer of 1992 that he finally came clean about meeting Linda at the pool and making out with her in her apartment. He told us what he had sworn to his father and offered us a heartfelt apology. Unfortunately, given the judge's exclusion of the "passion marks" grand jury testimony of Robert Hoehn and the Dykes brothers, Nugent had no credible way of offering the truth to the jury. The lie had taken on a life of its own.

Dobbs put Mayfield, Elfreide, and Louella on the stand. Mayfield testified for hours. Dobbs took him through his relationship with Linda from beginning to end. Mayfield assured the jury that his sexual relationship with Linda ended once he returned to his wife on May 19. From that point on it was akin to a father-daughter relationship, and he had encouraged her to get on with her life and start dating other men. He, of course, denied killing Linda. Under cross, he denied telling Ann White that Linda had ruined his career and couldn't recall if he told Olene Harned he was afraid Linda might follow him to Houston. Even if she did, he said, it would not have been a problem. He admitted that he and Linda would meet in Paula's apartment at night when Paula was away. He denied playing tennis a lot. He testified that Elfreide and Linda were on friendly terms.

Elfreide and Louella steadfastly provided Mayfield with his alibi. They said he never left the house the night of June 9–10. Elfreide denied telling her husband that Linda was not to live with them on Lake Palestine. She didn't remember feeling animosity toward Linda, testifying, implausibly, that even though Jim's affair had cost him his career, she didn't harbor resentment toward Linda. Linda moved in with them because they needed someone to clean the house. When her husband returned home after living with Linda in mid-May 1977, she and he did not discuss what happened because "it was over" and "I didn't think about it anymore." She didn't recall if, after Linda's attempted suicide, she exclaimed to Wanda Joyce, "When will it ever end?" For her part, Louella admitted to threatening to kill Linda if her affair with her father continued.

In Kerry's defense, Paul Nugent focused on developing Jim Mayfield as the more likely suspect. Unfortunately, given the judge's pretrial rulings, each witness was only permitted to tell the jury snippets of what they knew. Nine faculty members and staff testified for the defense. Olene Harned, Mayfield's successor at the library, had taken Paula into her home for a few days after the crime. While there, Paula told Olene more than once that she thought it was Mayfield she had seen that night. Olene also testified that Mayfield often wore white tennis shorts around campus and was worried that Linda might follow him to Houston.

Library staffer Ann White testified that the morning after the murder Mayfield angrily complained that Linda had ruined his career. Professor Andrew Szarka told the jury what he'd told the police on Friday afternoon, June 10—that the previous evening, mere hours before she was murdered, Linda had dropped by his house for a visit. Linda had been distressed about her relationship with Mayfield, saying that she had told Mayfield she wanted to date other men and that Mayfield had reacted badly to this. Professor Gary Mears was only allowed to testify that Mayfield played tennis a lot and fit the description of the man Paula had seen.

Doris Carpenter, manager of the Embarcadero, remembered Paula coming into her office several days after the murder and, when asked if she'd been scared when she saw the man in Linda's room, replying, "No, because it was Mayfield."

In his summation, Dobbs pointed out the connection between Linda's missing calf stocking and the scene in the movie when the little boy snuck into his mother's room after watching her play with herself. He reminded the jury how excited Kerry was while watching the movie, that he had started masturbating and climaxed on the carpet. In his closing remarks, Skeen repeatedly emphasized to the jury that the defense had offered no alternative explanation for the appearance of Kerry's fingerprints on the patio door other than that he placed them there the night he killed her. Skeen, of course, knew full well that an alternative explanation existed, and that the judge had simply ruled it out of evidence.

Two unbelievable things happened during jury deliberations. The first was the jury sending a note to the judge that said, "We have found the nylon stocking in the jeans of Linda Jo Edwards." Being good finders of fact, the jury had decided to remove the jeans from the plastic evidence bag in which they had been sealed for fifteen years. As they shook them to their natural length, the "missing stocking" fell out of the right leg. And lo and behold, it had no body parts in it! Somehow, neither the Tyler police nor anyone from the Smith County district attorney's office had ever thought to explore the legs and pockets of the jeans for evidence.

As the jury deliberations stretched into their third day, the second incredible thing happened. On December 16, Paul saw Dobbs reading the original copy of Hoehn's grand jury testimony. Not trusting him, he snatched it out of Dobbs's hands. To his shock, the transcript contained the missing four pages that Dobbs had repeatedly denied having. Nugent read the omitted pages in astonishment. When Hoehn had been asked whether Kerry was watching the movie on the night of the murder, Hoehn had said, "No, no, the movie was on and he wasn't paying any attention to it." Meanwhile, Dobbs had just gotten through arguing to the jury that the movie had so excited Kerry that he had decided to attack and butcher

Linda. Nugent immediately showed the missing pages and their highly exculpatory contents to Judge Tunnell. The judge denied his request to show them to the jury. Once again, he used his rulings to stack the deck against Kerry.

After five days, the jury informed Tunnell they were hopelessly deadlocked. He declared a mistrial, denied Kerry bail, and shipped him back to the Smith County jail to await his third trial. Afterward, Centurion interviewed seven of the jurors and discovered they were deadlocked at 6–6. The unexplained patio prints and Kerry denying he knew Linda were the primary reasons for the guilty votes. Those who voted not guilty strongly suspected Mayfield. They believed it was a crime of passion committed by someone who was intimate with, extremely angry at, and obsessed with her. Mayfield fit the bill. They also characterized Mayfield, his wife, and daughter as "liars." They were impressed that the university witnesses, who did not know Kerry but did know Mayfield, were willing to testify against Mayfield at great inconvenience, driving two hundred miles each way.

Paul had fought Dobbs and Skeen to a draw despite Judge Tunnell's restrictive and exclusionary evidentiary rulings and the prosecution's chicanery. In January 1993, Tunnell finally issued his ruling on double jeopardy. Tunnell found that Collard's aging of the fingerprints and A. D. Clark's insistence that he do so was calculated to mislead the court and the jury. He scolded the prosecution for not disclosing to the defense its agreement with Shyster Jackson in exchange for his incriminating testimony. He characterized Dobbs's jailhouse encounter with Kerry as "a serious breach of duty and protocol." Despite all of this, however, Judge Tunnell did not rule in favor of releasing Kerry on the grounds of double jeopardy. Instead, he allowed the district attorney's office to proceed with yet another trial.

Judge Joe Tunnell retired in June 1993. Kerry's third trial began on January 31, 1994, with Judge Robert D. Jones presiding. After being voted off the bench in Travis County (where Austin is the county seat) several years earlier, he became a visiting judge appointed by a regional administrator to assist those courthouses with a shortage of judges. The press dubbed this program "Have Gavel, Will Travel." Judge Jones adopted Judge Tunnell's evidentiary rulings in their entirety and secured the same courtroom in Georgetown for the third trial. With minor variations, all of the witnesses testified as they had in the second trial. What set the third trial apart was the participation of two expert witnesses from the FBI's elite Behavioral Science Unit in Quantico, Virginia, a department dedicated to the research and study of violent criminal offenders, especially serial and sexual killers.

The prosecution's star expert witness was FBI agent David Gomez. He had just completed two years of training as a violent crimes analyst for the agency's Behavioral Science Unit. One of his responsibilities was to serve as a consultant to local police agencies in Texas. On the defense side was Robert Ressler, a world-renowned specialist in sexual homicide. Ressler was one of the founding fathers of the Behavioral Science Unit, and had served as its supervisory special agent and top criminologist for sixteen years until he retired in 1990. He had coauthored the two bibles on violent homicide, *Sexual Homicide: Patterns and Motives* (1988) and the *Crime Classification Manual* (1992). Gomez conceded at trial that these two books were important resource materials during his recently completed training.

Gomez classified the Linda Jo Edwards murder as a "lust murder," which he defined as a homicide focused on the sexual organs of the victim up to and including the removal of body parts. He concluded this was done by a stranger who was not intimate with the victim; that the offender was motivated from a personal sense of sexual ambivalence, inadequacy, and immaturity. Linda's lust murderer destroyed her sexual parts to neuter her. Amazingly, Gomez did not see "overkill" in the attack—an excess of violence—only the amount of force needed to control and kill her. This is why he wouldn't classify it as a "domestic homicide," which is a killing that occurs between persons who are personally intimate and often involves overkill rooted in rage. Gomez believed the attacking of the vaginal area was the lust aspect of the crime, not overkill. In his conclusion he agreed with Dobbs's theory that voyeuristic activities could establish a fantasy phase of a crime and reflect the offender's sexual frustrations.

Ressler looked at this homicide differently. He classified it as a domestic homicide, most likely perpetrated by a former lover of the victim. He saw clear evidence of "extensive overkill," which is frequently present in domestic homicides. The wounds indicated extreme fury toward Linda. The heavy vaginal damage denoted a previous relationship that drove the killer to destroy the area of his interest in her that had caused his own destruction. Ressler rejected the idea that this was a lust murder motivated by sexual inadequacy or ambivalence, neither of which he had ever encountered as motivation for a mutilation murder. He was also prepared to testify that persons who engaged in voyeurism, or who were allegedly peeping Toms, were not confrontational and did not perpetrate violent sexual homicides.

But Ressler's crucial testimony would never be heard by the jury. During his voir dire, the preliminary examination by a judge to determine a witness's suitability to testify, Ressler told the judge that, as part of his preparation, he had read Gomez's testimony on the plane ride down from Virginia. Because of that, Judge Jones barred him from testifying, erroneously declaring that Ressler had violated the rule that prohibits witnesses from learning opposing witness testimony before they testify. Paul correctly pointed out that Texas evidentiary law prevented *fact* witnesses, not *expert* witnesses, from learning the opposition's testimony beforehand. It was perfectly acceptable as a matter of practice and case law for experts to review the testimony of their opposite number prior to testifying. Judge Jones, however, refused to concede the point. He dismissed Robert Ressler from the witness stand, leaving the jury with the impression that the FBI's Behavioral Science Unit had one opinion of Linda's murder—the opinion of Agent Gomez. Skeen took full advantage of this. In his summation he mentioned Gomez's name numerous times, wrapping up with the words "What Dave Gomez was telling you is the key to this case."

Judge Jones's outrageous ruling had disastrous consequences for Kerry.

Deadlocked after several days of deliberation, the jury asked the court to read back Agent Gomez's testimony. A half hour after this reading, on February 23, the jury found Kerry Max Cook guilty of capital murder.

The punishment phase lasted five days. Paul fought long and hard to save Kerry's life, but the result was predictable, considering the horrid nature of the crime. The day of reckoning came on March 3, 1994. Before sentencing, the judge asked Kerry if he had anything to say. He responded, "Yes, sir. With respect to the jury, with respect to the Court, I am an innocent man and the Lord forgive them, for they know not what they do." With that, Judge Jones sentenced him to death by lethal injection, just as Kerry had been sentenced sixteen years before.

After spending the last two years in county jails during the retrials, Kerry returned to death row a beaten and devastated man. He was one month shy of his thirty-eighth birthday, but his hair had turned prematurely gray. Meanwhile, Paul refused to give up. In the face of formidable odds, he resolved to appeal the conviction to the Texas CCA. At this point, he had been handling Kerry's representation pro bono for nearly four years. In recognition of Paul's unwavering dedication, Centurion was able to raise enough money to sufficiently compensate him for his labors in preparing the appeal.

One year later, in July 1995, Paul Nugent filed a mammoth 213-page brief detailing sixty instances of systemic prosecutorial misconduct and egregious judicial exclusions of exculpatory evidence throughout all three trials. Kerry couldn't help but be impressed by his attorney's efforts, but he had suffered one disappointment after another. The CCA was considered at that time to be a predominantly conservative court. The odds were heavily stacked against him.

The CCA, however, astonished everyone. On November 6, 1996, it reversed Kerry's conviction, excoriating the prosecution for its behavior and the trial courts for their exclusion of favorable evidence for the defendant. Judge Charles Baird, in his concurring opinion, argued that a retrial of Mr. Cook should be prohibited due to the fact that "prosecutorial misconduct has so tainted the truth-finding process that it renders a subsequent fair trial impossible." He wrote that the State had "allowed itself to gain a conviction based on fraud and ignored its own duty to seek the truth" and that "the State's misconduct in this case does not consist of an isolated incident or the doing of a police officer, but consists of the deliberate misconduct by members of the bar representing the State." He found that "the Illicit manipulation of the evidence on the part of the State permeated the entire investigation of the crime."

The majority opinion written by Judge Stephen Mansfield vacated the conviction but fell short of precluding a retrial. He found that "prosecutorial and police misconduct have tainted this entire matter from the outset." He rebuked the trial court for prohibiting the defense from introducing the "highly exculpatory" grand jury testimony of witnesses that offered an innocent explanation for how Kerry's prints got on the patio door. Perhaps most significantly, the majority ruled that if the prosecution decides to retry

Cook a fourth time, the court must exclude from evidence all statements made by the now deceased Robert Hoehn. Consequently, his tawdry yet mostly fictitious tale of steamy sex and graphic voyeurism on the night of the murder was now strictly off-limits.

So once again, this time to await his fourth trial, sheriff's deputies transported Kerry back to the Smith County jail from death row. It was August 6, 1997, twenty years and one day since his August 5, 1977, arrest.

A chastened, but increasingly hostile, Judge Jones set a $100,000 cash bond at a November 11 bond hearing, believing along with Skeen that this amount was well beyond Kerry's defense team's ability to meet. Two days later, Jay Regan, Centurion's board chairman and a Wall Street investor, wired $100,000 to the Smith County sheriff's office, much to the shock and dismay of Jones and Skeen. (Regan, trusting Kerry, knew he would get the money back so long as Kerry honored the terms of his release.)

Later that day, November 13, 1997, Kerry Max Cook walked out of the Smith County jail into the arms of his mother, Evelyn. His newfound freedom was exhilarating. But he was also scared, as he knew his battle with Smith County was far from over. Amid the sidewalk celebration, with reporters and cameras all around, Kerry, Paul, and I spotted David Dobbs standing across the street, glaring at us.

From prison, Kerry had developed a friendship with Dallas residents Mikaela and Richard Raine, who believed in his innocence. They generously invited him to live with them and their four children while he was awaiting trial, even giving him a Jack Russell terrier named Everton. Dallas criminal defense attorney Donya Witherspoon hired Cook as her paralegal. Soon he moved into an apartment on his own with Everton. Urinalysis drug tests in Tyler were a condition of his bail. His stomach churned every time he entered the town, fearing the police would set him up on some phony charge. Instead, life handed Kerry a gift. At a meeting of Amnesty International in Dallas, he met a lovely young woman named Sandra Pressey. Before long, the two of them fell in love. They have been life partners ever since.

On the eve of the February 1999 fourth trial, and despite the CCA ruling, prosecutor Skeen vowed not to rest until Cook was back on death row. Dobbs added that they "would never allow him to plea, not even to a life sentence." They wanted to put Kerry Max Cook in the ground. Centurion was equally committed to ensuring that Kerry's fourth trial would be his last. We knew he needed a well-heeled defense stocked with top-drawer forensic experts and a deep bench of legal talent to support Paul Nugent. This was no time to spare expense. A wealthy benefactor, David Gelbaum, stepped up and authorized a budget of $365,000. Dallas attorney Cheryl Wattley and Houston attorney Rocket Rosen joined the team. Eight different experts in the fields of eyewitness identification, visual environment, false confessions, forensic pathology, and psychiatry stood ready to offer their expertise. Among them was Robert Ressler, godfather of the FBI's Behavioral Science Unit. As 1998 sped by, Judge Jones picked Bastrop, a largely rural county thirty miles southeast of Austin, as the site for the trial. Jury selection would begin mid-February 1999.

The week before the trial brought potential new DNA evidence. For the first time in the twenty-two-year history of the case, the prosecution had submitted Linda's underwear to the state's crime lab for examination. Remarkably, the lab found semen stains large enough to obtain the donor's profile. With both sides agreeing, Judge Jones ordered DNA testing and the trial to proceed concurrently. We expected the DNA results sometime during the trial. Dobbs told the press that the semen "could only have been left by the killer." We agreed, confident it wasn't Kerry's and believing it was Mayfield's.

Then there was more: Just days before the trial, the prosecution broke its vow never to allow Kerry to plead out. Dobbs put a no-contest deal on the table, offering Kerry a forty-year sentence in exchange for a guilty plea. Kerry rejected it out of hand. Dobbs then proposed a deal that would give Judge Jones discretion to sentence Kerry to a term less than forty years. Again, Kerry dismissed it out of hand. There was no way he was going to entrust his future to Judge Jones. Finally, on February 16, 1999, minutes before jury selection was to begin, Dobbs offered a no-contest deal that included a lesser charge (murder, but not capital murder), no admission of guilt, and a sentence of twenty years. Since Kerry had already served the time, he could go home that day, a completely free man, with no supervision of any kind. The only downside was that he would be a convicted murderer. The judge gave him one hour to decide.

We all huddled back at the house Centurion had rented for the team. We told Kerry that it was his life. If he wanted to go to trial, we were ready. If he accepted the plea, we could understand that as well. He left the room and took a few minutes by himself. We waited.

Then he came back in and announced his decision. He was going to take the deal.

He had suffered so much trauma on death row that he could not face the risk of going back there to await execution yet again. He chose guaranteed and immediate freedom, home with Sandra that night, rather than taking the chance of another conviction in an extremely conservative county with a hostile and vengeful judge. That evening Kerry, Sandra, and the entire team celebrated at an upscale Austin restaurant. Many of us had been fighting for Kerry for nearly ten years. We took turns toasting each other. We couldn't wait to learn what the DNA results would be from the semen stains on Linda's panties.

At last, on April 16, 1999, the state crime lab spoke. The semen unquestionably belonged to James Mayfield, not Kerry Max Cook. Mayfield had testified at both of the retrials in 1992 and 1994 that he had not had sex with his former lover following her suicide attempt three weeks before her murder. While the district attorney's office was stunned, David Dobbs still tried desperately to salvage his dignity. He claimed that the DNA results didn't necessarily clear Kerry of the crime. Perhaps Mayfield's semen had been deposited when Mayfield claimed he'd last had sex with Linda three weeks before, and survived three weeks of wear and laundering, an absurd hypothesis. Before he had submitted the panties for DNA analysis, Dobbs had agreed, reasonably, that the semen had to belong to Linda's killer. Now, however, with the foundation of Kerry's plea deal—and his office's reputation—in question, he still insisted that Kerry was guilty, that the Tyler authorities had the right man, and that the new DNA evidence was "irrelevant."

The DNA evidence reinvigorated Kerry, though. It gave him new confidence and inspired him to take his exoneration to the world—literally. He spoke eloquently about wrongful convictions, the ills of capital punishment, and the flaws of America's criminal justice system to audiences in London, Paris, Rome, Geneva, and throughout America. He became a sought-after motivational speaker, telling his story to inspire others to never give up, no matter how dire the circumstances. Harvard, Princeton, and other universities welcomed him. He testified before the Texas State Legislature in favor of a moratorium on the death penalty.

His story was one of six featured in the theater production *The Exonerated,* which opened in New York in October 2000, and ran in venues across the country. His story was also adapted into a Hollywood movie by the same name, starring Aidan Quinn. In 2007, William Morrow published his memoir, *Chasing Justice*.

To Kerry, however, his greatest accomplishment during these years was the birth of his son, Kerry Justice Cook. "KJ," as Kerry and Sandra call him, will be twenty-four in 2024.

Despite all the adulation and accolades, Kerry struggled in his life after prison. He suffered from an acute case of PTSD and depression. The murder conviction still plagued him and his family, making it difficult to find work and keep it, and to sign leases and other legal documents. Occasionally, neighbors shunned him when they learned of his past. These problems and his long-held, deep desire for legal exoneration finally inspired Kerry to act. Exoneration by much of the public was not enough. He wanted the Texas criminal justice system to officially recognize his innocence.

In 2012, the Innocence Project took up his cause, bringing together a team led by Gary Udashen in Texas and Nina Morrison in New York. Three years later, in September 2015, they filed a writ of habeas corpus in Smith County, seeking to reverse Kerry's murder conviction and obtain a finding of actual innocence based on the 1999 DNA results and systemic misconduct by police and prosecutors.

Their investigation uncovered a suspicious decision by the Smith County law authorities regarding a bloody hair found on Linda's buttocks that was not Kerry's or Linda's. In 1999, when the authorities in Tyler submitted the hair to the crime lab along with Linda's underwear, the lab informed them that it, too, was suitable for DNA testing. But soon after the lab found the semen to be a match to Mayfield, the district attorney's office ordered the police to retrieve the hair follicle and not submit it for testing.

If this bloody hair had been tested for DNA and it proved to be Mayfield's, it would have blown the case wide open, because neither Mayfield nor the DA could have easily explained such results away. But they never had to. The Tyler authorities went on to destroy the hair follicle in 2001, in direct violation of a Texas statute enacted eight months before that barred destruction of evidence suitable for DNA testing. Jack Skeen was still the DA at that time. He did not leave office until 2003, when he became a Smith County judge.

In early April 2016, Skeen's successor as Smith County district attorney, Matt Bingham, at the request of Gary Udashen, surprisingly agreed to set up an on-the-record interview with Jim Mayfield at his Houston home. Bingham granted Mayfield immunity for whatever he might say, put him under oath, and allowed his longstanding attorney, Buck Files, to attend. The ever-faithful Elfreide sat in as well.

Forty years had passed since Linda's murder. Mayfield was now an eighty-three-year-old retiree who had served many years, ironically, as an assistant building manager of the Harris County jail. The unrestricted interview lasted two hours. Udashen took the lead in asking questions, with follow-ups by Bingham. The session yielded several significant Mayfield admissions. He admitted for the first time that he and Linda did have sex at lunchtime in Paula's apartment to celebrate his forty-fourth birthday on June 8, and that Linda had showered him with gifts, including a new tennis outfit.

He professed surprise that his semen was found in the underwear she was wearing the night of her homicide, because the last time they had sex was the day before. He couldn't understand why she would wear dirty underwear two days in a row.

He admitted that he was sexually addicted to Linda. Whenever he was around her, he was weak and couldn't resist the temptation to have sex. In fact, practically every time they were together, they had sex. "I'm not the strongest person when it comes to Linda," he said. He knew he "needed to stay away from Linda, best I could."

At the time of her death, the most important thing for him was to save his marriage; Linda "came second." He was trying to put his life back together, and "stop the sex with Linda." If he continued to see her, it would start all over again. His librarian career was destroyed. He had lost not only his job but also his house on the lake, and he had almost lost his wife because of her. He said he "wasn't going to destroy my marriage for Linda." He had promised Elfreide that it was over between him and Linda. If Elfreide had ever found out about what happened on his birthday at Paula's, that would have ended their marriage.

But Linda wouldn't let it go. She wanted to keep the relationship. After his birthday, she still wanted to be together. She "wasn't happy" he had decided to return to Elfreide. When she showed up at his house the evening of her murder, it was apparent that she was still trying to see him. She had visited him four times that day. He had to stop seeing her. He knew that somehow he had to end their relationship.

He admitted that he had angrily exclaimed to Ann White, while they were sitting in her car in the Embarcadero parking lot before Linda's body was brought out, that Linda had "ruined" his career. He had denied saying that at Kerry's trials. He conceded that he might have told Olene Harned he was afraid Linda might follow him to Houston, that Linda had that in her mind. He had also denied this at Kerry's trials.

Perhaps unknowingly, by making these admissions, Mayfield in effect laid out his motivation for killing Linda. To preserve that which he was desperate to hold on to—his marriage to Elfreide—he had to end his relationship with Linda. She had already destroyed his cherished way of life and a career perfectly suited to his ambition. He knew he did not have the will to overcome his sexual addiction to her, and that she would once again cause his ruination if she followed him to Houston. As he told Olene Harned several days before the murder, "If she [moves to Houston], I'll never be rid of her." Something had to be done to stop the relationship. Those who knew him well believed his explosive temper got the best of him and, in a fit of rage, he had cracked and uncontrollably destroyed those parts of Linda that had destroyed him.

In the interview, Mayfield also admitted for the first time that Professor Mears had confronted him about the illustrated mutilation book entitled *The Sexual Criminal*. At his depositions prior to Kerry's trials, Mayfield had denied having any knowledge of the book's existence. Because of his denial, Judge Tunnell and later Judge Jones prohibited Paul from introducing the book to the jury and questioning Mayfield about it.

Mayfield said he never saw or spoke with Paula after Linda was killed, and never tried to reach out to see how she was doing. When Udashen asked if he was aware that Paula was telling people he was the man she saw that night, he said he was. Curiously, during this interview he never said Paula was wrong in identifying him at the scene. As he always had, he claimed he was home that night with Elfreide and Louella. He never left the house. Standing by her husband of sixty-two years, Elfreide interjected, "Until I die, I know he was home with me that night."

Because Jack Skeen was now sitting as a Smith County judge, a judge from outside the county was appointed to hear Kerry's habeas claims—Judge Jack Carter from Texarkana. The hearing was scheduled for Monday, June 6. In the meantime, Udashen and Bingham negotiated behind the scenes for a settlement. David Dobbs, who had long ago left office, aided Bingham in these discussions. He and Judge Skeen wanted at all costs to avoid a public hearing that would subject them to a humiliating cross-examination. For his part, Kerry wanted a full-blown hearing, a reversal of his murder conviction, and a finding of actual innocence.

On the day of the hearing, the parties reached an agreement. Since it was clear from his recent interview that Jim Mayfield had perjured himself multiple times at the second and third trials, the district attorney agreed to recommend to Judge Carter that Kerry's murder conviction be vacated. But he would recommend that his claims of actual innocence be denied. For resolution of this final issue, rather than a hearing requiring witness testimony, the parties would make oral presentations to Judge Carter in the style of closing arguments at trial. The defense would argue for actual innocence, and the prosecution would oppose it, insisting on Kerry's guilt. Judge Carter agreed to proceed on that basis.

The only person who objected to the proposed settlement was Kerry. Even though the agreement included a long-sought and groundbreaking dismissal of his conviction, Kerry vehemently argued against it. He wanted his day in court to not only prove his innocence but to hold Dobbs and Skeen accountable for the physical and psychological distress he had suffered at their hands since they entered the case decades earlier. He believed this could best be done through an open, in-court evidentiary hearing.

Nevertheless, after a long and emotional discussion the night before the hearing, Kerry, with great reluctance, finally succumbed and agreed to the settlement. But a day or two after everything was in place, Kerry, still upset that the agreement did not include a public hearing, stunned everyone when he suddenly and without warning fired his legal team. Fortunately, a noted Houston attorney, Mark Bennett, who'd previously had no involvement in the case, stepped into the breach with only one stipulation. It would be impossible for him to spend time attempting to rescind the agreement. He now only had three weeks to prepare for the actual innocence argument.

On July 1, the attorneys made their arguments for and against actual innocence. The prosecutor regurgitated the State's evidence presented during the prior three trials. Attorney Bennett focused on the pervasive prosecutorial misconduct that led to Kerry's prior false convictions and made the case for Mayfield's guilt. On July 25, Judge Carter issued his opinion in the form of recommendations to the CCA. He recommended that Kerry's murder conviction be reversed, as agreed, but that Kerry's actual innocence claim be denied. He reflected that, for a convicted person to establish actual innocence, the CCA required that the new evidence must "unquestionably" meet a "Herculean" standard.

While he found that the DNA evidence was helpful to Cook's

defense, it "required a jury to make a deductive step" that Mayfield had left it in Linda's panties the night of the murder. He therefore concluded that the DNA didn't "unquestionably" establish Cook's innocence or Mayfield's guilt. In contrast, Kerry's defense believed it was an easy deduction to make.

To believe Mayfield didn't have intercourse with Linda on the night she was murdered, but rather thirty-six hours earlier as Mayfield claimed, the jury would have had to accept that Linda wore the same soiled underwear for thirty-six hours straight—from lunchtime on Wednesday, June 8, when Mayfield admitted they had sex in Paula's apartment, until very early on June 10, shortly after midnight, when she was killed. Linda had attended an art class for several hours that Wednesday night; returned home and slept in her bedroom; dressed the next morning to visit Mayfield at his office and have lunch with him; interviewed for a job at a local bank at 1:30; and played tennis with Mayfield after that. Several hours later, she drove down to Mayfield's Lake Palestine home to confront him about their relationship. Would it not be reasonable for any set of jurors, considering these facts, to have deduced that Linda must have put on a fresh pair of underwear at some point during that day and a half, whether dressing after sex with Mayfield on Wednesday or dressing the next morning for her interview, or showering after playing tennis on a hot summer afternoon and changing into clean clothes for her early evening trip to Lake Palestine to pop in on Mayfield? Yet, for whatever reason, Judge Carter didn't see it that way.

In August 2016, Judge Carter submitted his recommended findings to the Texas CCA for it to accept or reject. Eight years later and forty-seven years into his fight for justice, Kerry Max Cook was still waiting for the court's decision. Kerry couldn't help remembering that it took the CCA eight years to deny his original appeal in the 1980s. Why this court demonstrated such an extraordinary laxity in its handling of his case, no one can say. Nevertheless, holding on for dear life, he refused to give up hope that someday the court would do the right thing. Then, without any warning, it came like a bolt of lightning from heaven above.

Scripture tells us, "If you have faith, if you say to this mountain, 'Be taken up and cast into the sea,' it will be done." The long, long arc of justice finally found its mark on June 19, 2024, when Judge Bert Richardson of the CCA, in a blistering and comprehensive 106-page opinion, threw Kerry's mountain of injustice into the sea. He wrote, "This case is riddled with allegations of State misconduct that warrant setting aside Applicant's conviction. And when it comes to solid support of actual innocence, this case contains it all—uncontroverted Brady violations, proof of false testimony, admissions of perjury, and new scientific evidence."

With that, the CCA gave Kerry what his heart longed for during those interminable lost years—pure, unadulterated exoneration. His dream to be declared an innocent man by Texas's highest court had come true. The world now knows what he has always known—the *truth* that he was framed by Smith County law enforcement and its judiciary. Vindication is so sweet!

———

Note: The title quote is from Sir Walter Scott's poem Marmion: A Tale of Flodden Field, *published in 1808. Flodden is a hill in northeast England that was the site of a famous 1513 battle between the Scots and the English, won by England.*

THE FIRE DOES NOT LIE

JOHN GRISHAM

n 1976, the U.S. Supreme Court lifted a four-year ban on executions, and the thirty-five death states were off and running. Since then, 1,572 men and 15 women have been put to death by gas, lethal injection, electric chair, and one by hanging and another by firing squad. Texas proudly leads the pack with 586 killings. Oklahoma is second with 123, barely edging out Virginia with 113, a number that is unlikely to change since that commonwealth has now outlawed capital punishment.

The Death Penalty Information Center currently lists twenty executions, half from Texas, of men who were "probably" innocent. This number cannot be confirmed because there is no clear-cut, biological proof (DNA) of innocence, and, for obvious reasons, courts tend to lose interest in a case after the defendant is dead.

Journalists and innocence advocates do not. In the realm of criminal justice, there are few subjects more tantalizing than the possibility that an innocent person has been executed. Much has been written about these twenty executions, which are described by the DPIC as having "strong evidence" of innocence.

One case, though, has attracted far more interest than the others. Not surprisingly, it happened in Texas. Oddly, though, it is the only case in which the murder weapon was arson.

In 2004, Cameron Todd Willingham was executed for a crime that never occurred.

————

Todd, as he was known, was born in 1968 in Ardmore, Oklahoma. He died thirty-six years later in Huntsville, Texas, strapped to a gurney in the world's busiest death chamber. He spent the last twelve years of his life on death row and never stopped proclaiming his innocence.

He had a rough childhood. His parents split when he was an infant and his father remarried a woman he always considered his mother. He dropped out of school in the tenth grade and dabbled in petty crime—drugs, drinking, fighting, and small-time thievery. He liked heavy metal music, loose girls, beer, whiskey, nightclubs, and honky-tonks. He also liked fast cars and trained himself to be a decent mechanic, though his employment was sketchy. When he was twenty, he met Stacy Kuykendall in a bar in Corsicana, Texas, population 24,000. Her childhood had been more unsettled than his.

Stacy and Todd began living together in a small rental house in a blue-collar part of Corsicana, an hour southeast of Dallas. Their relationship was rocky and often violent. He drank too much, spent too much time in beer joints, and chased other women. They fought and he hit her more than once. She moved out, then came back. He moved out, and they patched things up. Life settled down when Amber was born. Todd and Stacy took parenthood seriously and doted on the baby. Before long, Kameron and Karmen arrived at the same time. With three little girls, all in diapers and his responsibility, Todd decided it was time to grow up. He and Stacy were married in Ardmore in 1991.

Both struggled to find full-time employment. Todd worked here and there in construction and as a mechanic while Stacy worked in a bar owned by her brother. The family was poor, usually broke, with barely enough essentials to get by. In December 1991, they were two months behind on their rent and other bills were due. Todd had been laid off again. Christmas was approaching and they were almost out of money.

On Sunday, December 22, Todd's stepmother, Eugenia, called and talked to him. She and Todd's father were planning a visit from Oklahoma in a couple of days to see the children for Christmas. Todd was in great spirits, ready for the holidays and enjoying his small children. He was pleased because he and Stacy had taken the kids to Kmart for family photos and couldn't wait to share some with the grandparents.

The following morning, Stacy left the house early to shop for Christmas gifts at the Salvation Army. Todd was babysitting the three girls. He gave the twins a bottle and they fell asleep in their usual spot, on the floor of their bedroom. Amber was napping, too. Todd stretched out on his bed and drifted away. Around 10:00 A.M., he was awakened by Amber screaming "Daddy! Daddy!" He bolted upright and was immediately hit with thick smoke. The house was on fire. He scrambled out of bed and as he was grabbing a pair of pants he yelled, "Oh God, Amber, get out of the house! Get out of the house!" He could not see her and she never responded. Staying low to avoid smoke, he headed for the children's bedroom but could see nothing but black smoke. He heard sockets and light switches popping. At the door to the children's bedroom he tried to stand but his hair caught on fire. The heat and smoke were too intense and drove him back. He managed to pat out the fire in his hair, got on all fours, and crawled and groped his way through the blackness. When he realized he was about to pass out, he scrambled down the corridor and burst out the front door, gasping for air. When he looked back at the house he was horrified. Smoke was pouring out of it.

A neighbor, Diane Barbee, saw the smoke and came running. Todd yelled for her to call the fire department, then found a stick and broke a window to the children's bedroom. Fire shot through the broken pane. He broke another pane and more flames escaped. A neighbor later told police that Todd was crying "My babies! My babies!" As the heat intensified, all five windows in the children's bedroom exploded and flames "blew out," as Diane Barbee described it. The first squad of firemen arrived and scurried around stretching hoses and spraying water. More neighbors gathered at the commotion and were aghast when they realized the children were still inside.

Todd became even more hysterical. A police chaplain, George Monaghan, grabbed him and led him to the back of a fire truck in an effort to calm him. He was crying and saying, "My little girl was trying to wake me up and tell me about the fire! I couldn't get my babies!"

When a fireman emerged from the house cradling the limp body of Amber, Todd broke and ran to them, then made a dash toward the children's room, with flames and smoke still roaring through the windows. Another fireman grabbed him and, with Monaghan's help, managed to restrain him. Todd was six feet tall, strong, and never shy about physical contact, and it took several firemen to hold him back. Monaghan received a black eye in the melee. A fireman later said, "Based on what I saw on how the fire was burning, it would have been crazy for anyone to try to go into the house."

Todd was taken to the hospital and treated for minor cuts and burns. While there, he was told that Amber had died of smoke inhalation. The burned bodies of Kameron and Karmen were found on the floor of their room.

News of the tragedy rocked Corsicana and there was an outpouring of sympathy and support. A fund was quickly established to pay for proper burials, and a large crowd gathered for a gut-wrenching funeral. Todd and Stacy clung to each other and managed to sleepwalk through the nightmare.

———

Four days after the fire, investigators arrived to examine the damage and determine its cause. Todd gave them permission to do their work, saying, "I know we might not ever know all the answers, but I'd just like to know why my babies were taken from me." The small, white-framed house was gutted but still standing. Half of the exterior was charred and blackened.

Douglas Fogg was the assistant fire chief of Corsicana, and he was soon joined by Manuel Vasquez from the State Fire Marshal's office. Vasquez was something of a legend among arson investigators and claimed to have investigated between 1,200 and 1,500 fires with a perfect record. He was once asked, under oath, if he had ever reached the wrong conclusion as to the cause of a fire. He replied, "If I have, sir, I don't know. It has never been pointed out to me." He was colorful, cocky, and enjoyed tossing out such maxims as "The fire does not destroy evidence—it creates it." "The fire does not lie." And, "The fire tells the story. I'm just the interpreter." And, "I'm just collecting information. I have not made any determination. I don't have any preconceived idea."

However, during his long career he had found arson in 80 percent of his investigations—an astonishing rate. The national average was around 50 percent.

Neither Fogg nor Vasquez had college degrees. Neither had scientific backgrounds. In Texas, as in most states, anyone could become an expert in arson investigation by taking a forty-hour course, passing a test, and getting a certificate.

Both men had learned on the job, by simply absorbing the tried-

and-true investigative techniques that were accepted and handed down.

They began their investigation by inspecting the outside of the house, taking notes and photographs. Then they went inside, entering the kitchen, which revealed only smoke and heat damage—signs that the fire had not originated there. In the master bedroom, where Amber's body was found, they again found only heat and smoke damage. In the narrow hallway, they noticed charring at the foot of the walls. Flames burn upward as heat increases, and this fire seemed to burn low, near the floor.

That was the first suspicious sign.

The second was in the children's bedroom, where they noticed burn patterns on the floor. An accelerant—gasoline, lighter fluid, paint thinner, etc.—poured on a floor and ignited will cause a fire to concentrate in what investigators call "pour patterns" or "puddle configurations." To Fogg and Vasquez, that was the first clear clue that perhaps an accelerant had been used. Then they noticed the metal springs under the burnt mattresses had turned white, a sign that intense heat had risen from the floor.

Most house fires involve broken glass, either from doors, windows, or dishes. For decades, investigators relied on a reaction commonly known as "crazed glass," a spiderlike pattern on some broken glass. Crazed glass was believed to be a key indicator that a fire had been very hot. It was also commonly believed that fires caused by accelerants burned hotter than fires caused by electrical wiring or burning wood. A hotter fire caused glass to fracture.

The fire left a trail, a "burn trailer," that Fogg and Vasquez tracked from the children's bedroom along the hallway and out the front door. At the door they were surprised to discover burnt wood under the aluminum threshold. The front porch had a concrete floor and on it they noticed brown stains, which they believed were caused by accelerants. Examining the fire patterns, it became evident, at least to Fogg and Vasquez, that the fire had originated in three separate places: the children's bedroom, the hallway, and the front door.

To fire investigators, multiple origins meant only one thing: The fire was intentionally started. Once again, Vasquez, the legendary arson sleuth, had found what he was looking for. Arson. Someone had poured accelerants throughout the children's room and down the hallway and all the way to the front door to create a barrier so the children could not escape.

Fogg and Vasquez sent samples of burnt items and materials to a lab for testing to detect the presence of an accelerant. In the sample taken from the threshold at the front door, a chemist found substances often used in lighter fluid.

Crime solved. A triple homicide. And Todd was the only suspect. The authorities did not hesitate to accuse him of perhaps the most heinous crime imaginable—burning his children alive.

———

Police went through the neighborhood searching for witnesses and left no doubt that Todd was now suspected of setting the fire. The crime was so horrific and shocking that people immediately believed it. The sympathy the town had shown only days earlier quickly turned into disgust.

Those who had witnessed the fire and given detailed, even dramatic, versions of Todd's efforts to save the girls now had second thoughts. Perhaps he didn't try hard enough. Perhaps he was just putting on a show. Even Father Monaghan, the chaplain who got a black eye trying to restrain Todd, said, "Things were not as they seemed. I had the feeling that Willingham was in complete control."

———

Two weeks after the fire, the investigators asked Todd to sit for a round of questions, strictly routine. He had no idea he was a suspect and was not advised of his Miranda rights. He readily agreed to the meeting and arrived without a lawyer. He told the story of the fire and walked them through his exact movements. When asked if he had any idea how the fire started, he said no, but it was probably in the children's room because that's where he saw the flames. He and Stacy used three space heaters to keep the house warm and one was in the children's room. It had been a cool morning and he felt sure the heaters were on.

Vasquez asked Todd if he had put on shoes before fleeing the house?

He said no.

That was the clincher. Vasquez knew then that Todd had killed his children. If the floor had been soaked with accelerant, as they believed, Todd could not have escaped without burning his feet. His medical exam that day revealed no injuries to his bare feet.

Todd insisted that the fire was near the ceilings and not the floors, but Vasquez did not believe him. He would testify later that, in his opinion, Todd lit the fire as he was retreating toward the front door.

———

A sensational crime demanded a sensational arrest. A man suspected of murdering his little girls could not be arrested simply by dispatching a couple of deputies with a warrant. Three weeks after the fire, Todd and Stacy were driving at night when SWAT teams suddenly appeared out of nowhere and forced them off the road. Heavily armed warrior cops surrounded the car with loaded guns and itchy fingers. Todd, unarmed, surrendered without getting shot. Stacy, also unarmed, was terrified.

She was also in disbelief. She later told investigators that, yes, she and Todd had had their battles and that he had hit her, but he had never abused his girls. The children had made them closer. "Our kids were spoiled rotten," she said.

Todd was jailed and charged with three counts of capital murder.

On the question of motive, the police at first had little to say. The children were covered by life insurance policies that paid a total of $15,000, but Stacy's grandfather had purchased them and was the beneficiary. Before long, though, the authorities began their efforts to control the narrative and destroy any semblance of the presumption of innocence. John Jackson, the assistant district attorney, chatted with a Dallas newspaper and described Todd as "an utterly sociopathic individual."

As an indigent, Todd was assigned two lawyers, both of whom were convinced he was guilty. Everyone was convinced he was guilty, and the trial should have been moved to a neutral site far away from Corsicana. It was not, and eight months after the fire the case was called for trial in the local courthouse.

Stacy remained loyal to Todd and knew he would never harm his girls.

Though her family felt otherwise, they wanted to avoid the spectacle of a trial. They approached the prosecutors, who agreed to offer an unexpected deal to Todd: a guilty plea in return for a life sentence.

Todd's lawyers were delighted with the offer. They knew he was guilty and that any random twelve jurors off the streets of Corsicana would quickly find him guilty and recommend death. One of his lawyers, David Martin, was quoted as saying, "All the evidence showed that he was one hundred percent guilty. He poured accelerant all over the house and put lighter fluid under the kids' bed."

Such was the public sentiment against the defendant.

His lawyers advised him to take the deal but Todd refused, saying, "I ain't gonna plead to something I didn't do, especially killing my own kids."

They wanted the case to be tried anywhere but Navarro County, and asked the court for a change of venue. At a hearing on the request, his attorneys introduced inflammatory statements the prosecutors had made to reporters. They showed a video of a pros-

ecutor chatting with the press and claiming, as a possible motive for
the murders, that "the children were interfering with Todd's beer
drinking and dart throwing."

The judge refused to change venue.

By capital murder standards, even in Texas, it was a quick trial.
The first witness called by the State was a surprise, a man named
Johnny Webb. Few capital trials are complete without the false testimony of at least one jailhouse snitch, and Todd's was no exception.
Webb had been convicted of car theft, dealing drugs, forgery, and
robbery. He was in jail on a charge of robbing a woman at knifepoint. He admitted to being a drug addict who started using at the
age of nine, and claimed he was traumatized after being raped in
prison in 1988. As a career criminal, he was well versed in the routines of snitching and fearful of another long stay in prison.

Webb happened to be in jail when Todd was arrested and spoke
to him briefly one day. Their encounter was seen by the sheriff, who
approached Webb and asked what they were talking about. The
sheriff told Webb to talk to Todd again about the fire; maybe he
would say something incriminating. The sheriff reported this to
John Jackson, the prosecutor in charge of the case. Jackson arranged
for Webb to come to his office in the courthouse. There, they talked
about the fire and Jackson was adamant that Todd had killed his
daughters. Jackson laid out photos of the dead girls, images that
Webb could never forget. The visit to Jackson's office was repeated
several times. Finally, Webb asked what kind of "deal" Jackson
wanted. Jackson promised to make the robbery charge disappear,
either now or later.

Webb told the jury his story: He walked by Todd's cell not long
after he was jailed, and, oddly enough, Todd wanted to talk about
his crime. Through a narrow food slot in the cell door, Todd broke
down and admitted to Webb, a total stranger, that he had deliberately set the fire by spraying lighter fluid on the walls and floors.

The alleged confession took place by a speaker system that allowed guards to listen to the prisoners.

Webb even juiced up his story with some additional fiction. He testified that Todd admitted a motive. It seems as though Stacy had been abusing the kids, had even hurt one of them, and Todd set the fire to kill the kids to cover up his wife's abuse.

The children's bodies were autopsied. The cause of each death was smoke inhalation. There were no additional signs of bruising or trauma.

Before Webb's testimony, not a single person had mentioned or suggested child abuse by either Stacy or Todd.

For good measure, Webb assured the jurors that he had not been promised leniency by the prosecution.

Jackson was later quoted as saying he didn't think Webb was a reliable witness. Seriously? Then why did the prosecutor call Webb as the State's first witness in such a sensational trial? Why use an unreliable witness to try to convict a man for the most horrible crime imaginable?

Next, the State called several neighbors to testify. At the time of the fire, they had portrayed Todd as a frantic father screaming for help as he knocked out windows and tried to re-enter the burning house to save his children. That was before the investigators began using the word "arson." Eight months later, testifying for the prosecution, they described Todd as being calm and indifferent, or perhaps he was acting, or in complete control.

The prime witness for the State was Manuel Vasquez, a veteran of the courtroom. He explained in great detail the twenty indicators of arson and walked the jury through his exhaustive investigation and analysis. In his opinion, the fire was deliberately started by Todd Willingham with the intent to kill his children.

As court-appointed counsel, the defense lawyers were on a limited budget. The only expert they could afford agreed with the prosecution. Todd insisted on testifying on his own behalf, but his lawyers were afraid he would make a bad witness. He did not testify, nor did Stacy. The white-flag defense called only one witness, a babysitter who said she did not believe Todd could have killed his children.

The trial lasted only two days. The jury deliberated for an hour before finding Todd guilty of capital murder. The following day, during the sentencing phase, Stacy and several family members testified in an effort to save Todd's life. When Stacy was on the stand, the prosecutor asked her about the significance of a large tattoo on Todd's left bicep. It included a skull and a serpent.

"It's just a tattoo," she responded.

"He just likes skulls and snakes. It that what you're saying?"

"No. Just had—he got a tattoo on him."

It was part of the State's strategy to portray Todd as a sociopath. To further prove it, the prosecution called two medical experts. The first, Tim Gregory, was a psychologist with a master's degree. His practice was devoted to family counseling. The prosecution had several photographs that had survived the fire. Two of them were posters of the heavy metal bands Iron Maiden and Led Zeppelin. Gregory was asked to interpret the images for the jury. In his learned opinion, they revealed a focus on death and dying. He stated, "Many times individuals that have a lot of this type of art have interest in satanic-type activities."

The second expert was a forensic psychiatrist named James Grigson, the infamous Dr. Death. His role was to convince the jury that the defendant, in every case, was a hopeless murderer who would murder again if given the chance; thus it was the jury's duty to stop him with the death penalty. He described Todd as an "extremely severe sociopath" who was beyond treatment. Three years after Todd's trial, Dr. Grigson was kicked out of the American Psychiatric Association, as mentioned previously in the Kerry Cook case, because he had repeatedly arrived at a "psychiatric diagnosis" without having first examined the individual in question; and for indicating, while testifying in court as an expert witness, that he could predict with 100 percent certainty that the individual would engage in future violent acts.

The jury unanimously recommended that Todd be executed.

———

Todd was taken to prison and began the long wait for his appeals to move through the system. He pleaded with his lawyers to rescue him, writing, "You can't imagine what it's like to be here, with people I have no business being around." He was not a criminal and didn't belong with a bunch of murderers. He fought with his cellmates and spent time in "The Dungeon," a black hole where troublemakers were banished. Child abusers are scorned in prison, and Todd fought back when he was called a "baby killer."

Todd liked some of his fellow inmates. Others he loathed. In the mid-1990s, Texas was killing prisoners so fast that he knew better than to develop friendships. Even so, it was difficult watching so many men he knew count down their final hours and disappear. Every execution reminded those left behind that their day would come.

One inmate Todd particularly liked was Ernest Ray Willis, one of the few others who insisted he was innocent. Contrary to popular belief, most men condemned to die do not claim innocence. Many are proud of their crimes and enjoy bragging about them, especially in prison.

Willis's case was unbelievably similar to Todd's. He was convicted of setting fire to a house in which he was sleeping. Two women died in another room. He barely escaped as the house exploded in flames. His bare feet were unharmed. Neighbors thought he acted suspicious. Fire inspectors found pour patterns and other clear signs of arson. There was no motive. Willis had no record of violent crime. Prosecutors decided he was a sociopath and charged him with two counts of capital murder. The jury quickly found him guilty and sentenced him to death.

Todd was stunned by the similarities. Willis, by the luck of the draw, had attracted the attention of a powerful New York law firm that entered his case as pro bono counsel. The lawyers were convinced he was innocent and were spending a fortune on experts and investigators.

Todd was stuck with his old team. He often complained to his parents of the burden of being represented by lawyers who thought he was guilty.

———

The Texas Court of Criminal Appeals rarely reversed a conviction, regardless of a paucity of real evidence or whatever happened at trial. In March 1995, it unanimously affirmed Todd's conviction. In doing so it found no problems with the trial, and said the trial court had properly denied Todd's motion for a change of venue. The ruling shoved him another step closer to execution. He managed to get another lawyer, Walter Reaves from Waco, and was thrilled when he realized Mr. Reaves had serious doubts about his conviction. He filed habeas corpus petitions in state court and they were denied. He filed them in federal court in 2001 and 2002, but they were denied. He appealed to the U.S. Supreme Court, but in December 2003, twelve years after the fire, the court refused to hear the case. An execution date was set for February 17, 2004.

On February 3, 2004, Walter Reaves filed for a temporary reprieve with the parole board and the governor's office. Ten days later, he filed again, in both places, an affidavit that included a report challenging the science behind the fire investigation. The report was prepared by Dr. Gerald Hurst, a well-known fire expert who lived in Austin, Texas.

The request for a stay was denied by both the parole board and the governor's office.

———

Dr. Gerald Hurst was a brilliant chemist who grew up poor in Oklahoma during the Depression. As a child he busied himself building radios from scrap iron, wires, and metals he found in junkyards. A teacher recognized his talent and steered him to college. He eventually received a PhD in chemistry from Cambridge University and worked for defense contractors building secret weapons. He designed bombs and other explosives and received some lucrative patents. With time he got tired of creating weapons that killed people and went to work investigating fires for insurance companies. His knowledge of fires and explosives was vast, and he became a leading expert in the field.

Criminal law got his attention, and as he began studying arson he was shocked at the methods used by state and local investigators. Most had only high school educations and had absorbed their knowledge by on-the-job training. They learned from the old guys, who had learned from the old guys. There were no enforceable national standards for arson investigation. In 1992, the National Fire Protection Association published its first guidelines, but they were routinely ignored. State and local arson investigators, for the most part, believed that their experience and intuition were more effective than the new scientific standards.

In the late 1990s, Dr. Hurst began investigating arson cases in which people had been convicted and sent to prison. His substantial income from patent royalties allowed him to devote time to his work without the need for getting paid, and he was generous with it. By the time he heard of Todd's case, his work had been crucial in ten exonerations of innocent people.

Two weeks before the execution, with the clock ticking loudly, Walter Reaves sent him Todd's file. He spread it out in the cluttered basement of his home in Austin and went to work. As he plowed through the voluminous materials, a few items caught his attention. The first was a statement by Manuel Vasquez that he had investigated between 1,200 and 1,500 fires and found arson in 80 percent of them. That was an incredibly high number, and Dr. Hurst simply didn't believe it. Nationwide, fire officials had for decades reported a 50 percent rate of arson.

Next was another statement by Vasquez, claiming that the fire burned "fast and hot" because of a liquid accelerant. It was an established belief among arson investigators that fires started by combustible liquids were hotter than those started by wiring, or space heaters, or wood, cloth, or other materials. This was a damning assumption, because it usually led to the suspicion that someone— the arsonist—poured or splashed gasoline or lighter fluid on the floor before lighting a match. But the theory was completely erroneous. Numerous experiments had proven that wood and gasoline fires burn at essentially the same temperature.

Hurst quickly became skeptical of everything Fogg and Vasquez said in their report. For example, they claimed that the brown stains on the front porch were evidence of a liquid accelerant that had not had time to soak into the concrete. The theory was that Todd sprayed fluid on the threshold of the front door to prevent his little girls from escaping. Dr. Hurst knew better. Brown floor stains were common in fires and seldom had anything to do with accelerants.

Another example was the "crazed glass" theory that the fire was so hot and fast that it cracked glass. Hurst knew better because he had tested various types of glass by heating them with a blowtorch, then cooling them suddenly with water. The weblike patterns in the glass were the same regardless of what caused the fire.

"Flashover" is a phenomenon that occurs when a room gets so hot it literally explodes with fire. Fogg and Vasquez assumed, as did most old-time arson sleuths, that flashover happened much faster when an accelerant was used. This, too, was erroneous. Once flashover occurs, the path of the fire depends on new sources of oxygen. When Todd escaped through the front door, the fire rushed toward it. When he knocked out the windows, flames shot out through them. Fogg and Vasquez concluded that it was impossible for Todd to run down the hall and through the front door without burning his bare feet. But with a flashover effect, the hallway was not yet on fire. The smoke was impenetrable, but the fire was contained, momentarily, in the children's room. After flashover, it becomes impossible to determine accelerant patterns.

Dr. Hurst conducted an experiment for each piece of evidence analyzed in the Fogg and Vasquez report. Vasquez had made a video of the house, and Hurst studied it. His experiments proved that each original conclusion was wrong. He methodically went through the Fogg and Vasquez list of the twenty indicators of arson and debunked each one. There was no evidence that the fire started in multiple locations. Because he had not visited the scene, he could not determine the cause. But he had no doubt that it was not arson—it was an accidental fire, probably caused by a space heater or bad electrical wiring. That explained why no motive for the fire had ever been established. He hurriedly typed his report. It began with: "A contemporary fire origin-and-cause analyst might well wonder how anyone could make so many critical errors in interpreting the evidence." He sent it to Walter Reaves, who immediately filed it with the parole board in hopes of a last-minute reprieve. The board refused.

Walter Reaves worked frantically to get the Hurst report in front of state and federal judges. He also sent it to the office of Governor Rick Perry, where it was received four days before the execution. The lawyer was hopeful that Governor Perry would grant reprieve in order to review the Hurst report.

Perry was a staunch, even noisy supporter of the death penalty and intervened in only one of the 234 executions carried out during his fourteen years as governor. In 2001, he vetoed a bill that would have banned the execution of inmates with very low IQs.

His aides verified that Perry had the Hurst report on February 17, the day of the execution.

Reaves called Todd and told him the parole board had voted unanimously against him.

———

During his final days, Todd asked Stacy if he could be buried next to his children. She refused. She had divorced Todd when he was on death row and remarried.

Her story, and it changed often, was that she had believed him for a long time after the fire, but doubts had arisen. She said she had looked at the original court records and arson reports (but not the one from Dr. Hurst) and had determined that he was in fact guilty. She told a reporter, "He took my kids away from me." Weeks earlier, she had gathered her family and informed them that Todd had confessed to her that he had deliberately set the fire with the intention of killing their children. After the execution, she denied he had confessed.

On February 17, Todd met with his parents and some relatives in the visitation room. Even at that last hour he was forbidden from touching them. He could not hug his parents because they were separated by a sheet of Plexiglas. Such was the procedure in all Texas executions.

At 4:00 P.M. he ate his last meal—barbequed pork ribs, fried okra, bean enchiladas with cheese, onion rings, and two slices of lemon cream pie. He received word that Governor Perry had refused to grant a reprieve. He told his parents, "In fifty-five minutes, I'm a free man. I'm going home to see my kids."

When it was time, he was carried into the death chamber by guards and strapped down with leather belts. A medical team inserted tubes in both arms. Though there were plenty of volunteers for the job, the team members wanted to deflect some of the responsibility. Each had a different role so no one member could be held solely responsible.

The warden asked Todd if he had any last words. He said, "The only statement I want to make is that I am an innocent man convicted of a crime I did not commit. I have been persecuted for twelve years for something I did not do. From God's dust I came and to dust I will return, so the Earth will become my throne." He looked at the witness room and saw Stacy, who was not expected to be there, and began cursing her. The warden pulled the microphone away, then pushed a remote control. Sodium thiopental, a barbiturate, was pumped into Todd's arm. Then pancuronium bromide, which paralyzes the diaphragm and stops the breathing. A third drug, potassium chloride, was sent in to stop his heart. He died at 6:20.

At his request, he was cremated and his parents secretly spread his ashes over his children's graves.

———

The execution was immediately controversial. Death penalty lawyers and innocence advocates complained loudly that Texas, and especially Governor Perry, chose to ignore the latest scientific findings from Dr. Hurst and rushed the execution. What was the hurry? Todd had been on death row for only ten years, not a long time in the byzantine world of post-conviction litigation.

Death penalty advocates, especially politicians, constantly complain of the endless appeals and promise efforts to kill people faster. The truth is that it often takes years, even decades, to find the evidence hidden by the police and prosecutors. Tragically, that evidence is often not found in time.

What happened to the Hurst report in Governor Perry's office? The official version is that the report was read and considered. A deputy press secretary said, "As with any execution, the governor was previously briefed on all the facts of the case. He was briefed on this [Hurst's] report once our office obtained it late that afternoon. After the document, which was four pages, was requested, obtained, and reviewed, the governor shared the opinion of the state and federal judiciary that the report was not enough to merit a stay of execution."

Questions about the investigation and the science behind it soon made the front page. Two reporters for the *Chicago Tribune,* Steve Mills and Maurice Possley, went to Corsicana to investigate. They also consulted with prominent fire experts and arson investigators, all of whom agreed that the work of Fogg and Vasquez was deeply flawed. Dr. Hurst, one of the experts, said, "There's nothing to suggest to any reasonable arson investigator that this was an arson fire. It was just a fire."

Even Texas agreed with him. Edward Cheever, a Texas state deputy fire marshal who had assisted Vasquez in the original 1992 investigation, admitted, "At the time of the Corsicana fire we were still testifying to things that aren't accurate today. They were true then, but they aren't now. Hurst was pretty much right on. We know now not to make those same assumptions."

Kendall Ryland was a fire chief and former fire and arson instructor at Louisiana State University. In his workshop he tried to simulate the conditions described by Fogg and Vasquez. When his experiments went nowhere, he told a reporter, "It made me sick to think this guy was executed based on this investigation. They executed this guy and they've just got no idea—at least not scientifically—if he set the fire, or if it was even intentionally set."

A year after Todd's execution, and in response to growing complaints about the shoddy forensics being used in Texas courtrooms, the state established the Texas Forensic Science Commission. The first cases to be reviewed were Todd's and Ernest Ray Willis's, the other arson case that was virtually identical to Todd's.

After seventeen years on death row, Willis was a free man, thanks to a talented legal team, and thanks also to Dr. Hurst, who had reviewed his case and concluded that the fire was not due to arson. The prosecutor believed the report and dropped the charges.

In both cases, Dr. Hurst concluded there was no arson. Todd

was dead. Willis was free. Different prosecutors, different court districts, same state.

The commission hired Craig Beyler, a noted fire expert and scientist, to conduct the review. His analysis followed that of Dr. Hurst, though his language was somewhat stronger. He concluded that Fogg and Vasquez had no scientific basis for finding arson. They ignored evidence, relied on discredited folklore, failed to eliminate potential alternative causes, did not understand basic fire dynamics, and violated "not only the standards of today but even of the time period." He criticized the findings of Fogg and Vasquez as "nothing more than a collection of personal beliefs that have nothing to do with science-based fire investigation."

When the commission was set to review Beyler's report, Governor Perry suddenly dismissed three members, including the chairperson. Perry, who was still confident that Todd was guilty and even disparaged the experts who said otherwise, replaced the chairperson with a Texas prosecutor. The shakeup of the commission delayed Beyler's testimony and other expert findings from his investigation until after the upcoming gubernatorial election.

Governor Perry was running for reelection in 2010 and planning a bid for the White House in 2012.

————

In 2006, the Innocence Project assembled five of the nation's leading independent arson experts to review the evidence in the case. The "Arson Review Committee" researched every aspect of the fire and picked apart the work of Fogg and Vasquez. Its forty-eight-page report concluded that the fire that killed the three Willingham children was accidental. It read, in part, "The artifacts examined and relied upon by the fire investigators in the case are the kind of artifacts routinely created by accidental fires that progress beyond flashover."

And: "The State's expert witnesses . . . relied on interpretation of 'indicators' that they were taught constituted evidence of arson. While we have no doubt that these witnesses believed what they were saying, each and every one of the indicators relied upon have since been scientifically proven to be invalid."

And: "Unfortunately for Mr. Willingham, while the fire may not have 'lied,' Mr. Vasquez misinterpreted what it was telling him. Such willingness to offer 'expert' testimony, while lacking the knowledge to present accurate information to the jury, may excuse Mr. Vasquez's many serious errors. The judicial system that allows such testimony to be presented, however, is in serious need of reform."

———

The conviction rested on two sources of evidence: the arson investigation and the testimony of Johnny Webb. Motive is not a requirement for capital murder. The State knew it couldn't prove motive, because there was none.

With the Fogg and Vasquez report and testimony taking heat from all directions, the prosecution worked overtime to keep its snitch, Johnny Webb, in line. He proved to be unstable and manipulative. His threats to recant and tell the truth routinely sent the prosecution into fits.

Every snitch wants a deal. They are in jail looking at more time in prison and they know how to play the police and prosecutors. At trial, every snitch lies when he or she tells the jury that there was no deal with the prosecution. There is always a deal. The prosecutor made it, and the prosecutor knows the snitch is lying. Suborning perjury is the act of inducing a witness to lie, but prosecutors are never punished when their snitches lie in court.

While reporters, lawyers, and innocence advocates assailed the bad forensics, they also hounded John Jackson. If there had been a deal with Johnny Webb, they were determined to find it. Oddly enough, they were aided by Jackson himself. Many of his efforts to protect Webb were documented by their own letters.

For example, two months after the Willingham trial, Jackson wrote to a prison official asking that Webb be transferred to a medical unit, a much better place than the protective unit he was in. He explained that Webb was a crucial witness in a capital murder prosecution, and, as a snitch, was at risk in the prison's general population. He wrote that he might need Webb again in court and wanted him in "an environment that guarantees the smallest risk."

A month later he wrote again, requesting that Webb be returned to the Navarro County jail in Corsicana for an even safer environment. He claimed that Webb had received death threats and needed to be protected. Having Webb closer to home, actually right down the street, would make things easier for Jackson. He wrote, "In the event of a reversal, I would also like to be able to count on Webb's continued cooperation." His request was denied.

The letters continued over the next three years as Jackson worked diligently to keep his snitch happy. Jackson leaned on a friend, a wealthy rancher named Charles Pearce, to funnel money to Webb's prison commissary account. In 1995, Webb wrote to Pearce with the story of a prison guard who was urging him, Webb, to recant his testimony to appease other prisoners who hated snitches. Pearce relayed this troubling news to Jackson, who wrote the warden and said, "I hate to keep bothering you with Johnny Webb problems. Webb is not exactly a model citizen, but I would be very concerned if prison personnel is leaning on him in an attempt to change his story."

In 1996, Webb wrote to Jackson and demanded a transfer to either a federal prison or the Navarro County jail. In the letter, Webb, inadvertently or otherwise, finally admitted the truth. He wrote, "Here the state offered me certain benefits in exchange for my testimony which resulted in sending a man to death row. Because I kept my end of the promise, the state is bound to uphold theirs until my release from incarceration."

Jackson worked behind the scenes to secure an early release for Webb. He lobbied Judge Kenneth "Buck" Douglas, the same judge who had presided over Todd's trial and also sentenced Webb to fifteen years, to reduce Webb's conviction to a lesser charge. He wrote to the parole board on Webb's behalf and covered his trail nicely by assuring the board that Webb had not been promised leniency for his testimony and that there had been no "expectation of leniency."

Jackson wrote to Webb to reassure him. Pearce wrote to Webb to reassure him. They promised they were doing everything possible to get him released. In spite of this highly unusual fawning over a career criminal, Webb kept threatening to go public with the truth. When his request for an early release was denied, Jackson himself asked the governor for clemency. He was denied. Jackson was determined to keep Webb happy as long as the lawyers for Todd Willingham were filing appeals.

In 1996, Jackson was elected to the bench, succeeding Judge Douglas. As the circuit court judge, he had far more power than as an assistant district attorney. One of his first moves was to issue a warrant to prison officials to haul Webb back to Navarro County for a hearing. There is no record of one taking place.

Two years later, Webb was finally paroled. He went straight to Pearce, who gave him money to buy a pickup truck. Pearce also agreed to cover the cost of a commercial driving course for Webb. He enrolled, then got busted on another drug charge and thrown in jail. He listed a $1,000-a-month stipend from Pearce as his only income. He pled guilty, got two years, but his parole violation locked him up until 2007. When he returned to prison, Pearce began sending him money again.

In March 2000, from prison, Webb prepared a nice piece of jailhouse lawyering, a handwritten document he called a "Motion To Recant Testimony." In it, he admitted lying about Todd Willingham, who "is innocent of all charges." He sent it to the district attorney, who sent it to Judge John Jackson. It was never sent to Todd's lawyers, nor was it included in Webb's court file. Webb eventually dropped the matter.

In August 2000, Judge Jackson wrote to Webb and assured him that he and Pearce were working hard to get him released again.

In 2004, as Todd's execution was getting closer, his lawyer, Walter Reaves, requested a ninety-day reprieve. Reaves had heard rumors of Webb getting a pickup truck in return for his testimony and wanted to investigate.

Judge Jackson opposed the request. It was denied.

—

Webb was paroled in 2007 and recanted again. In a series of taped interviews with the Marshall Project, a nonprofit news organization that covers the criminal justice system, Webb said John Jackson threatened him with a long prison sentence on the robbery charge if he didn't lie in his testimony against Todd Willingham. Jackson also promised to reduce his prison sentence if he testified.

—

David Grann is an award-winning journalist who has written for *The New Republic* and *The New Yorker,* among other publications. His books have been huge bestsellers. In August 2009, *The New Yorker* published a lengthy investigative piece by him titled "Trial by Fire: Did Texas Execute an Innocent Man?" The story was a shocking exposé of the Willingham case and sent it to the forefront of the debate about capital punishment. Impeccably researched, beautifully written, and remarkably balanced, it dug deep into the science of fires and arson investigations and concluded that the Fogg and Vasquez report was deeply flawed. Grann interviewed everyone who would talk to him: the families, neighbors, firemen, lawyers, police, prosecutors, witnesses, Johnny Webb, scientists, and even some of the jurors. The most important passages deal with the history of arson investigation and the need for more knowledge and better training.

In 2014, the Innocence Project, which had been investigating the Willingham case for a decade, filed a grievance against Judge Jackson with the State Bar of Texas, arguing that he should be investigated, sanctioned, or even criminally prosecuted for falsifying official records, withholding evidence from the defense, suborning perjury, and obstructing justice. The grievance claimed Jackson's conduct "violated his professional, ethical, and constitutional obligations."

The state bar took such complaints seriously. In 2013, it forced a judge to resign his position, surrender his license to practice, and serve ten days in jail in the well-known wrongful conviction of Michael Morton. The judge had been the prosecutor and had hidden evidence. Morton was accused of killing his wife and spent twenty-five years in prison before he was proven innocent by DNA testing. The judge served five days in jail and was released on good behavior. It is the only case on record in the United States where the prosecutor responsible for wrongfully sending someone to prison has been forced to serve time himself.

In 2014, the Texas State Bar successfully sought the disbarment of the district attorney Charles Sebesta for misconduct in the prosecution of Anthony Graves.

After an investigation, the state bar accused John Jackson of failing to inform Todd's lawyers that Webb had been promised favorable treatment in return for his testimony. Jackson denied everything and demanded a jury trial. In Navarro County! A special judge was sent in and twelve jurors were chosen. Attorneys for the state bar showed them a video deposition of Webb admitting he lied at Todd's trial after Jackson promised him favorable treatment. However, when Webb was put on the stand, he clammed up and refused to answer questions. He took the Fifth over fifty times and refused to incriminate himself. His memory wasn't working and he couldn't remember much. Almost a hundred times he said he simply couldn't recall anything.

The jury voted 11–1 in favor of John Jackson. It was a bruising defeat for the Texas State Bar and the Innocence Project, and a satisfying win for Jackson.

On April 3, 2014, the Texas Board of Pardons and Paroles voted not to recommend a posthumous full pardon for Todd Willingham. The Innocence Project, along with Todd's relatives and Michael Morton, had asked Governor Perry to order the parole board to investigate whether the state should pardon Todd. The parole board did investigate but refused the pardon.

———

A final word from Johnny Webb. In a 2015 interview with Maurice Possley on behalf of the Marshall Project, Webb regretted getting involved in the trial. He said, "Now I'm stuck in this Willingham thing for the rest of my life."

ACKNOWLEDGMENTS

JOHN GRISHAM

After writing every single word of the first fifty books, I'm sure I'll be asked why I finally decided to work with a coauthor. The sarcastic answer is that I am tired and lazy. Why not let someone do half the work?

The real answer is that Jim McCloskey is a true American hero. He began his lonely quest to find justice when he was a young divinity student at Princeton. He dedicated his life and career to freeing the innocent. He built Centurion Ministries into a powerful innocence group. Most important, though, is that Jim tells great stories. I am honored to share the dust jacket and title page with him. It's not every day you get to work with one of your heroes.

In spite of the fact that I've written far too many books, Doubleday has always been eager to publish them. That enthusiasm continues today. Many years ago, I realized how fortunate I am to be able to do nothing but write the books and not worry about how they make it all the way to the stores. This is because I have a great team at Doubleday, and I have not thanked them in a long time.

Suzanne Herz has been my publisher for thirty years. She's had various titles along the way—every publishing company is awash in titles—and I stopped trying to keep track last century. What it means is that Suzanne receives the manuscript from me, and about three months later she sends me, hot off the press, a beautiful hardback that I proudly place on a special shelf with all the others. I don't know everything that happens during those three months, but I know that she is in charge. We discuss and often debate the artwork for the jacket. We've had disagreements over titles. She often prods me to go here or there to speak and promote the books. On the creative side, she is quick to say she loves a story, and almost as quick to say she does not. She is free to question anything, even down to a single word in the manuscript, and I always listen. I don't always agree, and the bickering is often enjoyable. She knows the business, and in her quiet and steady way knows how to spot a good book, get it in the stores, and make it sell. Her writers are fiercely loyal.

The trust is implicit and grounded upon our long friendship. Thanks, Suzanne.

Todd Doughty is Suzanne's close friend and sidekick. The three of us have hit the road together for mini-tours and still laugh about our adventures. Todd handles publicity—again, his official title escapes me—and he knows more about publishing and bookselling than anyone in the game. He knows every reporter, journalist, producer, editor, and newsperson in the business. He has close relationships with booksellers and has visited hundreds of stores across the country. He reads everything and follows dozens of writers, not only in-house but throughout the industry. He watches every television show and every movie, and can wipe out an entire Double Jeopardy! board in a matter of seconds. Thanks, Todd.

Around Suzanne and Todd are the other members of the team: Judy Jacoby in advertising, Lauren Weber in marketing, and Eddie Allen in production editorial. Vimi Santokhi is the managing editor. Jaci Updike handles sales for all of Penguin Random House.

Kris Puopolo is our marvelous editor, who effortlessly juggled the ten different narratives arriving at different times from two very different writers.

Thanks also to Neil Rosini, my longtime literary lawyer. Neil specializes in copyright and libel law, and he read the manuscript, as always, with a sharp eye, searching for potential problems. Hopefully, the writers fixed the ones he found.

Thanks to Eric Brown for his steady legal advice over the years. As a former lawyer, I still try to remember how to be a good client. Eric is always a pro to work with.

Thanks also to Claire Leonard, Ana Espinoza, and David Litman.

And, as always, thanks to David Gernert, my agent and close friend. In 1990, when he was an editor at Doubleday, David had the wisdom and good fortune of buying my second novel, *The Firm*. A good move for both of us. He published my next five novels, all to a growing market. In 1995, David left Doubleday and became a megastar agent. I was his first author. We've had a ball ever since and, as we approach our twilight years, have no plans to slow down. We talk virtually every day, and rarely about books. We catch up with family news, discuss last night's basketball game, dread our next joint replacement, and I usually manage to take a cheap shot or two at his beloved Mets when they're losing, which is most of the time.

JIM McCLOSKEY

The idea for *Framed* is the brainchild of John Grisham. The book's concept, title, and structure of ten astonishing true stories of wrongful conviction originated with him. John's vision for this book is rooted in his compassion and strong empathy for those who suffer from this kind of injustice, and his outrage that such things take place so often.

I felt honored and humbled when he invited me to join him as co-author in early 2021. I'm still pinching myself. Although the work has been challenging, John has always been a pleasure to work with. He is affable, generous, and very collaborative. When we finished our work on this project, I soon developed withdrawal symptoms. My partnership with John, writing *Framed,* was the highlight of my professional career.

I am hugely indebted to the Doubleday editorial team, who with great tact and skill made these stories as readable as they are. The lead editor with whom I worked very closely was Kristine Puopolo, a Doubleday VP and editorial director for nonfiction. She made the editing process almost enjoyable as she deftly and significantly improved what I handed her. I will miss you, Kris. She was ably assisted in various matters by her assistant, Ana Espinoza, who was instrumental in managing the collection of photographs used in my five chapters.

I am especially beholden to my literary agent, Deborah Grosvenor, who has had my back in many ways. She has become a good friend over the years since our association began in 2014. Debbie sold and negotiated the publishing rights to my memoir, *When Truth Is All You Have,* to Doubleday. She also edited each of my five *Framed* chapters before I sent them to Kristine Puopolo, with whom Debbie stayed in close touch on a variety of issues. She advised me on the different contracts needed to formalize my joint authorship with John and Doubleday/ Penguin Random House. I'd feel lost without her. Thank you, Debbie, for doing what you do for me so effectively and with patience and good humor.

John and I would certainly be remiss in not recognizing Corban Addison Klug, fact-checker extraordinaire and an accomplished nonfiction author in his own right. He meticulously and thoroughly went through all ten chapters to fact-check and create endnotes tying important statements to source documents. He also, at my request, offered editorial comments and suggestions for my five stories.

Tyler Spikes, Centurion's staff archivist, went the extra mile many times over, organizing and selecting prospective photos related to the subjects of my five chapters. His efforts included tracking down images, identifying their owners, and securing the rights to use them, a challenge given the photos' age and geographical dispersion.

Now I turn to the men and woman whose cases I profiled, without whom there would be no book called *Framed*. Thank you for allowing us to tell your stories. Hopefully, doing so will give you some solace and help ease the unimaginable suffering you went through many years ago, suffering that marks your lives even today. You are Clarence Brandley, who died in 2018; codefendants Mark Jones, Kenneth Gardiner, and Dominic Lucci; Ellen Reasonover; codefendants David Alexander and Harry Granger; and Kerry Max Cook.

In writing your story, I revisited in-depth what happened to you. This gave me an even greater appreciation and respect for the courage and grace that enabled you to miraculously endure the unendurable. I am reminded of what Saint Paul said in his letter to the Romans (5:3–5), "Suffering produces endurance, and endurance produces character, and character produces hope, and hope does not disappoint." No one exemplifies this more than you.

———

Because there are so many, I cannot mention here by name all the attorneys, investigators, judges, and witnesses who were instrumental in the effort to exonerate the innocent inmates featured in my chapters. Instead, they are all cited and named in their respective chapters. I would, however, like to give an honorable mention to a few of these brave souls:

Paul Henderson joined Centurion in 1988 as a staff investigator after a Pulitzer Prize–winning career as an investigative reporter at *The Seattle Times*. Paul worked selflessly with me on three of these cases— Reasonover in St. Louis; Alexander and Granger in Louisiana; and Jones, Gardiner, and Lucci in Savannah. He passed away several years ago at the age of seventy-eight. All of us at Centurion will never forget his unflagging energy and hard work on behalf of these folks, as well as for many other Centurion "clients."

Peggy Woodward and Steve Woodring deserve special recognition for standing up for Alexander and Granger in Iberia Parish. Woodward heroically faced off against a hostile and unrelenting district attorney's office and the entire Louisiana judiciary in her ten-year fight to free these men. Woodring, much against the wishes of his former law enforcement colleagues, became an outspoken advocate, stating unequivocally his belief in their innocence to anyone who would listen, including CBS's *60 Minutes*.

Bill Srack caused a mistrial in Clarence Brandley's first trial as the lone juror voting "not guilty." His fellow jurors ridiculed and mocked him for being "a nigger lover." In the ensuing months he and his wife received threatening anonymous phone calls nonstop, day and night. All because he voted with his conscience. Mary Johnson paid a heavy price when she testified against her boss, Judge Martin, at the hearing before Judge Perry Pickett. He fired her as his court reporter, and she became persona non grata in the Conroe courthouse. As a result, she lost her career.

Finally, I want to thank my brother, Richard, and my sister, Lois, for giving me their encouragement and moral support during the last two years of writing. My warm gratitude also extends to my Centurion family, headed by Executive Director Corey Waldron, all of whom did the same.

A NOTE ON SOURCES

JOHN GRISHAM

Unlike my coauthor, I did not live these stories. Jim made them happen. He was in the trenches—the streets, alleys, bars, jails, prisons, and courtrooms—digging for the truth. He was the main character, the protagonist, the center of the plot, dealing with the large and unruly cast of witnesses, informants, lawyers, prosecutors, judges, families, and, of course, the innocent men and women themselves. And he pushed them hard until he found the truth.

I simply read about them. They came to me, in newspaper and magazine articles, books, legal briefs, court opinions, even documentaries. I relied on the work of others, and here I'd like to give credit.

THE NORFOLK FOUR

In August 2007, *The New York Times Magazine* ran an article titled "What Happened in Norfolk?" Though I live in Virginia, Norfolk is far away and I'd never heard of the case. The article, by Alan Berlow, is a fascinating account of the unbelievably botched murder investigation by the Norfolk police. By then, the four sailors had been in prison a number of years and plenty of lawyers were working to get them out.

I knew a couple of the lawyers and made contact. They shared their files and even sent me a copy of a clemency petition that was on the governor's desk.

Richard Leo is a professor of law at the University of San Francisco and an expert on police interrogation tactics and false confessions. Tom Wells has written extensively on wrongful convictions. In 2009, they published a remarkable book, *The Wrong Guys: Murder, False Confessions, and the Norfolk Four.* The book exposes the abusive behavior of the Norfolk police and leaves no doubt that the confessions were coerced and fraudulent. There is a copy of it on a shelf behind my desk. On its cover are the four faces of the young sailors in uniform, almost thirty years ago. I look at it every day.

A small army of lawyers labored for over a decade to free them. I will name a few who helped me, and in doing so I will inevitably neglect someone. My apologies in advance. George Kendall, then of Holland & Knight, Des Hogan of Hogan & Hartson, and Don Salzman of Skadden Arps opened their files. Don was especially helpful in reading the manuscript and flagging my mistakes.

AUTOPSY GAMES

In 2007, I had a small role in the founding of the Innocence Project at the Ole Miss Law School. Tucker Carrington was hired as the executive director and we have been friends since. My son, Ty, also studied law at Ole Miss, and worked in Tucker's innocence clinic.

In 2014, Tucker and Radley Balko, a fearless investigative reporter, published a book titled *The Cadaver King and the Country Dentist.* It is an exposé of the terror campaign of Dr. Steven Hayne and Dr. Michael West. I was honored to write a foreword. Years ago, Tucker and I talked of writing a book about the wrongful convictions of Kennedy Brewer and Levon Brooks, but couldn't find the time. His and Radley's book is an excellent account of a story that still amazes me.

UNKNOWN MALE #1

Paul Casteleiro is the litigation director for Centurion Ministries and has been slugging it out with prosecutors and attorneys general for decades. During one of his reports to the board of directors he summarized the bizarre case from Chester, Pennsylvania. He and Centurion represent Sam Grasty, and he encouraged me to investigate the case.

Vanessa Potkin is the top litigator for the Innocence Project in New York and has many notches in her belt, probably more exonerations than anyone except Jim McCloskey. She represents Morton Johnson and was of great help.

In Chester, attorney Guy Smith gave me enough local color to fill several books. He represented Morton at trial in 2001, and has been fighting for his clients in Delaware County and Philly for over fifty years.

THE ABSENCE OF MOTIVE

Pamela Colloff is an award-winning reporter for ProPublica and a staff writer for *The New York Times Magazine*. In 2018, she published an exhaustive two-part report titled "Blood Will Tell." It is about the bad forensics that convicted Joe Bryan and sent him to prison for thirty-four years.

One of his lawyers, Jessica Freud, answered all the questions I could think of. She met me at the prison when I visited Joe.

Walter Reaves, of Waco, represented both Joe Bryan and Cameron Todd Willingham (whose story is told in "The Fire Does Not Lie"), and was always eager to answer my questions.

THE FIRE DOES NOT LIE

In 2009, David Grann, a writer for *The New Yorker,* published the astonishing story of the Willingham execution and the role bad forensics played in it. That was my first introduction to the case.

I have not found another case with as much coverage as Willingham's. There are literally hundreds of newspaper and magazine articles.

The final report of the Texas Forensic Science Commission is nine hundred pages long. I relied on in-depth reporting by David Grann, the Marshall Project, *The Texas Tribune, Chicago Tribune,* and *Houston Chronicle,* as well as online reporting by the ACLU, the Innocence Project, and Time.com.

The story has inspired at least two feature films and one documentary. *Frontline* has produced a series of videos on the case. And the story goes on and on.

JIM McCLOSKEY

As I stated in the preface, the five cases chronicled by me in *Framed* were ones I personally managed and investigated from the beginning to the end of Centurion's involvement. It is our custom at Centurion to collect and study the case records before our work on a case, and we inevitably add many more to our files as the investigation matures. We conduct extensive correspondence with prospective clients as well. In writing these narratives, I relied on this wide assortment of Centurion archival material, which includes, but is not limited to, transcripts of trials, pre- and post-trial evidentiary hearings (federal and state), legal briefs, police reports, judicial opinions, court and criminal history records, and Centurion investigative memos and contemporaneous interview notes. In each case these various records amounted to thousands, and in some cases tens of thousands, of pages. These source materials, and my ongoing consultations with the subjects of these stories, have enabled me to present them as accurately as I can to the reader.

GUILTY UNTIL PROVEN INNOCENT

In telling Clarence Brandley's story, I am highly indebted to the book *White Lies* by Nick Davies, published by Pantheon Books in 1991. As the author points out in the prologue, starting in the fall of 1987, Davies, a seasoned British investigative journalist, spent two and half years in the United States researching and writing the book, including conducting interviews with main characters on both sides. Davies provides an account of how the case against Clarence unfolded and then how his conviction unraveled, resulting in his exoneration in early 1990. He also provides a vivid description of Conroe's culture and racial history.

In September 1987, the prestigious *Texas Monthly* magazine published a comprehensive feature story by Tom Curtis (deceased) on Clarence's case, titled "Guilty Until Proven Innocent." I adopted that title for the Brandley chapter because it so perfectly captures the thinking of local law enforcement that led them to put Clarence on death row. This article was informative and helpful source material as well.

I joined the defense team in early 1987 and spent most of that year in search of new evidence and preparing for the evidentiary hearing held that fall. My personal involvement in Clarence's case and my review of its entire written record were of great value in enabling me to write this story.

60 Minutes, with correspondent Harry Reasoner, broadcast Clarence's story in 1987. Information developed by the producer team provided material for this chapter, too.

LAST NIGHT OUT

A Centurion volunteer, Jock McFarlane, spent close to six years, from 2003 until 2009, accumulating the record of this 1992 Savannah crime and conviction from family members and the former trial attorneys of the three soldiers, Mark Jones, Dominic Lucci, and Kenneth Gardiner. He was aided in his case development work by Deborah McGill, Mark Jones's mother, who gathered an enormous volume of case records and sent them to Jock.

The Savannah-based trial attorneys of the soldiers, believing in their clients' innocence, helped the Centurion investigation immensely by sharing their files and knowledge of the case's characters and all that had transpired prior to and during the 1992 trial.

I was able to write this story based on my multi-year personal involvement and by relying on Centurion's archival files, which include the 1992 trial and 2013 evidentiary hearing transcripts, six hundred pages of police reports, Centurion investigative memos and interview notes, judicial decisions, extensive Savannah newspaper coverage, and legal briefs submitted by both sides from the beginning of the case.

TALE OF THE TAPES

Centurion staff person Kate Germond took several years to obtain and carefully study the trial transcripts, the legal history, and many other documents related to Ellen Reasonover's case, which I relied on for this chapter. Her case development work included a long correspondence with Ellen, getting her side of the story as well as a detailed autobiography. A 1984 *Washington Post* feature story resulting from its investigation of Ellen's case was very informative as well.

In addition to numerous Centurion investigative memos and interview reports, I relied on the transcripts of the original trial and the federal hearing before Judge Hamilton, legal briefs prepared by State and defense, judicial decisions (notably Judge Hamilton's seventy-five-page decision vacating Ellen's conviction), and numerous police investigative reports, including transcripts of taped police interviews with a variety of witnesses.

THROUGH THE LOOKING-GLASS

Twenty years after the convictions of David Alexander and Harry Granger, all appeals had been summarily denied in state and federal courts without benefit of a hearing. When Centurion picked up the ball and began to work for David and Harry in 1996, no Louisiana criminal defense attorney would touch the case, believing it was a lost cause since all judicial avenues had been exhausted twice around. That is, none but one—New Orleans attorney Margaret "Peggy" Woodward.

In shaping this complicated thirty-year saga into a short chapter, I was helped tremendously by Peggy's meticulous and lengthy writings. In 1999 she submitted a 178-page legal narrative in support of an application for post-conviction relief, detailing the absurdity of the State's case and the evidence of actual innocence of all six indictees. Attached to it were 146 exhibits consisting of numerous court documents and countless investigative reports and witness statements collected by Peggy and, after we joined forces, Centurion. Sadly, this petition, too, was dismissed out of hand by state and federal courts.

Peggy's unpublished 436-page book about the case, titled . . . *And Counting,* which she permitted me to use as I saw fit, was of enormous benefit in writing this chapter. It tells the whole story of these wrongful convictions in plain and superbly written prose.

60 Minutes, with correspondent Ed Bradley, broadcast a compelling story on the Alexander and Granger case titled "Who Killed Louis Gladu?" It, too, provided insight into the case that proved helpful in writing the story.

"OH, WHAT A TANGLED WEB WE WEAVE / WHEN FIRST WE PRACTICE TO DECEIVE"

Kerry Cook's chapter is twice as long as the other nine. I apologize for that, but it couldn't be helped. His story is a forty-seven-year roller coaster that finally ended in the summer of 2024 when Texas's highest court vacated his conviction on the basis of actual innocence. I am eternally grateful to John Grisham and Kristine Puopolo, Doubleday's VP and editorial director for nonfiction, for allowing me the space to tell it. There is much to say.

Centurion jumped into Kerry's case in 1991 and, together with Houston attorney Paul Nugent, saw him through two retrials in 1992 and 1994 and the advent of his fourth trial in 1999. In writing this chapter, source materials were endless. They included transcripts of three trials, important grand jury transcripts, detailed police investigative and interview reports, forensic reports, forty years of legal briefs and judicial opinions, extensive newspaper and magazine feature stories, and Centurion's own investigative memos, reports, and contemporaneous interview notes that were produced throughout the 1990s.

The 1996 Court of Criminal Appeals opinions vacating Kerry's 1994 conviction were quite helpful in preparing this chapter. Another important resource of great use was Kerry's memoir, *Chasing Justice,* published in 2007 by William Morrow. If you want to know what it is like being an innocent man on death row for twenty years, I highly recommend this well-written true story. Several *Texas Monthly* feature stories written by investigative journalist Michael Hall, particularly his lengthy April 2017 story entitled "The Trouble with Innocence," were insightful as well. And David Hanners, in addition to his numerous and invaluable *Dallas Morning News* articles written throughout the tortuous history of Kerry's case, wrote an important special article for *Texas Monthly* in March 2015.

Post-release, Kerry filed a writ of habeas corpus in 2015 asking that his murder conviction be erased and that he be found factually innocent based on DNA results. Subsequent to a 2016 hearing, the judge recommended to the Court of Criminal Appeals that Kerry's conviction be vacated based on new evidence—but that his claims of actual innocence be denied. After eight long and tortuous years, the CCA stunned Texas's criminal justice system when it issued a 106-page opinion excoriating the Smith County authorities for falsely convicting an innocent man, Kerry Max Cook. The extensive record of these 2015–2016 legal proceedings and the CCA's comprehensive opinion exonerating him enabled me to provide an up-to-date account of Kerry's legal standing for this chapter.

It is of paramount importance that the reader has full confidence in the accuracy of each case narrative. I have done my best to write in such a way as to not betray or violate that trust.

Coming soon from

JOHN GRISHAM

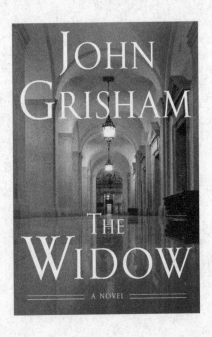

From the #1 *New York Times* bestselling master
of the legal thriller: his first-ever whodunit.
The Widow is even more suspenseful than his
courtroom dramas. This time a small-time
lawyer accused of murder races to find
the real killer to clear his name.

Learn more at jgrisham.com